AF361327

# Daring to Run

# Daring to Run

## How I Ran an Outsider's Campaign for Mayor of Elmira, New York, and Won

JOHN S. TONELLO

excelsior editions

State University of New York Press
Albany, New York

Published by State University of New York Press, Albany

© 2026 State University of New York

All rights reserved

Printed in the United States of America

No part of this book may be used or reproduced in any manner whatsoever without written permission. No part of this book may be stored in a retrieval system or transmitted in any form or by any means including electronic, electrostatic, magnetic tape, mechanical, photocopying, recording, or otherwise without the prior permission in writing of the publisher.

Links to third-party websites are provided as a convenience and for informational purposes only. They do not constitute an endorsement or an approval of any of the products, services, or opinions of the organization, companies, or individuals. SUNY Press bears no responsibility for the accuracy, legality, or content of a URL, the external website, or for that of subsequent websites.

EU GPSR Authorised Representative:
Logos Europe, 9 rue Nicolas Poussin, 17000, La Rochelle, France
contact@logoseurope.eu

Excelsior Editions is an imprint of State University of New York Press

For information, contact State University of New York Press, Albany, NY
www.sunypress.edu

**Library of Congress Cataloging-in-Publication Data**

Name: Tonello, John S., author.
Title: Daring to run : how i ran an outsider's campaign for
mayor of Elmira, NY, and won / John S. Tonello.
Description: Albany : State University of New York Press, [2026]. | Includes
    bibliographical references and index.
Identifiers: ISBN 9798855807202 (epub) | ISBN 9798855805703 (PDF) | ISBN
    9798855805697 (pbk. : alk. paper)
Further information is available at the Library of Congress.

*For Gina, because when one adventure ends, another begins.*

# Contents

# Prologue

For some Americans, the initial impetus to run for public office comes from watching the news, listening to radio shows and podcasts, franticly scrolling websites and social media, and getting mad as hell.

For others, it can be all that *plus* local leaders and issues that drive them batty and make them feel less safe or less neighborhood pride or less certain their property taxes aren't being wasted.

Or just feeling unheard.

The angst that results can be debilitating. Recent American election history bears that out. Some well-meaning citizens simply unplug, refuse to discuss politics at any level with anyone, or just roll their eyes at all the latest political antics, hoping it'll all just go away. Those human fears and frustrations are real, the outcomes uncertain. Many find it easier to simply look away. Many choose not to vote at all.

For others, the angst can be motivating, perhaps transforming into outright anger that tips the scales just enough to lift them off the sidelines and onto the playing field, fraught as it is. Instead of merely reeling from a state or national election, watching a neighborhood deteriorate, or waiting for local governments to respond, some decide to take matters into their own hands.

Indeed.

That's where I landed.

It wasn't just one thing that drove me to enter the race of a lifetime, but a combination of frustrations and, yes, anger. A disappointing presidential election, a neighborhood crack house ignored by local police and city hall, an albatross urban-renewal project that was doing more harm than good, a sense that local leaders weren't listening, and my desire to step up into public service all drove me to act. I was also at a personal low following the collapse of my brief marriage. I felt adrift and depressed, and I needed to climb out of my personal hole and discover new ways to motivate myself and find happiness and purpose again. I'd hit bottom, and that forced me to pull up my big-boy pants and step into the fray.

I didn't know what I was in for.

## A little history

My bright idea came when I was thirty-eight and living in Elmira, New York, a city of about 30,000 in a part of the state that hugs the Pennsylvania boarder to the south, the foothills of the Appalachian Mountains to the east, and the Finger Lakes to the north. In New York, the region is generally known as the Southern Tier, and Elmira is perhaps most famously known as the place where Mark Twain did some of his most notable writing. He enjoyed the moderate Elmira summers, sequestered away in the Octagonal Study on the sprawling Langdon family farm overlooking the Chemung River valley.

Twain, who famously worked on the Mississippi and traveled the world, ended up in Elmira because it was the place his wife, Olivia Langdon Clemens, called home. Her father had prospered in the lumber, coal, and shipping industries, built a Greek Revival mansion in downtown Elmira, and, as a strong abolitionist, became a conductor on the Underground Railroad. Twain married Olivia at the family home, spent twenty summers in Elmira working on *The Adventures of Tom Sawyer* and *Adventures of Huckleberry Finn* and other books, and today is buried in the Langdon family plot in Elmira's Woodlawn National Cemetery. As my friend Craig Palmer always says, "Many places claim Mark Twain, but we've got the body."

Before Twain, Elmira was, among other things, a mustering point for Union soldiers heading south to fight the Civil War and, before the war ended, the site of a notorious Civil War prison camp. It was there along the banks of the Chemung River that nearly 3,000 of the 12,000 Confederate soldiers imprisoned there died. Despite the horrors of the camp, the prison idea became permanent when the Elmira Reformatory, later known as the Elmira Correctional Facility, or just "The Hill," was built a dozen years after the war. The imposing brick and stone prison on Davis Street came to house some of New York's nastiest criminals and became a model for prisons aiming to reform, not just incarcerate, criminals. It housed upward of 1,800 inmates and was a big local employer, offering correction officers jobs that were among the highest paid in the state that didn't require a college degree.

During Twain's time and later, Elmira also was home to the headquarters of the American LaFrance fire-equipment factories, responsible for churning out tens of thousands of fire trucks and firefighting apparatus before the local plant closed in 1985. Elmira was home to Heisman Trophy winner Ernie Davis, who played football for Syracuse University after earning All-American honors as a high school player for Elmira Free Academy. Later, Elmira became the birthplace of internationally known fashion designer Tommy Hilfiger, who in the early 1970s opened the People's Place, his first clothing store. Other famous Elmirans include NASA astronaut Eileen Collins, the first woman to command a US space mission, and filmmaker Hal Roach, who produced the classic *Our Gang* short films featuring Spanky and Alfalfa.

Elmira has a remarkable historic record but arguably reached its peak in the late 1940s, when manufacturing jobs were plentiful. The railroad that still cuts through the heart of the city carried goods and passengers to all points of the compass, including Buffalo to the northwest and New York City to the southeast. But like other Northeast cities in the forty years after World War II, Elmira was well into a steady decline. The population shrank, good-paying jobs disappeared, and with them went any permanent sense of growth.

The region also had more than its share of devastating natural disasters, including the 1972 Chemung River flood blown in by hurricane Agnes. The slow-moving storm dropped twenty-two inches of rain on the region and drowned much of downtown Elmira and nearby downtown Corning under rushing water that swept away bridges, businesses, and homes. Ever resilient, residents rebuilt, but as the floodwaters receded, the two cities' fortunes diverged. Corning Glass Works, later Corning Inc., helped rebuild Corning, while many Elmira businesses used their federal disaster aid and insurance money to leave the city for good.


## Elmira's political history

Throughout much of the twentieth century, Elmira was something of a blue dot as the seat of Chemung County, where registered Republicans outnumbered Democrats by nearly two to one. The year I ran, Republicans outnumbered Democrats countywide 24,300 to 17,475, or 48 to 31 percent, with another 2,200 voters registered as members of the Independence

Party, a conservative line created in 1991 by former gubernatorial candidate Thomas Galisano and others. Those Independence Party voters—not to be confused with *independently* registered voters—generally cast ballots for Republicans too. At the time, some 9,800 registered voters in Chemung County had no party affiliation, known on the voter rolls as Blanks and, more generally, as independents. Despite these voter enrollment numbers, turnout for local elections was generally low.

In Elmira itself, the voter registration numbers were different. Some 5,700 voters were registered Democrats and 4,400 were registered Republicans, or 56 to 43 percent. But despite the Democratic voter registration advantage, Elmira had its share of Republican mayors and councilmen, including Stephen Fesh Jr. and former police captain Howard Townsend, who held the mayor's office in the mid-1980s and mid-1990s, respectively. The city certainly wasn't a lock for Democrats.

As a kid, I was barely aware of these political metrics. My mother and stepfather were Republicans. My father, who still lived in Buffalo, was a Democrat. As a teenager, I wasn't exactly clear on the differences, though I'd become a fan of presidential history and understood from reading biographies like Arthur M. Schlesinger Jr.'s *A Thousand Days* that John F. Kennedy and his brother Bobby were Democrats and Richard Nixon was a Republican. I discovered I liked what I read about the former much more than the latter.

The fact that the Southern Tier was one of the most conservative parts of New York State never quite registered with me when I was younger. Like many teenagers, when it came to local politics, I was clueless. Politics was a vague idea that came to the forefront every four years for presidential elections. We'd moved several times in my youth, from Western New York to Connecticut, back to New York, to Ohio, and finally back to New York's Southern Tier, where I found myself almost completely unaware of the region's politics. Landing in a rural area between Corning and Elmira when I was just starting high school mostly meant I was, in many ways, an outsider looking in. I was far more interested in fitting in with other kids at school and in our suburban neighborhood than figuring out who was who in local, state, and national government.

Unlike some who run for public office, I had no long-standing roots in the Southern Tier. I hadn't grown up in Elmira or even gone to school there. I had just turned thirteen when my stepfather landed a job that took us from the flat farmland of Delaware, Ohio, to the rolling hills of New York's Southern Tier. The river valley parted low hills covered with maples, oaks, and other trees that turned magnificent colors each fall. That natural beauty was a pleasant change from the nearly infinite flat farmland of central Ohio but, politically, I saw no difference.

In 1980, just a few months shy of my fourteenth birthday, my mother, stepfather, brother, and two stepbrothers moved into a white, five-bedroom colonial house in a suburban neighborhood located on the far eastern edge of Steuben County, roughly halfway between Corning to the west and Elmira to the east. It was an area on the western edge of Chemung County near two towns with unusual names: Big Flats and Horseheads. Other than a small pizza shop, a gas station, and a mini-mart, there was little for miles, just subdivisions, farms, and the coal-fired Hickling power plant that dusted our homes with fine black ash.

My brothers and I attended what was then Corning West High School in Painted Post, a nine-mile school bus trip west that took about forty-five minutes each way. Though we lived miles from Corning itself, as residents of the town of South Corning, we considered ourselves Corningites, not Elmirans.

In high school, I was a new kid, rather shy, and not active in sports, theater, or other extracurricular activities. I helped manage the varsity basketball team my freshman year, briefly played cello in the high school orchestra, and sang in the West High Concert Choir, but I wasn't active in student government, the yearbook staff, or the school newspaper. I basically lived on the periphery—not popular, not unpopular—earning grades that ran mostly to Bs.

As a recent transplant from Ohio—and a year younger than most of my peers because I'd started kindergarten in Connecticut at age four—I never felt fully connected with my classmates, and I found my high school years challenging. The school district covered a large geographic area that scattered my classmates far and wide, making it difficult for those of us too young to drive to gather outside school.

That disconnect was a big part of the reason I decided to leave West High after my junior year to attend Corning Community College, where I could simultaneously complete both my senior-year academic requirements and my college freshman requirements. Though I'd be just sixteen when college classes started in the fall, my high school guidance counselor and my parents agreed to let me go.

It was during my time in college, high atop Spencer Hill in Corning, that I developed a deeper understanding of national politics, thanks in part to my freshman English professor, Hank Moonschein Jr., who happened to loathe President Ronald Reagan.

At the time, Reagan, who'd won a landslide victory over Jimmy Carter in 1980 (489 electoral votes to 49), was well into his third year as president. Unlike many of my college classmates, I wasn't yet old enough to vote, but Moonschein offered my classmates and me a starkly different take on the Great Communicator than I'd heard from my mom and stepfather at home. I didn't feel strongly one way or the other about Reagan, but my professor's positions awakened in me a new political awareness that would persist well after college.

I'd also soon come to learn that liberal voters were dramatically outnumbered in the Southern Tier. Reagan had carried the region and won the entire state in both 1980 and 1984, but despite the left-leaning nature of New York City, New York State at the time was anything but a "blue state."

After earning an associate's degree at Corning Community College, I left home to attend Syracuse University to get my bachelor's. I figured I wasn't just going off to school, but leaving the Southern Tier for good. When I finished my degree it was anybody's guess where I'd end up. I figured I'd probably work at a daily newspaper somewhere in New York State, perhaps even the Elmira *Star-Gazette* or the Corning *Leader*, but with any luck I was aiming to land at a larger city paper somewhere beyond the Southern Tier.

That turned out to be the case. After a successful internship my senior year, I landed a job at the Syracuse *Post-Standard*, working as a reporter in the newspaper's Cortland bureau, located about thirty miles south of Syracuse. Cortland also sat in a river valley surrounded by tree-covered hills, and it was home to SUNY Cortland, a state school specializing in training teachers. Like the Southern Tier, Cortland County was pretty conservative, but the small city of 17,000 leaned Democratic. As a young reporter in a two-person bureau, I got to cover everything from the college and schools to crime and fires to the county legislature and city council.

It was there in 1987 that I covered my first local political campaigns, including a close mayoral race between local attorney Marty Mack, a Democrat, and incumbent city councilor Gerald Duffy, a Republican. They were competing for an open seat, and the race came down to the wire, with Mack winning by about two hundred votes. As a *Post-Standard* reporter, I was an eyewitness to the campaign, and covering the mayor's race—and other local campaigns—was one of most interesting things I'd ever done. I'd been right there for the ups and downs, and, when Mack took office, I had a front-row seat from which I was able to see how he worked with city council, city staff, and the public and witness firsthand his approach to running the city. Over the next few years, I learned even more by watching the thirty-four-year-old first-time Mayor Mack turn his progressive, often nonpartisan ideas into action.

## A strange illness

In my nearly four years in the *Post-Standard*'s Cortland Bureau, I'd learn a lot about city and county government, but the job started to wear on me. My stomach was mess, and on my desk I kept a bottle of Maalox I could drink to cool the burning in my gut. Over the course of several months, my condition worsened, and I was diagnosed with ulcerative colitis, which led to three weeks in Cortland Hospital and, when my condition got even worse, three more weeks at Arnot-Ogden Medical Center back in Elmira. Though I had no active desire to leave Cortland and return to the Southern Tier, my illness forced the issue. I left Cortland to convalesce at my parent's home in South Corning and didn't return.

This strange illness, which had caused me to rapidly lose thirty pounds and half my body's blood, had no cure. That staggered me and gave me a new appreciation of my own mortality, which prompted me to consider what I *really* wanted to do with my life. I was just twenty-four years old, but I knew I never again wanted to waste my time on earth doing a job I hated. I spent the next six months at my parent's home regaining my strength and thinking a lot about my future—with ulcerative colitis along for the ride.

When I received a bill for nearly $30,000 for my three-week stay at Arnot-Ogden Medical Center, it got me thinking about the state of politics. Suddenly, the cost of health care was my primary concern, and I wasn't sure what help, if any, I might get from the government. There wasn't yet an Affordable Care Act, and the hospital bills scared the hell out of me; I didn't have thirty grand just sitting around. Fortunately, I had health insurance to cover most of my health care expenses, but I'd now have to take expensive medications for the rest of my life. I was genuinely terrified.

This new fear came at a time when I'd become newly aware of several other political issues that raised alarms for me. During the Reagan years, the country had shifted to the right, and unions were losing support and muscle to influence the health care debate. Democrats, not Republicans, were championing the value of unions, equal pay for women, and programs to help impoverished mothers and families. Democrats also were supporting efforts to help end discrimination and assist the vulnerable. I was now a member of that vulnerable group, and it became abundantly clear to me that Republicans weren't likely to help me or others like me.

I emerged from my self-reflection as a committed Democrat. I'd become socially liberal and economically conservative, which to me meant allowing people live their lives as they wanted, helping Americans in need, and operating government at every level with sound, professional financial stewardship. My illness had left me afraid for my future, and I was going to need government to be on my side. I wasn't looking for handouts, but I *did* want support. Without it, my future with a chronic illness was in doubt.

It took me months to get back on my feet, but when I did, I found work in media relations at Rochester Institute of Technology, a prominent engineering university located in Rochester, New York, and, later in university communications at my alma mater, Syracuse University. It was there that I began to experiment with coding and web development, which was so new that there weren't yet books available on the subject. The internet was just starting to take off then, and it turned out that working in higher education—where computer and network technology were well ahead of other industries at the time—was the perfect place to explore my newfound interest in the web.

It was around this time, too, that Bill Clinton came out of Arkansas and defeated incumbent President George H. W. Bush and Ross Perot in the 1992 presidential election. I remember watching television alone in my Rochester apartment that November night, jumping up and down as the returns came in. Clinton was young and a fresh face after twelve years of Ronald Reagan and George H. W. Bush, and it all felt like a new beginning, which in many ways it was. I respected Bush and his long government service—and I'd voted for him in 1988 over Democrat Michael Dukakis—but, like many Americans, I'd had a political epiphany that opened my mind to change. I wasn't alone. My adopted counties of Monroe (Rochester) and Onondaga (Syracuse) went for Clinton in 1992, while back home both Steuben (Corning) and Chemung (Elmira) counties went to Bush. I was proud of Clinton's Democratic win and my many neighbors who'd voted for him. The right-leaning tilt of voters back home made any desire I had to return to the Southern Tier fade all the more.

That would soon change, however. Despite my eagerness to live in places where Democrats dominated, politics took a back seat to my career when my mother mailed me a small newspaper clipping for a job at the Elmira *Star-Gazette*. The newspaper wanted to launch its first web presence and was looking for its first online manager. The web was the newest thing, and I dearly wanted to be part of it, wherever it might take me. So when I applied and landed the job, I swallowed my political pride and moved back to the Southern Tier.

## Making the Southern Tier home

The job at the *Star-Gazette* would be my first real opportunity to work full-time in Elmira, but it took me another three years to finally settle on the idea of living there permanently. I had always believed if I ever did happen to return to the Southern Tier, I'd live in Corning, not Elmira. I found Corning charming, with its historic Market Street shops and riverfront views, but after working as the *Star-Gazette*'s online manager and a short stint as the newspaper's metro editor, the now-older me realized Elmira had more to offer in the way of restaurants, businesses, politics, and general activity. It wasn't a one-company town or conservative like Corning, and I'd grown fond of Elmira and its plucky history. It also didn't hurt that the city was affordable for a first-time home buyer.

After leaving the newspaper and joining a small web-development firm before going on to work for Accenture, Corning Inc., and Cornell University, I decided I should stop renting, sink some roots in Elmira, and buy a house. After some hunting, I found a two-story, 1,800-square-foot bungalow built in 1868 that sat on a deep, wooded quarter acre in Elmira's Near Westside and paid $63,000 for it. I'd soon discover my new neighbor had purchased the duplex next door just a month earlier, and I became friends with Chrissy Brown, a smart, pretty civil engineer with a lopsided smile. We discovered we both liked the historic single- and multi-family charm of Near Westside homes, their shaded lots, the ready access to shops and restaurants, and the idea of living in the city itself. We felt part of a new generation of young homeowners looking to invest in Elmira, and we were.

Unlike me, Chrissy had grown up in Elmira and had deep roots in the city. At times, it seemed as though everyone knew her. By contrast, I was a true transplant with very little personal history or knowledge of the city beyond the Near Westside. Despite the different paths that led us to become West Gray Street neighbors, we became close, always finding time to have a beer, share a meal, help each other with yard work, and talk about the general ups and downs of life. It also helped that she was a fellow Democrat. Over the next dozen years, Chrissy taught me a lot about the city and its people.

As we began projects to update our newly purchased historic homes, the city of Elmira was aiming to remake itself too. It had a fundamental problem: jobs. The city was home to consistent employers, such as Arnot-Ogden Medical Center, Elmira College, the Elmira Correctional Facility and its companion maxi-max prison in nearby Southport, Hardinge, Hilliard Corp., Howell Packaging, Kennedy Valve, nearby Anchor Glass, and others, but the really big manufacturers, like American LaFrance, had long since left the area.

The result had been economic stagnation, and downtown streets, once bustling with nearly 50,000 residents and later drowned under feet of water and muck from the 1972 flood, lost buildings to demolition and apathy. Many beautiful brick and stone facades dissolved into parking lots, and newer retailers often brought generic, low-density suburban architecture to Elmira's historic neighborhoods, a transition that wasn't new. Nearly sixty years earlier, the city okayed the demolition of the historic Langdon Mansion—the Greek Revival home on Main Street where Mark Twain married Olivia Langdon—so the site could be turned into a shopping plaza. Back then, historical preservation and history-based tourism weren't a thing.

Despite its challenges, Elmira had a lot of appeal to a young homeowner like me. It was affordable and walkable, had a professional minor-league baseball team called the Pioneers (which I briefly covered as a part-time stringer for the *Star-Gazette*), beautiful views of the Chemung River valley and surrounding wooded hills, a slight Democratic lean, and a rich history beyond Mark Twain.


## The arena


Not long after I'd moved in, however, city leaders leaned not into Elmira's historic roots, but into a different sort of project to bolster the city: a new downtown hockey arena. The 125,000-square-foot, 3,700-seat facility, originally planned to have an accompanying hotel, was meant to house a professional hockey team, offer public skating and soccer, become a concert venue, and ultimately draw conferences and spur downtown redevelopment.

Unfortunately, the project included the demolition of more historic buildings on Main Street not far from what had been the Langdon mansion. It would also end up saddling the city of Elmira with enormous debt. The hotel part of the project never happened either, diminishing the hoped-for economic impact. The urban planning principal of build-it-and-they-will-come wasn't panning out and mirrored urban development failures like Buffalo's subway, which tore up Main Street there, shuttered dozens of businesses, and left an urban scar that took that city nearly forty years to heal.

It was no accident that the idea of a big, bold public project found its way to Elmira from Buffalo. City Manager Samuel Iraci Jr., hired to run Elmira in early 1994, had been deputy mayor under Buffalo Mayor Jimmy Griffin, who spearheaded Buffalo's subway project. Such expensive, broad-stroke urban redevelopment efforts were popular ways to energize flagging downtowns in the 1970s and 1980s, and twenty years later, many in Elmira supported the arena idea, including *Star-Gazette* editorial writers, who had at first struck a cautious tone before giving the project their blessing.

I couldn't. I felt far less certain that a build-it-and-they-will-come project would pay off. Such projects often left white elephants behind and, sure enough, within a few short years, it was clear the Elmira arena was struggling. It wasn't profitable, it was failing to draw substantial new business to downtown, and the city had yet to recoup any monetary return on its investment.

Some on the Elmira City Council openly blamed and publicly battled with the arena's owner/operator with whom they'd partnered to run the place. The public-private partnership behind the arena required the City of Elmira to commit federal Housing and Urban Development funds—money typically used to revitalize neighborhoods—to pay its share of the debt on the arena. More than an albatross, the arena was sapping efforts to revitalize other parts of the city.

When the arena was first conceived, there was a lot at stake for city leaders. If it was a success, it would draw people and new tax revenue to the city. If it failed, the impact would be felt in neighborhoods around the city in fewer paved streets, less investment in stressed housing, and fewer low-income residents getting help.

As a city taxpayer, the whole project stuck in my craw. The new Jackals hockey team drew fans, but not enough to make a difference in regular downtown foot traffic. A few bars and restaurants opened downtown near the arena, and existing businesses saw a slight uptick in foot traffic on game nights or during concerts, but it was never enough—or consistent enough—to bring lasting new business and patrons or trigger true economic growth.

I wasn't the only one grumbling. Chrissy and other city residents I spoke with were moving beyond mere skepticism for the arena to disgust, and it marked the first moment, as a homeowner, when I felt the city leaders were out of step with their constituents. Sure, politicians make promises all the time, but it wasn't just the project that was failing. We felt city leaders were failing to explain why they were doing what they were doing (or not doing) to make the arena work.

## The crack house

Around the same time, the city's issues suddenly came much closer to home when drug dealers set up a crack house in a first-floor apartment in the middle of our Near Westside neighborhood. Chrissy; my neighbors across the street, Bonnie and Ralph Gestwicki; and I were quick to report the criminal activity and the all-hours visitors who were turning our block of West Gray Street into a shambles, but the crack house persisted.

Each day, we would watch helplessly as drug users pulled up to the deteriorating house that had long since been cut up into three apartments, enter the rear apartment, smoke some crack, and drive off buzzed. They paid no attention to driveway cuts, one-side-only parking regulations, or the people who lived in the neighborhood. They had simply found a supplier and did their business without regard to anyone but themselves.

City police expressed sympathy when we reported the activity, but given the scale of other drug and crime problems in the city, they largely ignored our pleas for help. We decided to turn to our First District city councilman, Bill Hopkins. With his help, we felt the odds were good we'd get better results. As a group, we neighbors were college-educated, responsible taxpayers and knew a problem when we saw one. We weren't nattering nuts looking to pick a fight with the city. We were concerned citizens looking to do what we could to help solve our local drug problem, and we wanted the city's help.

Councilman Hopkins responded quickly and took our concerns seriously by setting up a meeting with Elmira's mayor, city manager, and police chief. We were impressed that such a group of city leaders would all agree to sit down and discuss the crack house with us, so we were optimistic. Surely they would quiet our fears, drive the drug dealers from our neighborhood, and restore our sense of pride in the historic city we all called home.

Not a chance.

Instead of easing our anxiety, the city leaders added to it. Mayor Stephen Hughes offered vague pleasantries and took the time to list some of his accomplishments as mayor of the city, including the downtown hockey arena and new jobs he'd helped bring about. The police chief told us his department was more interested in arresting big drug dealers, not chasing away minor characters selling crack hits in our neighborhood. We should be patient, vigilant, and avoid confrontation, he told us. After all, he said, crack houses can be dangerous places.

During the meeting, my neighbors and I eyed each other in disbelief. Why were the mayor and city manager boasting about the arena and job creation and not talking about our crack house problem? We felt unheard, and when we tried to speak, our words came in fits and starts. We were dumbstruck.

A year passed, and not much changed in our West Gray Street neighborhood. The crack house activity faded on its own when the roof over the drug-dealer's apartment gave way, and the landlord had to boot the drug-dealing tenants. So-called slumlords were common in Elmira, carving up tired old houses and turning them into apartments, charging market-rate rents, and rarely reinvesting money back into the sagging properties. This was a larger, citywide issue that came into focus during our ordeal and helped me better understand that our relatively isolated crack house problem was really the not-so-faint edge of a bigger issue dragging down the city. Again, my neighbors and I couldn't understand the city's inability or unwillingness to act—or effectively communicate—about the problem and how they might address it.

Despite our frustration with the city, my attention turned to my personal life. My two-year-old marriage was ending. Ours had been a bit of a whirlwind romance that went from a workplace flirtation to living together in my West Gray Street home to a Lake Placid elopement—all in about seven months. Our schedules had fallen out of sync, our arguments had become more frequent, and after just thirty months, our marriage was over. The divorce left me feeling empty, lost, and rethinking my core beliefs. One day I was married, the next I wasn't, and it left a gaping hole in my world.

My ex-wife and I had purchased a new home in Elmira before our divorce, but my West Gray Street bungalow had never sold. I repainted the rooms, sanded the oak-plank floors, and made some minor renovations, happy that, if nothing else, I still had this piece of the American dream. By not selling my home, I had a ready place to return to and start over. It also meant I was still a city resident, and that fact would make a big difference in the shape of my life over the next twelve months.

1

# Deciding to Run

### A chance meeting at a hardware store

When I started renovating my West Gray Street home after my divorce, I spent a lot of time driving back and forth to the local Ace Hardware store on the corner of Broadway and Pennsylvania Avenue in Southport to buy paint, tools, and whatever else I needed to stay busy brightening up my house.

On one of those shopping trips in late November, I recognized a fellow customer as Jim Hare, a former Elmira mayor and current Sixth District city councilman who'd just lost a competitive race for New York's 137th State Assembly district. Jim, then fifty-eight, was easily recognizable. He sported thinning white hair, wire-rimmed glasses, and a ready smile. I knew him by reputation only, but I'd learned he'd been active for years in local Democratic politics, had taught American history at Southside High School, served in the army during the Vietnam era, and been a regular on the stage of Elmira's amateur production company, Elmira Little Theatre. Though I didn't know all that much about him personally, he projected an easy confidence. He seemed familiar because of all the media coverage he'd received during the recent campaign, and I didn't want to miss the chance to meet him.

I approached Jim, and by way of introduction said, "There's the guy I voted for!" Jim turned from what he was doing, smiled and shook my hand. He was immediately friendly and engaging, and our conversation soon turned from his failed race for state assembly to the recent presidential election, which saw Republican George W. Bush returned to office. We commiserated, and, because he was always eager to engage new people in politics, Jim asked if I'd like to attend the upcoming Chemung County Democratic Committee meeting. He explained it was the party's annual organizational meeting and I'd be welcome.

For someone who'd just lost an election—and didn't know me from Adam—Jim came across as upbeat and positive. Maybe it was the politician in him, but I, too, was eager to get involved in Democratic politics, and he was *the* guy to help me do just that. Jim asked where I lived (always thinking about Democratic committeeman assignments), gave me a card with his phone number written on it, and urged me to come out to the meeting. I told him I would.

That chance encounter was a true turning point for me. Just as I was pondering the city's problems and the idea of getting off the sidelines, here was a guy who could help make that happen. I doubt he would remember our meeting as fondly because, though neither of us had any sense of it at the time, we soon would be working at cross-purposes. Still, it was a positive and uplifting introduction that started my wheels turning. Perhaps I could be in on local efforts to get more Democrats elected to office in a region dominated by Republicans. Perhaps I could see up close how it all worked and could be truly involved. I was grateful to Jim for opening the door.

That brief introduction got me thinking that, just maybe, becoming active in the party would help ease the frustration—and even guilt—I felt following the presidential election. I hadn't lifted a finger to help get Democrat John Kerry elected president. I'd done a little campaigning for the Democratic candidate for Congress, but I hadn't done much at all to help any other Democratic candidates get elected. Sure, I'd voted for them, but I mostly just watched from the sidelines and hoped. Clearly, that hadn't been enough.

Though I'm not a big believer in omens or signs, that random meeting at the hardware store—and Jim's invitation to join the efforts of local Democrats—seemed like serendipity. It would prove to be a great place to start remaking my life—and my involvement.

I ruminated about that chance meeting throughout the early winter and looked forward to the Democratic Committee meeting, set to take place in downtown Elmira's Steele Memorial Library, a modern two-story building that stood alongside the railroad tracks in an area of the city rebuilt after the 1972 flood. The meeting would be my first chance to see how the local Democrats operated, meet fellow party members, and begin to understand the people and mechanics of it all. I wasn't yet thinking about running for local office, but the idea wasn't exactly absent either. Public service was something that ran in the family.

## Some political blood

When I was a kid, my uncle Carmelo Parlato, one of my mother's four brothers, had served two terms on the Buffalo school board before being elected in 1972 to serve a ten-year term as a Buffalo city court judge. Later, when he ran a losing battle for a seat on New York's State Supreme Court, I remembered stuffing envelopes and helping to put up signs. I'd been just nine years old at the time.

Though he'd been active in Republican politics—including campaigning in Buffalo with Pat Nixon during Richard Nixon's 1972 reelection bid—my uncle never had the airs of a politician. As a kid, I remembered the lively political discussions that took place each holiday when his siblings gathered around the dining room table at his Porter Avenue home in Buffalo, but publicly—and to his extended family—it wasn't something I ever heard him talk about.

Having a judge in the family always gave me a sense of awe, but Uncle Melo wasn't the only politician in the family. My great-uncle Frank Gugino, my mother's uncle, also was an attorney and politician. After serving in the army during World War I, he earned his law degree in 1922 and worked as deputy state attorney general before winning a seat and serving in the New York State Assembly from 1935 to 1948. During his time as a Western New York assemblyman, he'd helped establish and secure money for what became known as Buffalo's Roswell Park Cancer Institute.

My uncle and great-uncle had stepped up and into public service, and I thought just maybe it was in my blood too. I wondered about the possibilities of following in their political footsteps the day I stepped through the doors of the Elmira public library for that mid-winter Democratic Committee meeting.

## The Democrats' planning meeting

The Chemung County Democratic Committee gathered in a large, window-less library meeting room painted in muted colors and lit by neon ceiling lights. Tables had been set up in rows, and behind them sat a surprising number of men and women, not the modest few I'd expected given the Republican dominance in county politics. I'd soon learn all these people were city and county committeemen—men and women who represented specific election districts in Chemung County and the City of Elmira—and many had been at it for years. They were business people, union members, artists, public servants, and a true cross-section of the community. Before the meeting was over, I'd become a committeeman too.

Though the room was filled, most of the committee members were strangers to me. I didn't recall any of them knocking on my door or campaigning in my neighborhood. Jim Hare was there along with other active members of the city council; the chair of the Chemung County Democratic Committee, Cindy Emmer; and the chair of the City Democratic Committee, Steve McNamara. Notably absent was then-Mayor Stephen Hughes, whom I was told didn't actively engage with the Democratic Committee at the county and city levels.

Among the veterans were other newcomers like me, including Andy Patros, a thick-bearded Greek guy with glasses I'd first met years earlier when I was working for the *Star-Gazette* developing the newspaper's website. Andy, now in his forties and living in Southport just outside Elmira's city limits, was a former letter carrier who co-owned a web-development firm in nearby Corning. Like me, Andy was disaffected with the outcome of the November presidential election and wanted to get involved in local politics. At the meeting, we struck up a conversation, and it didn't take long to discover we were much more eager than the party regulars to shake things up. I spoke, he spoke, and we both agreed we wouldn't be satisfied with the same-old, same-old that left most seats in local, state, and national government filled by Republicans or out-of-touch Democrats. After the meeting, we immediately started to exchange phone calls and emails.

Getting reacquainted with Andy and our deepening friendship turned out to be another life-altering time for me. In Andy, I'd found an ideological brother. We were both new to the party committees, but we'd both left the Democrats' meeting with the sense that many longtime members, good people that they were, were resigned to Republican dominance in local politics. Andy and I were hungry to change the status quo and shake things up in ways that could get more Democrats elected countywide.

Chemung County had long been the bastion of Republicans, who were repeatedly elected to town supervisor seats, the district attorney's office, the county legislature, and the state assembly and senate seats—often unopposed. The region was conservative to be sure, repeatedly voting for Republican presidential candidates and Republicans all the way down the ballot. Though registered Democrats outnumbered registered Republicans in the City of Elmira, the rest of the county was deep red, much like the rest of Upstate New York. Except for urban pockets—Elmira, Ithaca, Syracuse, and Rochester, to name a few—the region was, and remains, overwhelmingly Republican territory. Some who don't know New York might think it's true-blue from the shores of Lake Erie and Buffalo to the tip of Long Island and Montauk. The reality is much different. New York City and upstate cities are places where Democrats abound. Everywhere else, not so much.

Andy and I felt a real sense of disappointment in the Democrats' inability to change that in mostly rural Chemung County. Many local Democrats seemed to see the party as a permanent underdog, particularly in county, state, and national races. That hadn't really been borne out in Jim Hare's recent—and relatively close 26,108 to 22,213—loss to Republican Thomas O'Mara in the state assembly race, but it was plain as day in the county legislature's overwhelming Republican majority. We figured the status quo—the predominant thinking that Democrats didn't have a shot at any of these races—was the wrong approach. Andy and I both felt the local party needed to think and act in new ways if it wanted to get more Democrats in office.

The Elmira and Chemung County Democratic parties seemed to be in a rut, but they certainly weren't alone. Democratic Committees in other rural parts of New York State were struggling, too. Andy and I believed only a new approach could change things and inject new life into local races.

We felt a keen sense of urgency because it was now a local election year, with the city council and mayor's races due to kick off soon. In City Hall, Democrats held a six to one majority that included the mayor, but Andy and I both felt that, despite city government's Democratic majority, decision-making was opaque and headed in the wrong direction. With frustration growing over the hockey arena and other local issues, we felt the Republicans had a good chance of flipping the city council in the fall, something we wanted to avoid at all costs. But with the same slate of incumbents planning to run, we were worried. There didn't seem to be a lot of compelling reasons for city voters to give all the incumbents a free pass—and their votes.

It didn't help that the mayor and council had voted four to three the previous September to place a referendum on the November ballot to extend council terms from two years to four. The referendum passed citywide by fewer than 100 votes out of 4,700 cast. Those in favor argued it would provide better continuity because incumbents could focus on governing, not running for office. Those opposed said it would make the mayor and council less accountable. The new lengthened terms would take effect in two years, perhaps not impacting any of the current incumbents, including the mayor, but the slim margin on the referendum suggested to me and others that many voters didn't hold a strong desire to give city leaders longer terms or less accountability.

Not all the local Democratic Committee members were complacent, but those of us clamoring for change were certainly in the minority. The city was stagnating, the arena was not a winning election issue, and issues with drugs and slumlords were contributing to the decline and general shabbiness of many neighborhoods. We figured voters of all stripes were seeking change, and we feared the Republican dominance of county, state, and national races would seep into the city. The status quo wasn't enough, and as Andy liked to say, we needed to "stir the pot."

In the weeks ahead, our concerns would take on even greater meaning because of a major shake-up in city government leadership, but for now, we weren't happy. We'd joined the party because we wanted to make a difference and give voters more choices. We didn't have anything personally against anyone in the party, but we weren't willing to have our energy and enthusiasm quickly tempered by party machinery that seemed resigned to Republican dominance.

Instead, we took a radically different approach: We would seek elective office ourselves.


## Talking with friends and neighbors

I began to form a clearer idea of becoming a candidate not long after the winter Democratic Committee meeting. I figured holding public office would give me a chance to be *really* involved, inject a more communicative and open approach to local government, and provide me with a soapbox for Democratic issues. By serving in a way that was based on common sense and transparency, perhaps I could bring forward issues my neighbors and I felt were important. Perhaps I could also use an elected position to weigh in on larger political issues of the day.

After seeing how the committee and its members worked, there was no longer any lingering hesitation about the prospect of running myself. Any deference I'd paid to incumbent politicians evaporated. Elected officials were just ordinary men and women with ordinary day jobs and families and mostly folks with an urge to give back to their communities and serve. If they could run for office, why couldn't I?

But which office should I seek? My first impulse was to challenge sitting Mayor Stephen Hughes in a Democratic primary because I wasn't a fan of his approach, particularly after our encounter over our neighborhood crack house. Still, a primary against an incumbent would be a gutsy move. Perhaps too gutsy.

Just the same, I thought I should float the idea to a few people in the know to feel them out. One of the first people I approached was a former neighbor and fellow Democrat who seemed to know the local players. As we stood on his porch and chatted, he made it clear where his allegiances lay. He told me he thought Hughes was popular, had a good record, and would be hard to beat, particularly by an unknown newcomer. I told him I sensed others were just as disaffected as I was with Hughes, but my neighbor seemed adamant. Others agreed a primary would be a difficult hill to climb and that I'd be better off running for something more feasible, like a city council seat. I thought about it for a few days and reluctantly decided to shelve the idea of running for mayor.

The most obvious opportunity for me, then, was the First District City Council seat. Each member of Elmira City Council represents one of the city's six wards. These were geographically much smaller than county legislature districts, which represented fifteen regions across Chemung County. Four of the city wards were north of the east-to-west-flowing Chemung River. The remaining two were on the south side. I lived in the city's northside First Ward, where Hopkins was first elected in 1999 over Republican incumbent David Brown.

Fellow Democrat Bill Hopkins, the same guy who'd helped my neighbors and me get a meeting with the mayor, city manager, and police chief more than a year earlier to talk about the crack house, had been reelected twice. Still, the margins showed a Republican could win the district, suggesting a more moderate Democratic registration advantage.

Hopkins was a self-employed artist in his early fifties, but I didn't know much else about him or his record on the city council. Others I asked didn't know much about him either, but if I wanted to run for council, his was the seat I'd have to pursue. He'd been quick to pull together that meeting with city leaders a year earlier and I had no animosity toward Hopkins, but the First District council seat represented my only way into city government—and the path of least resistance.

I briefly contemplated other offices, including the 10th District county legislature seat held by longtime incumbent Ted Bennett. He'd been there since the county legislature was transformed from a board of supervisors to a stand-alone legislature in 1974—more than thirty years earlier. No one else had ever held the seat, and though Bennett often sided with the Republican majority over the years, he was a familiar incumbent I thought would be difficult to defeat. Thirty years of representation and favors, I thought, made him a more formidable opponent than Hopkins.

After doing more research on the mechanics of running for office, I learned the council race would be a far easier entry point for a political newcomer. Each city council race required candidates to collect just a few dozen signatures on nominating petitions to get on the ballot, and the ward itself was basically a single square mile. Meeting voters and campaigning in such a relatively small geographic area seemed doable, especially considering I had a day job at Cornell University in Ithaca that would limit the time I had available to campaign. Ithaca is about a forty-five-minute drive up Route 13 from Elmira, which meant I wouldn't be able to just run home at lunchtime to knock on doors and campaign.

The First District seat also represented the area I was most interested in: my Near Westside neighborhood. The area was filled with single- and multi-family homes built in the last century, and I certainly understood the challenges of parking, crime, and other issues facing the historic Elmira neighborhood where many single-family homes had been converted to apartments by absentee landlords. I felt I could speak to district voters in terms they could understand and, with work, get elected.

Of course, this was all still just conjecture on my part. Taking on Hopkins would likely mean a Democratic primary, something pretty rare and no doubt fraught with peril. Surely the Democratic Committee would not like the idea. Neither would Hopkins, a decent public servant who hadn't done anything bad enough to set up a challenger, particularly one from within his own party. The threat of a primary might lead him to voluntarily decide to step aside, but that seemed like wishful thinking.

To get a better sense of what I was in for, I reached out to some friends, neighbors, and Democratic Committee members. My neighbors Chrissy Brown and Bonnie Gestwicki liked the idea of me running for the council seat, both suggesting that Hopkins was nice, but not well-known, which matched my thinking and supported the idea that he might be vulnerable to a competitor.

I also reached out to First District resident Sharon Mitchell, an artist I'd met at the Democratic Committee meeting who owned a boutique and studio in a home once owned by Jervis Langdon, Mark Twain's brother-in-law. She'd grown up in Elmira but had lived most of the past twenty years in Maine, where she'd been appointed by the governor there to do economic development work. She'd moved back to Elmira three years earlier, in 2002, and was now an active member of the Elmira Democratic Committee. I soon learned that she, too, was frustrated and saddened by the state of Elmira's decline over the past two decades.

She told me she was shocked by how badly the city had been treated. She also told me she liked that I was willing to toss my hat in the ring because leadership at all levels needed to change before the city could move forward.

In addition to Sharon, I talked about my idea to run for city council with a few friends at Horigan's Tavern, my favorite local watering hole. As a local attorney, Bill Ogilvie knew a lot of the players in city government and became my regular sounding board when we bumped into each other at the bar. We discussed different scenarios for a possible political campaign and he provided many facts about the active players. Bill told me the kind of campaign I envisioned wouldn't be easy, but he didn't rule out success. Given the state of affairs in the city, he believed such a race was feasible. I took that as a good sign.

These meeting, conversations, and email exchanges with Sharon, Bill, Andy, and others were crucial to my decision-making process because I felt that once I committed to running for the First District seat—and made a public announcement—there would be no turning back. I was thinking about taking on a fellow Democrat and party regulars, putting my political beliefs to the test in the most real way possible. I couldn't tackle it half-assed or purely from a position of anger or ego. I needed objective voices willing to give me their best gut feelings before I took the leap.

But any decision I was about to make hit a sudden fork in the road when Mayor Hughes announced he was resigning. With the incumbent mayor suddenly out of the picture, my original thought of running for mayor was back on the table, turning that Elmira spring into one of the most challenging of my life.

2

# Councilman vs. Mayor

### Pulling together a committee

Throughout late winter and early spring, one thing was clear: I was super motivated to run for office, even if it meant taking on political veterans with plenty of experience. Though I'd never run a campaign, I found myself full of confidence—and some motivating anger—that made me want this more than anything.

So far, I had talked with friends and family about my new ambition so they could tell me the unvarnished truth—and help assure me I wasn't crazy—but the time had come for me to formalize my approach. That meant forming a committee. At the state and national levels, political committees are usually filled with professionals who know the game, how to raise money, and how to shape winning strategies. At the local level and in places like Elmira—particularly in city council races—that's far less common. I never considered professionals as a real option and figured any committee I'd assemble would be filled by volunteers with little or no political experience.

The rationale for bringing together a political committee was, first and foremost, to create a sounding board for my ideas and, later, form the foundation of a formal campaign organization—if I got that far. If possible, I wanted this first informal committee to be a mix of Democrats, Republicans, and independents, people with different backgrounds and talents, and people I could trust.

I immediately thought of Andy; my neighbors Chrissy Brown and Bonnie Gestwicki; my mother, a lifelong Republican who held a PhD;

and even my ex-wife, Nicola Pytell, a libertarian-leaning communications professional with a master's degree. Though it's uncommon, my ex-wife and I maintained a mostly friendly relationship, and I considered her for the committee because she was definitely someone who wouldn't pull any punches when I asked for feedback.

So far, my fledging committee was mostly made up of women, Andy, and me. I also pulled in my stepbrother, Tom Krajci, a graduate of the US Air Force Academy and a smart guy who lived out West. Andy had deep roots in the community and knew people. A lot of people. I always marveled at his ability to come up with names from the not-so-dark recesses of his vast memory. Maybe it was his background as a letter carrier and having to remember one house after another, but he definitely knew who was who in Elmira, and he made a great addition to the team.

From the start, my ad hoc committee weighed in on what was shaping up to be my near-certain run for city council. I emailed them my ideas and got their feedback on a press release I was working on to eventually announce my candidacy. Everyone believed the First District council seat was winnable despite being held by fellow Democrat Bill Hopkins. At this early stage, I was keen to leverage my own communications background to maximize campaign coverage in the local newspaper and on local television news. In my work at RIT, Syracuse University, and Cornell, I'd written hundreds of press releases, produced glossy publications, and done plenty of marketing. Social media was relatively new then—Facebook was just a year old and Twitter wouldn't launch until the following year—so I fundamentally believed that mass media was the best way to spread my message. The only question was when?

By late February, I started putting together a website and talking points about my intent to run for city council even though many political veterans considered the heart of winter too early in the election cycle to make any sort of campaign announcement. Jim Hare and others expressed tentative support for my plan to run for council and challenge Bill Hopkins, but they suggested I hold off on announcing until late spring. With the prospect of a primary, I thought that was a long time to wait. I wanted to get out in front and be the first to announce because I believed it would make news and spark curiosity about my campaign. If I had any advantage at all as a newcomer, it was my media experience. I fundamentally knew that being first was big. Very big. I didn't want to miss out, and I felt any delay in announcing for city council would close an important window of opportunity.

Despite my better instincts—and with a bit more thought—I decided to heed the suggestions of Jim and others and wait until March to make my announcement. That would still be early, but waiting a few weeks seemed reasonable.

The delay gave me some time to more deeply consider my strategy. Instead of announcing my plan to seek the First District council seat outright, I thought it might be more useful to announce I was forming a committee to help me *decide* whether or not to run at all. Admittedly, this was a bit of obfuscation, but by announcing my exploratory committee of Democrats, Republicans, and independents, I'd give the whole idea of my newcomer run a nonpartisan push and simultaneously give Hopkins the news that I was serious about taking him on. I also wanted people to know that it wasn't my ego driving me to run, but a group of similarly concerned citizens who were helping me decide, all while making my intent known. This was an unusual step in local election races, frankly. Politicians on the state and national stages often announce exploratory committees, but not so much on the local level. Most local candidates just announce and move forward. But with the possibility of a primary and the infighting that might result, I wanted to show that I could gather nonpartisan support that could arm my later efforts.

I ran the "exploratory committee" idea by my fledgling committee members, who agreed with the approach, and I prepared to issue a press release on March 13 after our next team meeting. I finished building my website, put the final touches on the announcement, and braced myself for what was to come.

Before that could happen, though, I came down with a case of pneumonia, which quite literally knocked me on my ass. I had never had pneumonia before, and I was surprised by how it made me feel like a weak little old man. I'd been hospitalized for six weeks because of my ulcerative colitis a dozen years earlier, but this was a whole different thing. When I drove to my doctor's office, the car felt heavy, my legs rubbery. I thought maybe I had a bad flu, but my doctor told me otherwise. I was seriously ill, and the pneumonia forced me to miss a week of work at Cornell University.

Instead of going to work or thinking about my council run, I sat in an easy chair in my living room, watched television, and gave my cats more daytime love than they were used to. I continued to think hard about my candidacy, but I didn't have the strength to work on anything at all. Hell, I could barely make dinner for myself, let alone announce a campaign launch.

Though I started to feel a little better after a week or so, I came to the sad conclusion that there was no way I could make my announcement on the mid-March date I'd set. If I didn't have the energy to climb the stairs to my bedroom, how could I possibly handle the inevitable media inquiries? It killed me to postpone for a second time, but pneumonia was clearly in control.

It turned out to be a good thing.

## A sudden twist of fate

As I convalesced at home, some startling news broke. On March 16, Mayor Stephen Hughes announced he was resigning, and his decision to leave Elmira City Hall dominated the *Star-Gazette*'s front page the next morning. Hughes told the newspaper and local television news that March 18 would be his last day in office. For most, it was a sudden and stunning turn of events, but the surprise move had been quietly in the works for weeks.

It actually started back in December, when MT Picture Display Corp., known locally as Toshiba, closed suddenly, leaving about 900 without jobs, including Hughes. With his experience as mayor and at Toshiba, he was able to land a new job as development director for Catholic Charities, a local nonprofit that supports low-income residents and others. Unfortunately for Hughes, Catholic Charities received some of its funding from the City of Elmira's federal Housing and Urban Development (HUD) Block Grant, and under federal law, public officials cannot simultaneously work for an organization receiving HUD funds and hold a public office that decides how that money is spent. Hughes sought a waiver that might allow him to keep the mayor's job, but a March 8 letter from HUD's regional office in Buffalo confirmed it wasn't possible. When presented with the choice of keeping the mayor's job—and the annual salary of $10,350—or the much higher-paying Catholic Charities job, Hughes chose the latter. He had a family to support, and it was the only way to go.

"As far as I'm concerned, he made the proper decision," Third District Councilman John Corsi, the lone Republican on the city council, told the *Star-Gazette*. "Your wife, family, and home come first. I want to wish him well."

Other council members and the city manager said they'd miss Hughes and his leadership, but I wasn't nearly as distraught. Hughes had been in local government nearly half his life, but the meeting he'd had with us about the crack house more than a year earlier had left a bitter taste in my mouth. I wasn't a big fan.

The reality of Hughes's decision slowly started to sink in. After nearly eighteen years in city government—the last seven and a half as mayor—Hughes was out. The next question was who would fulfill the final nine months of his term? Might it be a sitting council member? An interim mayor with designs on running in the fall? According to the newspaper, the Elmira city charter required the city council to name a replacement within thirty days or call a special election. It was anybody's guess what the council would decide.

Immediately upon Hughes's announcement, Deputy Mayor and Fourth District Councilman Terry McLaughlin challenged the wording of the city charter, which said a sitting council member could not fill the interim mayor's job. Despite the city attorney weighing in, Terry argued a sitting member *could* hold the job, and although he didn't put it in so many words, perhaps his role as deputy mayor made him the obvious choice. Other council members were less certain of his argument, and stories about this legal controversy were included in the *Star-Gazette*'s coverage of Hughes's resignation. It was clear to me based on the newspaper's reporting that two or even three sitting council members—including Jim Hare and Terry McLaughlin—had visions of running for mayor that fall.

Still, the fact the incumbent mayor was out and the seat might be open made me belatedly thank pneumonia for keeping me from announcing my run for the First District council seat. The news of Hughes's resignation gave me a renewed flash of possibility: Could I run for mayor myself? For months now, I had committed myself to the smaller council race, but this turn of events was clearly an opportunity. If I'd gone ahead with my original plan to announce a run for council, I'd have been more or less stuck with that decision. Now I still had options. Ironically, pneumonia had opened the door to other options, and I needed to think about what to do. Certainly, any plans I had to announce a run for the city council seat needed to be put off until the dust settled on the mayor's race.

Over the next month, city council members privately huddled over what to do about the open mayor's seat. Hughes had left almost immediately to start his new Catholic Charities job, so the vacancy was real. There wasn't much news coverage of the process, but many were certain the city council members were having a lot of closed-door conversations to come up with a decision within the thirty-day deadline. Calling a special election just seven months ahead of the regular November election seemed like a nonstarter, particularly because it would cost the city as much as $15,000, money it didn't have to spare. But given the jockeying happening on the city council, it was hard to imagine that any current member would give another member a leg up by appointing an interim mayor from among their own. The outcome was anybody's guess.

## Talking it up, again

The mayoral drama added new distraction to my own pending council race, so I pushed out a lot of emails to my team. I wanted to make the best choice and get everything right. I'd already postponed my city council announcement twice, and I felt a sense of urgency to get on with it, if that was what I was going to do. Once the city council made its decision about the open mayor seat, I wanted to be ready to act.

I also used that time to exchange emails with Jim Hare about my plan to run for the First District seat, but I'd given no indication yet that I was pondering a run for mayor. Jim and others in the party suggested I should reach out to the Green and Working Family parties about simultaneously running on those party lines, a common practice that allows a candidate's name to appear on multiple ballot lines.

I wasn't keen on the idea because I wanted to run and be elected as a Democrat, but the multi-line idea was common among many local candidates, as it offered voters reluctant to pull the lever on the main party line an opportunity to support them on one of the others. A vote was a vote, regardless of the party line on the ballot.

The other advantage of running on those party lines was that it would be easier to get on the ballot in the first plate. In New York State, getting on the November ballot requires candidates to collect nominating petition signatures, the required number of which varies based on the number of votes garnered by each party in the previous election. The number for getting the Democratic line for the council seat was not onerous—just a few dozen signatures—but getting the Working Families line for the city council seat would require fewer than ten. That seemed like a low bar to clear to help ensure I got on the ballot at all.

My email exchanges with Jim were particularly helpful because of his vast experience with local politics and elections. He was supportive of my candidacy for the First District seat and told me he thought I could bring a lot of energy to the race. As someone who had been active in Democratic politics for years—and served two terms as mayor—Hare was always strongly motivated to put Democrats in power and energize the party.

"When I say I want to make government work for people I really mean it," Jim told me in an email. "I enjoy the whole process. But I am also aware that we are in a heavy Republican area and as Democrats, we must show our presence, we must put good candidates forward and challenge the power structure. Over the years, I have worked for many candidates and have had many people work on my behalf. I believe I can still motivate, energize, and work."

He said a potential primary in the Chemung County sheriff's race that year was likely to create public competition for the seat in the Republican Party, a competition he saw as an opening for Democrats. The incumbent wasn't running again, and things were heading for a summer showdown. Like many in local, state, and national politics, Jim told me he believed primaries were bad for parties, even relatively minor ones over a city council seat like mine.

"It is interesting to watch the Republicans," Jim wrote. "Absolute power may be affecting them. The potential primary over sheriff is another major rift. Politically, we need to be accentuating the rifts among Republicans, questioning county government decisions rather than competing among ourselves in a primary. Republicans are successful for a number of reasons. They have enrollment, money, and a sympathetic press. But the fact is they are able to keep their disagreements and rivalries behind the scenes. They project competence and organization. I really believe it is the wrong time for us to have an intra-party competition. Quite frankly that is why I have worked for a committee decision on the mayor's race. And I have counseled my council colleagues to handle our disagreements behind the scenes, not at the council table."

It was abundantly clear that Jim didn't like primaries, and he would be certain to use his influence to avoid a Democratic one, regardless of the seat. I knew he wouldn't be shy among fellow Democrats, and I thought he might even put a bug in Hopkins's ear to encourage him to step aside in favor of my candidacy. Whether anyone would listen to him was another story, but while the Republicans grappled with their own sheriff's primary, Jim wanted Democrats to present a united front.

I'd always heard that primaries weren't good for parties, something that's become even more prominent in the modern political era. In Washington, the threat of facing a primary challenge is often enough to get a recalcitrant lawmaker to toe the line. I've since adopted the opposite belief. If you're a good, capable, and communicative incumbent, you shouldn't fear a primary. After all, you're running on your record. If you've done your best, explained your decisions, and worked for your constituents, what do you have to fear? The answer, of course, is a flood of money for your opponent and a fall from power. But in a representative democracy—a concept that's become frayed in the United States—keeping voters front and center should usually mean reelection. If you're out of step, shouldn't that mean someone in the same party with the same core political beliefs who has a closer bond with voters would be better than losing a seat to the opposition? Elective offices shouldn't be sinecures, and to me, primaries represent a powerful way to retain seats, not lose them.

Jim wanted to bring new blood to the Democratic Party, and he saw me as someone who could be energetic and enthusiastic, so he gave me tips on getting out into the community to gain some visibility, including joining a new group of volunteers who were working to clean up litter along the Chemung River. He also suggested I get close to party officials who coordinated things like the Democrat's float in the annual Grove Street Festival, a community event that drew residents—and voters—from the First District and surrounding neighborhoods.

Jim was a great help during this time when I was frankly a bit frantic. His long experience in politics and local government enabled him to offer me concrete local issues to raise and deep insights into how everything worked. In some ways, I was overthinking the whole process, and Jim helped tamp down my anxiety.

Despite Jim's help, I still felt I needed more information about how the whole process worked and what exactly the role of the Democratic Party would be in my council race. Maybe it was the former newspaper reporter in me, but I needed more sources, particularly inside sources like Jim. To that end, I swallowed my pride and decided to approach now-former Mayor Stephen Hughes for advice.

I drove to his home on the city's south side to ask his opinion about the timing of my announcement to run for the First District seat and other aspects of local campaigning.

First, rather than delivering a "pre-announcement," Hughes suggested I simply announce I was running. Though the pre-announcement technique is common in national and state campaigns, he told me a direct announcement is a more genuine, up-front approach in a city council race. He made a good point, though I didn't see my approach as disingenuous, and I felt the "traditional" approach local candidates employed wasn't everything it was cracked up to be.

Second, Hughes said the nature of the city campaigns meant there were built-in blackout periods—weeks and months with little or no media coverage of local candidates. He suggested I shouldn't worry too much about staying in the news from the day of my announcement to the day of the election, but should use that time to get out to meet people. Again, I felt my communications experience gave me a better perspective. There aren't media blackouts, just periods when candidates stop making news. I was a complete unknown, and the longer stretch of media coverage I could get, the better. Yes, it would take work, but I was going to bolt myself to the news no matter what—*and* meet people. To me, the two ideas went hand in hand.

Hughes also suggested I make a call to Bill Hopkins as soon as possible to inform him of my plans to announce my run. He said he anticipated a full slate of Republican contenders this year, and the sooner I could announce, the better. On this point, I agreed. It would be better to face Hopkins and tell him my intent rather than surprise him with a public announcement. It would be a difficult and uncomfortable conversation, for sure, but it needed to be done sooner rather than later.

In my quest for information, I decided to attend a few Elmira City Council meetings to get a handle on what went on, how the meetings were run, and the types of issues they addressed. Before then, I'd never been to City Hall for any reason. I didn't even know where the mayor's office was inside the three-story Beaux Arts building, which stood on the corner of Church and Lake streets.

Council meetings were held in the main City Hall courtroom, a big space on the second floor with a high ceiling, tall windows, wood-paneled walls, and old-fashioned radiators that made distinct knocking sounds when steam was rising. The mayor and council members sat behind tables more regularly used by prosecutors and defense attorneys during court sessions. The tables were pushed together end to end for city meetings, and behind them was the elevated judge's bench, which had wing desks for the clerk and court witnesses. Standing between the tables and gallery was a low wooden rail with two swinging gates.

I tried to picture myself working on the business side of the rail in this stately room, but I couldn't quite do it. I sat quietly and watched the clerk call the roll before the mayor and council set to work, but despite having a copy of the agenda in my hands, I often found the meetings hard to follow. Council members voted by some predetermined order, not in the order in which they were seated, and they voted on a consent agenda—all the items they agreed on—in one fell swoop. I thought if I had a chance to run the meetings, I'd try to ease some of the confusion by explaining council actions in a way audience members, many of whom were first-time attendees, and the young reporters could better understand.

Most city council meetings were conducted before sparse gatherings of spectators, usually residents or people with business before the city. The clerk read aloud each agenda item, the mayor led discussion, and the clerk called the role for council votes. As a reporter, I'd covered many such municipal meetings, and each has its own unique feel and cadence. The officials were comfortable and familiar with what was going on, but as a spectator I was a little lost, like someone going into the theater for a movie that was already half over.

I'd been curious to see how Hughes, who was still mayor then, the council, and city manager interacted with each other and the audience members, and found them to be an interesting bunch. There was the occasional descent into minutiae that the mayor shut down with a terse "Let's move on." Some members of the council remained mostly silent; others took the opportunity to use the floor to give short speeches or even admonish the owner of the hockey arena, the county, or their peers, playing a bit to the newspaper and television reporters who sat listening.

When I went to those meetings, I often had the sense that my silent attendance made some on the council curious and wonder who I was and what I was up to.

Strategically, I considered attending council meetings a good thing. It helped make me visible, and I felt the need to show the council members, city manager, and others I was serious, not just a crank.

## Challenging an incumbent

It was now mid-April, and though Hughes had left the mayor's office vacant less than three weeks earlier, there was little news about a replacement until the thirty-day deadline for the council to act was nearly up.

A story appeared in the April 10 *Star-Gazette* about the mayoral drama, and the article confirmed that city council members would not appoint one of their own to replace Hughes. A close reading of the charter by the city attorney made it clear that wasn't an option, though Deputy Mayor McLaughlin continued to argue his case.

In the same story, Fifth District Councilman Daniel Royle, a three-term incumbent and a Democrat, told the newspaper he was considering a run for mayor, and many weren't counting out Jim Hare either. There was still no decision on who might become interim mayor.

Still, it was well into April and no one from the Democratic or Republican parties had formally announced his or her intent to run for mayor or any other city council seat that fall. Regardless, I felt the clock ticking on my own announcement for the First District council race. I wasn't sure if I should invite the media to an event or if I should just send a press release and follow up with calls. In retrospect, this was part of my hedge. I was intimidated by the idea of holding a press conference and being on the other side of the podium. As a reporter, I'd covered plenty of press conferences, but I'd never been the subject of one. I eventually decided a press conference was best and knew it would've been a massive mistake to miss out on a chance to appear in person. A press release might be fine for the newspaper, but television news wanted video too. Since I was going to rely on the media to become better known, I needed to maximize whatever coverage I'd get.

For many local candidates announcing election bids, the press release was their whole ball of wax. They'd send out an announcement, and the newspaper and television stations would pick it up and run a short item. The problem with this approach is that it gives the candidate much less visibility. If the newspaper has an older stock photo, they'll maybe use that with a candidate's announcement. On television, there might be no video or picture at all, just an anchor reading an item and moving on. I didn't want that.

Instead, I planned to issue a news advisory, a very short release that only hinted at what was going to be announced without giving away the full story. News reporters would either have to attend or miss the story entirely.

Before any of that happened, though, I needed to put in a call to Bill Hopkins to let him know I was looking to challenge him for the First District seat. This was one of my first big challenges: telling a sitting elected official I was gunning for him. I admit, it was pretty bold, but I was eager and motivated. I held no personal animus toward Hopkins, but he was standing in the spot I wanted. I knew the professional thing to do was to confront him, but the thought of it made me nervous. I assumed

Hopkins would not be happy about an upstart like me horning in on him and downplaying his record—and the city's record—so I braced myself for a tough conversation. I thought about what I was going to say, framing in my mind the same arguments I would use in my campaign. I would be polite, but make clear that I wanted to make city government more open and accountable.

I started by trying to reach Hopkins by phone, leaving messages asking him to call me back, but several days passed without any response. If I'd been him, I probably wouldn't have been too quick to call me back either. Still, it made me wonder if he was too angry to call or perhaps was using the time to weigh his options.

While I waited, I spoke to the head of the City Democratic Committee, who told me he thought Hopkins *would* run. The more time passed without word from Hopkins, the more I got that feeling too. My pessimistic side assumed the worst: that Hopkins would not bow out quietly.

With my phone not ringing, I decided to confront Hopkins in person after the next city council meeting. When I approached him, he remembered me from the crack house meeting, and I thanked him for his efforts back then before quickly shifting the conversation to his reelection plans. By then, I'd been making some noise about running with Hare, Hughes, the Democratic Committee chairs, and others, and Hopkins didn't seem too taken aback by my question. He'd certainly heard rumblings.

Surprisingly, he told me he would probably *not* run for a fourth term, hedging a little by explaining he still had issues he wanted to address before leaving office at the end of December. Though he didn't come out and say for certain, I was happy with his "probably." I'm not sure he was happy with the pressure I was putting on him, but our exchange was cordial, and I left feeling that if Hopkins bowed out, I could pursue the First District seat without a primary and maybe even with his support.

As it happened, that was too much to wish for.


## Changing horses

Timing of my First District council race announcement remained an open question, and now that I had recovered from pneumonia and made Hopkins aware of my plans, I thought April 18 would be a good day to announce. It was still considered a little early, but I'd postponed twice already. I wanted to be first out of the gate, put pressure on Hopkins to make a decision one way or another, and beat any Republican to the punch.

The third time would *not* be the charm.

As foreshadowed by the *Star-Gazette* story the previous Sunday, the Elmira City Council announced April 15 that it would, indeed, appoint an interim mayor. They would make it official by voting to approve their choice at their April 18 meeting. I just could *not* catch a break. Each time I chose a date to announce my run for the First District seat, something outside my control blew it out of the water.

It had taken a full month since Hughes's resignation for the council to announce it would not call a special election and instead would appoint an interim mayor. William O'Brien, a local municipal attorney whose father had served as a city councilman years earlier, was their choice. O'Brien, a Democrat, was in his early fifties and had deep ties to the city. He knew how local government worked and had served as attorney for the villages of Elmira Heights and Wellsburg, jobs he gave up to become Elmira's interim mayor.

O'Brien was a solid, safe choice to fill out the remaining months of Hughes's term, and he was especially appealing to council members who were considering their own runs for mayor because O'Brien had made it clear he would not run in the fall to make the job permanent.

That little nugget was big news to me. The council had telegraphed it would opt to appoint an interim mayor, but I hadn't connected the dots to someone like O'Brien serving now *and* ruling out a run later. In retrospect, given the mayor's race chatter among three sitting council members, it should've been obvious to me they'd choose a placeholder for the job, not a permanent replacement who might later emerge as a candidate. I was pretty naive and wrongly presumed whomever they chose would be the standard-bearer in the fall election and difficult to challenge. But now there was no standard-bearer. The mayor's race was wide open.

It still didn't fully sink in. I mostly thought of it in terms of my announcement, and I agreed when Chrissy reminded me that the city council's mayoral drama and its upcoming vote on appointing an interim mayor would overshadow my small race.

"The mayoral stuff WILL DOMINATE," she wrote to me. "If this is the case, it seems you must announce this week."

Jim Hare and Cindy Emmer, the county committee chair, advised the opposite. They said mayoral news would bury any announcement I might make and that I should announce after all that. I was facing yet another delay, but I knew the timing was out of my control again, and waiting was the best option.

Then it finally dawned on me. Could all these delays be a *good* thing?

Given all that had happened since Hughes resigned, perhaps my original intent of running for mayor could be taken off the back burner. After all, a big part of my aim in running for office in the first place was to have a soapbox to more openly promote the city, its work, and my Democratic ideals. Sure, one or more of the sitting councilmen would likely put themselves forward, but now they wouldn't be able to carry the added political benefit of actually holding the mayor's job in the meantime. Of course, Jim had been mayor before, but none of the other council members had—and would not be able to claim that mantle now.

As I thought about it, I didn't think any of the likely Democratic candidates would represent the change I was after and would really just represent the status quo. Despite my almost overwhelming inexperience, I felt certain the political winds were blowing away from the incumbents. People wanted change. Putting forward a candidate with incumbent baggage might very well hand the mayor's seat to an as-yet unnamed Republican.

I was about to put off announcing my First District run for a third time, but now I had an even bigger decision to make. Should I run for the city council seat, which seemed a safe first foray into politics, or go right for mayor? It was a tall order. I was a complete unknown with few ties to the party, no name recognition to speak of, and no direct experience running a political campaign. Unlike Hopkins—who was still on the fence—the other councilmen with eyes on the mayor's seat surely wouldn't just voluntarily withdraw, clap me on the back, and wish me good luck. No, this would be very different—and much easier to lose.

I wanted to hear what my committee thought of me switching horses.

"If Bill O'Brien is indeed an apolitical choice—meaning he won't be seeking to run for the mayor's office in the fall—it sets up a wide open field," I wrote to my team. "That's *very* tempting to me and, as you know, fits with my original intent. It's a lot more work, though, and represents a whole different kind of campaign."

That last bit was an understatement.

After spending months giving singular focus to the First District seat (and patiently putting up with my indecision and sometimes misplaced verve), it was a bit of a shock to my committee to start thinking about the much larger mayor's race. I'd been hesitant to run a primary against

Hopkins, and now I was considering running against one or more experienced incumbent councilmen, perhaps even former Mayor Hare himself. Was I crazy to even think it?

"My gut reaction is to run for City Council first," Bonnie wrote to me. "I believe you can win against [Hopkins] in the primary and that you will be a formidable candidate against a Republican."

Others expressed similar feelings, and I knew switching to a much larger campaign would be a challenge. But I also believed that rarely had the stars aligned in such a way to give an outsider like me a serious chance of becoming mayor. Regardless of what I'd decide, I knew my friends, family, and team would support me, so I asked myself, "What do *you* really want?"

The answer was clear: I wanted to run for mayor.

I was completely bullheaded when it came to shaking up the Democratic Party, and I wasn't going to let Jim or others dissuade me on party grounds alone. Though going from zero to mayor was a tall order, I just could not shake off the idea. I'd learned a lot about local politics over the past few months, and instead of discouraging me, it did the opposite. I'd gotten to know many of the players and felt I had just as much to offer voters as anyone else. The work didn't frighten me either. I was going to do it, damn it. I was going to run for mayor.

My mom and stepfather were among the first to hear my news when I took the opportunity to tell them over dinner at their place one evening in late April. They'd known I was planning to run for city council, but this was new. I'd never told them about my earlier desire to run for mayor, so my decision came as a shock. Still, they calmly and warmly expressed their support, and I knew I could count on them. It wasn't until a few years later that my mother told me what she was *really* thinking when I told her the news.

"You could've knocked me over with a feather," she said.

3

# Wooing the Party

## A conversation with a Democratic heavyweight

Shortly after making my decision to run for mayor, my mother offered me the name of prominent local attorney Carl Hayden, who had served as chancellor of the State University of New York State Board of Regents and was well connected in state and national Democratic politics. Just a few years earlier, he had hosted then-First Lady Hillary Clinton at his Elmira home before her first run for US Senate. Though I didn't know him, I thought Hayden might have a few insights on my local run for mayor.

I met Hayden at his Elmira office, and I was impressed by his confident yet somehow laid-back style. He was tall, trim, and had a shock of gray hair that gave him an air of sophistication. He was welcoming, but that first meeting felt a little stilted to me. While we chatted about my potential race for mayor, I got the sense Hayden was looking me over and studying the type of person I was. I figured that as an attorney, he was used to sizing people up, and I mostly sensed ambivalence. He offered me neither great support nor grave doubt, but he did provide one piece of advice: Get out from behind my mother.

I took Hayden's suggestion to mean I shouldn't be seen having my mother open doors for me. It struck me as an odd way to end the conversation. Yes, my mother worked on my campaign, but she was by no means shaping it—or my actions. She'd merely given me Hayden's name and suggested I have a chat with him. I certainly wasn't hanging onto her apron strings. She had been head of human resources for the local Aetna

Life & Casualty payment processing center and a respected professional in her own right. I valued her advice, but Hayden made me feel that any amount of reliance on her—at least publicly—would be a bad thing.

Hayden was a powerful guy with lots of powerful connections, but I didn't exactly feel charmed after our conversation. I'd thought it was a good idea to talk with powerful people like him, but I couldn't help feeling that he thought I "wasn't the guy." Later, I'd learn that Hayden was the attorney for the City of Elmira police union, which would potentially place us on opposite sides of the bargaining table if I were to become mayor. I was a naive newcomer, Hayden was connected, and what I was witnessing was the real-time reaction of one of the local power brokers to my upstart candidacy. I was an unknown, a wild card, and I was a long shot.

Of course, that chess-like way of thinking about politics wasn't my thing at all. I wasn't completely unaware of the political swirl, but at the same time I didn't want to become a maneuvering political operator. My approach was straightforward, and I was uninterested in gamesmanship. Yes, I wanted to be mayor, but to me it was about public service, not political power. I certainly was no threat to Hayden, but I was an unknown quantity. I suppose that made me a bit of a curiosity and, for some, the face of a potential shift away from the status quo.

Hayden certainly wasn't alone in being seen as an Elmira power broker. Though he wasn't active in the local Democratic Committee, it was well-known that he had connections and money. On the Republican side, a lot of political power lay at the feet of the O'Mara family and patriarch John O'Mara, another prominent Elmira attorney. He had connections with then-Governor George Pataki and had, among other thing, gotten his thirty-five-year-old son, Thomas, appointed as interim Chemung County district attorney to fill a vacancy. John O'Mara also supported other local Republican candidates and elected officials, including Assemblyman George Winner, and was generally known as the kingmaker on that side of the aisle. O'Mara had helped his son run for district attorney, a race he lost to longtime Assistant DA John Trice in what would become a major intra-party feud.

I'd never met John O'Mara, but I knew he would be working behind the scenes to help elect as many local Republicans as possible. Despite that—and his real or perceived power—I avoided dwelling on men like him and Hayden. In many ways, O'Mara was the type of political operator I was trying to get rid of. As a political observer, I saw the damage political wheeling and dealing had done to the city. I hated gamesmanship or horse-trading for favors at work, in politics, or in personal relationships.

To me and others, that sort of governing smacked of a few powerful people sitting in private rooms making decisions for the entire community. That sort of thing is all too common in politics, of course, but I was damned if I was going to play that game.

In those early days of the campaign, Andy and I actively decided not to pay much attention to these guys. I wasn't naive enough to think there wouldn't be hurdles to leap over in dealing with what we called the local Powerful White Men, but we also put them in the "one vote" category. That is, they were likely to pour energy and money into efforts to defeat us, but each of them had only one vote—like the rest of us.


## Jockeying for position

What concerned me more were the other potential candidates for the Democratic nomination for mayor. By now, it was clear that both Daniel Royle, a three-term city councilman and store manager from the city's south side, and Jim Hare, a former two-term mayor and current city councilman, were interested. Taking them on in a three-man primary didn't seem workable, but it was shaping up that way.

In early May, Andy thought it would be a good idea for us to sit down, graciously, with Jim to talk about the mayor's race. Andy knew Jim better than I did, so it made sense for him to reach out for an in-person meeting. Jim agreed, and we went to his home on Elmira's south side to chat.

Jim welcomed us in his usual affable way, and Andy started the conversation by saying he and I had an ambition to make Democrats more prominent and successful. He also said we weren't happy with the status quo and wanted to inject some new blood and new ideas now, not later. I gave Jim my elevator speech, telling him I planned to leverage my background in communications to mount a strong, visible campaign and that I had the right experience for the moment to keep a Democrat in the mayor's seat.

Jim listened and told us he thought it would be better if we formed an alliance—him running for mayor, me running for the First District council seat—to create the best of both worlds. His experience and my newcomer energy, he said, would make us hard to beat. He'd like the idea of my running for city council, but clearly he was not keen on me running for mayor. He wanted it, and he was the professional in the room. Andy and I also knew that, despite Jim's ability to repeatedly get elected to the Sixth District council seat, his stock wasn't as high for a citywide mayor's race. Yes, he'd run a close race for State Assembly, but when it came to city voters, many felt he'd been there and done that. Many people we talked to didn't think he was ripe for a comeback.

Neither Andy nor I thought it would be an easy meeting, and it wasn't. Jim was not going to bow out quickly or gracefully. We'd made our points, but they weren't enough to convince Jim to forfeit his own ambitions. As a result, if I were to make a run for mayor, Jim would be right there too.

After the meeting, Jim and I exchanged a few emails in which we each laid out our feelings on the mayor's race. I respected him, but I was determined to make the case for change. It was ironic because when he challenged four-year incumbent Mayor Stephen Fesh Jr. in 1987 and won, Jim had run on the idea of change too.

Jim had won that election 4,915 to 2,942, or 63 percent of the vote, by sweeping twenty-seven of the twenty-nine city election districts. More than 8,200 voters turned out, and Jim told the *Star-Gazette*, "There were people who liked Jim Hare, people who didn't like Steve Fesh, and people who may have liked both of them, but felt it was time for a change in the city."

Twenty years later, Jim perhaps envisioned similar success and reiterated the benefits of my seeking the First District seat, with him as mayor. He saw that combination as the best way to leverage our strengths while avoiding what he thought would be a destructive Democratic primary. He staunchly believed a primary would be bad for the party, but I had my doubts when I emailed him afterward. His reply told me I'd gotten it right.

"I appreciate the note and the talk," he wrote. "I do believe we could make a strong team. I have followed up our talk with a number of conversations. I sincerely believe I am the strongest candidate and that a primary would be unhealthy. I have always welcomed new ideas, fresh blood, and enthusiasm. We should build an effective and exciting team. But I do value your friendship."

I thought the cordial nature of our exchanges was a good sign, and they continued when he wrote me a longer follow-up email the next day:

> After my response to your e-mail I had some other thoughts. Let me share them. As you may realize, I am passionate about politics and government. When I say I want to make government work for people I really mean it. I enjoy the whole process. But I am also aware that we are in a heavy Republican area and as Democrats we must show our presence, we must put good candidates forward and challenge the power structure. Over the years I have

worked for many candidates and have had many people work on my behalf. I believe I can still motivate, energize and work.

It is interesting to watch the Republicans. Absolute power may be affecting them. The O'Mara people are watching Trice closely, keeping track of his record, I have that on good authority. The potential primary over sheriff is another major rift. Politically, we need to be accentuating the rifts among Republicans, questioning county government decisions rather than competing amongst ourselves in a primary. Republicans are successful for a number of reasons. They have enrollment, money and a sympathetic press. But the fact is they are able to keep their disagreements and rivalries behind the scenes. They project competence and organization. With Trice and O'Mara and now the sheriff's race, that aura breaks down a bit. I really believe it is the wrong time for us to have an intra-party competition. Quite frankly, that is why I have worked for a committee decision on the mayor's race. And I have counseled my council colleagues to handle our disagreements behind the scenes not at the council table.

Nothing breeds success like success. Winning and building is what we need to do. Quite frankly, I have urged Cindy [Emmer] to write a letter or two pointing out the dispute in the Republican Party. Wish we had a sheriff's candidate. If we have a primary, we distract from Republican disarray when we could be projecting that we have it together. The Republican mayoral candidate is right in the middle of that fight having publicly endorsed one candidate. Well, those are some thoughts.

In reading Jim's words, I couldn't wholly disagree with many of his points. I'd always heard that primaries were bad for a party, but not having been through one, I wasn't fully convinced. *Not* having a primary struck me as more backroom dealing, where a few party insiders made choices that should be left to voters. Jim even alluded to this approach by mentioning how he and party insiders on city council were maneuvering to put forward a mayoral candidate.

I wrote back to Hare, laying out my approach:

You raise some great points about the Republicans. I completely understand your call for unity. In fact, the Republican schism is well worth exploiting. Many in the community wonder why it hasn't been exploited already. We should be hammering them, and people want us to be hammering them. Rarely has the opportunity been greater to take them on—not because of their party, but because of their lack of leadership and progress.

With that said, I have no doubt that you have strong party support. I can't fill the seats at the committee meeting later this month like you can, and I can't point to years of party involvement, or even a record of service on the council. All I can point to is the future, my own experience, what I believe is possible, and my deeply held belief of what people tell me they want: something new. People are just itching for change—big change. And as I said Tuesday night, though people see you as motivated, energetic and hard-working, they know the one thing you're not is new. In the Assembly race, yes, and they tell me so; but for mayor, no. I honestly wish it were different.

Here's what I envision: I see a Hare-Tonello partnership that plays to each of our strengths. I am new, energetic, and I think you'll agree, capable of capturing people's attention and articulating a clear message. I have nearly 20 years of experience working for large corporations, small businesses, and universities. I'm a media veteran, having worked as a reporter, editor, and media relations professional. I understand and rode the technology boom of the 1990s to great success. I have been a change-agent all my life and I have hard evidence to point to real successes and risk-taking.

You are a master politician, an astute observer of the local scene, and an experienced public servant. Your resume on that score is hard to match. With me as mayor and you as councilman, we get to work that mix to its greatest effect. If I were to become mayor, you would be my closet advisor and ally, the man standing closest to me, both literally and figuratively. We would not only strike a powerful balance, but also show that the Democrats are willing to put the city before personal ambition. That's a powerful notion that will do more to boost us than anything else we or the Republicans might do in this campaign season.

I haven't asked for your support before, but I am now. Your support for my bid for mayor will help avoid a party split and deliver the unity you speak of. I believe we can retain the

Democratic seat in the First District, take a hard run at the Second and Third and keep a lock on the rest. Turnover this year is inevitable; minimizing it, as you suggest, should be a top priority.

I'm asking a lot and we'd be taking a risk, I know, but I believe it's what city residents of all stripes want.

I was making a big ask, particularly knowing that Jim was *the* guy in local Democratic politics. He'd just run for state Assembly and was well-known. He wasn't a wealthy attorney like Hayden or O'Mara, but he had his thumb on the scale when it came to pushing the committee and his ideas about local races. I was focused, however, and I was determined to break up the clubby local politics that kept most Elmirans on the sidelines.

Jim wrote a brief email back.

"Unfortunately our competition for this office will result in the elimination of one of us from the scene," he wrote. "I am sorry that will happen. A primary serves no positive purpose for the cause."

I could not agree with him there. I definitely didn't feel the same way Jim and others did about potential ill effects of primaries, and, as a newcomer, I saw only the upside. Yes, it would be a lot of work, but I was tired of hearing from long-standing party members that this was the way things were done. Unity was everything, they said. For whom? The approach served party insiders, not voters, and I wasn't going to give in.

## Refusing to "wait my turn"

All this chatter about a primary started to stir up Democratic Committee members, and people started taking sides. Some were on my side, and allies like Andy, Sharon, and others did not want the so-called veterans to be forcing their agenda. Most, however, wanted the old ways to prevail. After all, many had served as committee members for years, waiting their turns to move up to council and even county legislature races. They'd put in their time, and my candidacy was as much an unknown as it was a breakdown in the way things always were. If I was able to come in and blow that up, they wouldn't be happy. All the time they'd spent toeing the line—reluctantly or not—would mean change and new rules. As a result, many told me to "wait my turn," to get in line and wait for the party gears to continue their slow turn.

Despite the pressure, I refused. I'd read my high school civics book back in the day, and nowhere did it say citizens looking to effect change must wait to run for office or kneel down to the party regulars. Besides, party committees—Democratic, Republican, or any other—represented the feelings of a few dozen people, not thousands of registered voters. Who made up the rule that the party, not average citizens, were in charge? It frustrated me to no end, and it left Andy and me feeling even more undeterred. We were digging in for a fight because our frustration with the national Democratic Party had pushed us to make changes *now*, not in a few years. Our single-minded determination was making people in the party mad, but as far as we were concerned, the local party was not just holding us back, but holding back the entire city.

By mid-April, it was clear that Jim was not going to quietly step away, and it was clear, too, that Fifth District Councilman Daniel Royle, also a Democrat, was planning his own campaign for mayor. That made three of us, but even at this early stage, I felt the incumbents were on the wrong side of the issues. After talking informally with so many different people, it was clear in my heart that voters wanted change. I didn't have the incumbents' experience, but the more Andy and I talked and listened, the more we felt Jim and Dan couldn't win.

Dan Royle had apparently won the favor of many in the Democratic Committee's internal jockeying, with Jim Hare popular among many too because he not only had been around—and had been successfully elected—but had personally recruited many of the local party's members. Again, they had followed his lead and patiently waited their turns. Royle was completing his third term on the city council, and though he was by no means well-known as a result, he had a track record. In the eyes of the committee, he'd put in his time. I'm sure some were unhappy that Jim was getting in Dan's way too, but they deferred to him and the well-known party rules.

In a late April committee meeting, acting Mayor Bill O'Brien attended, a welcome contrast to his predecessor. It was the first time in years that the siting Democratic mayor had participated in a meeting, and I was impressed that he made the effort. O'Brien was well-spoken, calm, and even-keeled, but he, too, didn't like the idea of a primary. He voiced the same reasons Andy and I had heard repeated time and again: A primary would be bad for the party. Without throwing his weight behind Jim, Dan, or me, he urged us to work it out. Others at the meeting agreed. Hell, I agreed too. I wanted Jim and Dan to step aside and let me run, but that was a mere pipe dream and way too much to ask. Egos were at stake along with pride and ambition. Including my own.

## A sudden dropout

Over the next few weeks, Jim and I exchanged more emails, each becoming more heated. It was getting close to crunch time, when the party would announce its slate of candidates. A few days after that, committee members would start canvassing neighborhoods to collect signatures for nominating petitions. With three of us vying for mayor, the party was unsettled, but I had my heels deeply dug in, and I wasn't going anywhere. I was convinced either Jim or Dan would lose to the as-yet unnamed Republican candidate.

I tried not to dwell on the turmoil and instead used my time to overhaul my campaign website and announcement. Gone now was my Tonello for Council site, replaced with a new Tonello for Mayor site. I hadn't yet made any of it public and kept it all very quiet and viewable only by members of my own team. My news experience told me that any leak or trickle would be bad, so I needed everything to remain on the down-low until the day I announced.

In planning the website and my announcement, I was careful not to make specific reference to any of my potential competitors or the six Democratic incumbents on city council. I did make it clear, however, that I represented a change. I also recast the job of mayor from political leader to community leader. I argued that the mayor's primary job was to communicate, and who better to serve as mayor than a professional communicator? I was working to redefine the role around my strengths and experience, feeling I needed to give voters a good sense of how and why I'd be the best choice.

This proved to be an effective strategy that helped my team and me frame my differences and highlight my credentials. I was a former journalist with lots of experience with the media, corporate communications, publications, and more, and I wanted to cater to voters who shared my frustrations with the city's lack of transparency. If I could get that message across, I'd have a fighting chance.

As spring bloomed in Elmira, with trees sprouting leaves and daffodils and other flowers poking out of the ground, it was clear that the May 19 meeting of the full Democratic Committee would be a rollicking affair. They would endorse a candidate for mayor—despite a potential primary—and committee members would get their packets of nominating petitions for the canvassing that started in June.

Jim and I continued to talk, and I spoke with Dan Royle too. He clearly wasn't going anywhere, but my main concern was Jim. He had the experience and party leverage behind him.

A few weeks before the committee was set to meet, we had one of our last calls of the pre-campaign season. I happened to be back at the Euclid Avenue home I'd shared with my ex-wife, feeding her cats while she was away. After dishing out food and scooping litter boxes, I was playing with the cats when my cellphone rang. Jim was calling to offer a last-ditch truce of sorts, urging me to run for the city council seat. I wandered into the yard, pacing back and forth and giving the cats apologetic looks as we argued, but I again refused what Jim was asking. I was going to run and primary him and Royle if necessary.

Jim grew angry. Though it had been less than six months since we'd first met, I was going toe to toe with him, and that affable first meeting in the hardware store was now a distant memory. Who the hell did I think I was? The angrier he got, the calmer I got, a technique I developed growing up as one of seven children with three siblings and three stepbrothers. I'd come to learn to moderate and time my responses in that crowd and also learned I could win arguments by simply remaining calm. When my brothers lost their tempers, I worked to hold mine. I did that now with Jim.

In the heat of the call, he finally paused and told me that, for the good of the party, he was out.

I was stunned. I mean, we'd gone at it hammer and tongs for more than a month, and Jim had suddenly—just like that—taken himself out of the race for mayor.

Before hanging up, Jim also told me he'd be backing Dan Royle in the race. I'm sure he also told me my ambition was doing damage to the party, but I was too taken aback by his decision to drop out to remember anything more. I'd held my ground against the former mayor and a political veteran, and I was still standing.

When the call with Jim ended, I dialed Andy to tell him the news. I was still pacing among the cats wandering around my ex's backyard, simultaneously feeling the thrill of Jim's decision and an all-new sensation: I might actually be able to win this thing. I hadn't really admitted to myself until that moment just how formidable a race against Jim would've been. I'd been dreading it without expressing it out loud or in so many words. Without him in the race, I saw a much clearer path to victory. Dan was a three-term councilman, but he was a relative unknown. I felt sure he'd be easier to defeat in a primary than Jim. Whether or not that was true was debatable, but I'd apparently harbored real doubts about challenging Jim. Now that wouldn't happen, and I was elated—and filled with an overwhelming thought: Be careful what you wish for.

4

# Announcement Days

## The campaign season heats up

With Jim telling me he was out of the race, I would avoid taking on *the* man, but not his political power. He'd told me he'd be backing Dan Royle, and I knew he would push the Democratic Committee to endorse Dan at the May 19 meeting. Jim knew how to work the levers to make things happen, and he was convinced—and able to convince others—that a primary would be bad for the party. I knew he'd do everything he could to avoid that, including encouraging the city committee to endorse a candidate, even though it was clear there would be a primary. Not only was he looking to nip my candidacy in the bud, but now he'd become angry with me. To him, I was an ambitious upstart, and I felt certain any misgivings he had would only add to his determination to defeat me and, perhaps, put me in my place.

Jim remained publicly undecided on the mayoral race as late as May 9, when Republican Daniel Mandell Jr. announced his candidacy. Dan Mandell was superintendent of the Chemung County Jail, which was part of the Chemung County Sheriff's Department, and he was chairman of the city's Republican Committee. He had apparently given the *Star-Gazette* his full campaign announcement because the story about his candidacy appeared on the day *of* his announcement, something I always tried to avoid. As a result, there was no coverage in the paper the following day from his actual press conference. Still, television had covered the story, and an item appeared at the bottom of the front page of the newspaper in which Mandell said he'd been planning to run even before Hughes dropped out months earlier.

"Actually, I was going to run against Steve," Mandell told the newspaper. "I've been tossing it around the last couple of years, actually. The city needs a change. I feel I can lead us in the right direction, not only now but in the future."

The article also quoted Jim, who told the paper he hadn't yet made up his own mind about running, but added, not surprisingly, that Mandell wasn't the best man for the job.

"Danny's a nice guy," Jim told the paper. "I think he's got built-in conflicts, being in a paid supervisory position with the county. I think he's at a disadvantage. I am available, and I've made that clear to people. It's just a process of sorting things out. There have been other people interested."

It was interesting to read between the lines of this and other stories, and I read and reread each one as candidates started to announce their runs. Jim's "sorting things out" comment struck me as more insider baseball, with Jim intimating that Democratic incumbents and party members were jockeying and deciding. I'm sure the Republicans had done the same thing, though Dan Mandell had been the standard-bearer for some time as head of his party's city committee. It also didn't hurt that his father—ironically, a registered Democrat—owned Mandell's Restaurant, a popular place on Elmira's south side. As a result, Dan Mandell had much more name recognition than Royle or I did, that was for sure.

Two days later, Democratic members of the Elmira City Council rallied around Dan Royle, and he announced his candidacy for mayor at Brand Park, a large, tree-filled twenty-two acres along the Chemung River on Elmira's south side. It was also in the Fifth District, where he'd successfully run for council three times. The lead paragraph in the story that appeared in the next morning's *Star-Gazette* said, "The Democratic members of Elmira City Council have chosen their next mayoral candidate, sending 5th District Councilman Daniel S. Royle to claim the seat."

With Mandell coming forward, my team hadn't quite anticipated Royle's announcement, and I was surprised by how the newspaper story was framed. First, Dan Royle made his announcement well before the Democratic Committee meeting and any potential endorsement. I figured it was a tactic to force the issue, and not a bad one at that, but it sounded like insider politics to say the council members had essentially chosen one of their own. That felt pretty arrogant to me and seemed like something I could exploit later on. Royle told the newspaper his agenda would include revitalizing downtown, improving infrastructure, and finding new ways to increase city revenue without raising taxes. He also made a pitch for running a clean campaign. "Finally," he told the newspaper, "we must pull together, try not to personalize this election, but share ideas and ways to move the city forward."

I thought he positioned himself well, and I agreed with that last bit, but I also felt it was a roundabout way to downplay a primary. It wasn't surprising that Jim was quoted in the same story, stating that he'd previously expressed interest in running for mayor, but he "called himself a team player and felt Royle was the right choice for Democrats."

"There is a freshness about Dan," Jim told the newspaper. "He has a fresh enthusiasm as he takes on a new challenge."

This, too, I read as a dig against me, though there was no mention of any dissension among Democrats or hint of a potential primary. However, the reporter also reached out to city Republican Committee Chairman David Brown, who told the paper, "Dan Royle is personally responsible for last year's 3 percent (property) tax increase."

Not surprisingly, Jim was quoted in both newspaper stories about the mayoral announcements. It definitely spoke to his recognition as a party insider and someone to reckon with.

Two days later, Jim made it official that he was out of the mayor's race when he announced his plan to seek another term representing Elmira's Sixth Ward. "In my 22 years on the council," Jim told the *Star-Gazette*, "I have fought to improve the quality of life in the neighborhoods and in our city. I want to be involved in making Elmira a better place to live."

Around the same time, Bill Hopkins made it public that he would not seek a fourth term, and Bill Knapp, a Democratic committee member from the First District, announced his plans to run for the seat I'd been targeting. If I'd known Bill was dropping out, it wouldn't have changed my mind. I was determined to run for mayor.

Still, Jim's long experience and standing in local politics could not be taken lightly. Twenty-two years was a long time. Hell, I was just a teenager when he'd started. Still, he'd backed down from running for mayor, and that at least was something for my team to savor.


## Working the phones and committee members

To blunt some of Jim's efforts to support Dan Royle, Sharon, Andy, other members of my team, and I agreed I needed to make a personal pitch to the nearly forty city committee members who could vote to endorse a mayoral candidate at the May 19 meeting. I'd give them my elevator pitch, listen to their perspectives, and try to garner as much support as I could ahead of the meeting.

With Royle already an announced candidate, my goal was to shift support to my side for the committee's endorsement vote. Failing that, the next best thing was to encourage the committee to vote against endorsing any candidate. After all, I reasoned, why should a handful of party members make a decision better left to voters? By endorsing only one of two primary candidates, wouldn't voters see that as more divisive than not? What message did they want to send? I believed the Democratic Committee should be seen to favor voters' opinions over their own and not put their thumbs on the scale before the race even began. Of course I was pretty naive and idealistic, but I truly wanted this approach to succeed, not simply politics as usual.

I got the list of committeemen and women, sat down at my dining room table, and started making calls. Most were polite conversations, and it was clear that I had some support, but even clearer that most sided with Dan Royle. He'd put in the time, they told me. It was his turn. Jim was behind him, and Jim knew best. It was frustrating, for sure. The party machinery was doing the opposite of what Sharon, Andy, and I believed was right: They were shutting down newcomers, and they were doing the same old thing over and over again, expecting a different result.

Still, I pressed on into the evening of May 18, with the few waning hours before the Democratic Committee meeting offering my last chance to change minds. Each call was lasting about ten minutes or less, and I did the math. I'd need these calls to be brief and to the point if I was going to get to everyone. I wouldn't shut anyone down who wanted to talk longer, but time was finite and the urgency real. With that in mind, I went down the list, building some momentum, honing my pitch, and being as agreeable as possible. I wasn't out to tar the incumbent elected officials; I just wanted to breathe some new life into the Democratic Party and the city.

It was a delicate dance, but mostly I just had to prove to these folks that I was two things: qualified and not insane. That last bit was no joke. Many people who come forward to run for office are, sadly, cranks or a little off their rockers. Being seen as reasonable and sane—as in *not* crazy—was important.

Midway through the evening, I felt the tide might be turning when committeeman Jeff Etkind listened to all I had to say, asked some tough questions, and kept me on the phone for forty-five minutes. He was a teacher, active in his synagogue, and a friendly guy. By the end of the call,

I thought for sure I'd won him over. But when I asked for his vote, Etkind equivocated. He liked what I had to say and how I said it, but he told me if Dan Royle wanted to run, he would support him. I was flabbergasted. I'd just spent a long time—time that was in short supply—talking with Etkind, and he'd agreed with almost everything I said. I thought he'd become an ally, and that my time on the phone with him had proved to be well spent, especially if he talked me up among the other wavering committee members, but in the end it was all for naught. He was going to support the other guy.

We ended the call, and I sat there at my dining-room table roundly pissed off. If I couldn't get someone like Etkind to swing my way, how could I convince other committee members? In my mind, I called Etkind all sorts of insulting names, but he didn't deserve them. The problem lay not with him personally, but with the party committee system and its long-standing ways of doing business. Folks like Etkind saw it as Royle's turn. Royle had put in the time and had earned the right—from the committee's point of view—to be the Democratic Party's nominee for mayor.

Regardless of how the Democratic Committee meeting turned out the next evening, I'd come to understand that the party was the path most candidates took to get support, get on the ballot, and get into office. If I couldn't get the committee on my side and get the kind of support it typically gave other Democrats, I'd have to go around it.

In lobbying committee members, I started to see party support as a nice to have, not a need to have. There was nothing legally preventing me from getting myself on the ballot without the party's help, but instead of having nearly four dozen committee members carrying my nominating petitions and gathering voter signatures from around the city's six wards—and more than thirty election districts—I'd have to do it myself with a much smaller team. That would mean gathering a minimum of 286 unique signatures in less than five and a half weeks, between June 7 and July 14. Under New York election law, that was all the time any candidate had to collect signatures to appear on the primary ballot.

There wouldn't be any campaign funding from the party during the primary either. In fact, under state law, political committees could not give primary candidates money, so at least Royle would be in the same boat. Still, I now knew the primary would be as much about beating the party as about beating Royle. Instead of being deterred, I took a deep breath, stepped out onto my back deck for a cigarette—which was becoming a more and more common way for me to calm my nerves—and dug in for the fight.

## Developing a strategy for greatest impact

I'd known from the beginning that to be successful, my campaign needed to develop a great strategy, stick to it, and keep it to ourselves. So far I trusted only a few city Democratic Committee members—Andy, Sharon, and a few others—but for the most part I saw city committee members as allies and conduits to Jim and Dan. If my campaign team projected what we were doing before we did it, I saw the results being only negative. We didn't know what we didn't know, so we didn't want to telegraph any of our plans. Fortunately, my team was as tight-lipped as I was. Of course I planned news coverage and public announcements, but we agreed that we would try our best to avoid undercutting ourselves by holding our cards not just close, but inside our vests.

In developing a strategy, I wanted an approach that would provide maximum visibility and impact, at least when we were on offense. But defense was something we'd have to play too. We never knew when Jim, Dan, or their Democratic supporters might call us out, either among the committee members or in the news media. We wanted to control the narrative as much as possible, stay on offense, keep the campaign clean, and never be seen as reacting.

The core idea was to project the fact that I was running *for* mayor, not *against* Dan. We felt the entire theme of the campaign—the way all of us felt—was similar to how many other Elmirans felt. We were frustrated with city government—the lack of openness, the lack of clarity, the insider politics. Many people we spoke to already echoed the same frustrations. Even Dan Mandell had preached change in his own mayoral announcement. We felt we were not alone, and we aimed to bring that broader discontent to this fight. There was no way we could be certain, of course, but our guts told us this was a winning formula. It was the incumbents who were out of touch with residents and voters, not us. They were wrong and we were right. And if Mandell and I were right, if there was going to be a change, I wanted the Democrats to come out on top.

I translated that into my campaign phrase, "New face. New energy. New ideas." I had it printed on white business cards that said "John Tonello for Mayor of Elmira" along with a picture of my smiling face and my website address. I also had round red, white, and blue stickers with "John Tonello Mayor" printed on them. We'd wear these, not buttons, wherever we went, and we'd use the "New face. New energy. New ideas." phrase over and over again, determined to link positive change to my campaign and my candidacy.

With our strategy in place, we knew we had to stick to it and stay focused on the central premise. We would be flexible enough to shift and modify our tactics as necessary, but we committed ourselves to our core philosophy and went all in. Andy and I would regularly remind each other to deflect as much of the flak as possible and "stay on target," much like Luke Skywalker did when he flew his X-wing starfighter toward that exhaust port to destroy the Death Star. In fact, that movie phrase echoed in my mind again and again in the weeks and months to come as we set off into our own gauntlet.

My journalism background told me we should avoid reacting to our opponents. We didn't want to get into any sort of public back-and-forth. As a former newspaper reporter, I knew that reacting quickly to something your opponent says was a great way to be seen as playing catch-up. Unless there were some truly unfair or inaccurate statements made, we'd just ignore them, reiterate our talking points, and focus on our plan.

Of course, this is easier said than done. The natural human reaction to negative personal attacks or media reports is to deflect them and fight back. If you hear or read something negative about yourself, the impulse is to push back fast and hard. As good as this might feel in the moment, experience had taught me that knee-jerk reactions would be the worst reactions. In campaign terms, reacting allows your opponent's storyline to become *the* storyline and, in newspaper terms, gives a story *legs*. A story with legs goes beyond one news cycle and can extend for days or weeks or months. By not reacting, we would be actively working to literally cut the legs off any opposing narrative. We'd play rope-a-dope like Muhammad Ali, and we'd let our opponents tire themselves out until we were ready to strike.

This required us all to grow thick skins, at least publicly. Among ourselves, we could shout and swear all we wanted—and we did. It was cathartic and, frankly, a necessary way to vent our frustrations. But outwardly, we would do our best to remain cool.

Another key part of our strategy was to work the media as much as possible to gain positive news coverage. In this, I felt pretty confident we could time press releases and announcements to good effect, get cameras on me, and create a tone that didn't just appear to be open and honest, but actually was. We were going to run the campaign as I would govern as mayor: I would communicate, communicate, communicate. I would also stay positive and avoid personal attacks. We felt it was fair game to attack the work record the incumbents had amassed, but we wouldn't make it personal. Strategically, we wouldn't be taking on just Dan Royle or Dan Mandell. We were taking on how the city had been run. I wanted to change the whole discussion and get voters to believe, as we did, that it was important to blow up the old ways of doing things.

This approach served us well because it kept us all focused on a single, perhaps idealistic, goal. This primary race would be bigger than a one-on-one matchup or a battle with the party. This was going to be about the future of the city and its residents. When we kept that top of mind, it was clarifying and helped us deflect criticism. Of course today things in politics are a little different, particularly at the national level, where politicians and candidates for office like to immediately set fire to everything their opponents say and do. Social media makes it even easier to do that. We didn't want any part of that approach. We preferred to take the high road and lose than wallow in the gutter and win.


## A bold announcement at noon

We discussed our strategy at length, but finally it came time to put it all into action. I'd delayed my announcement for the First District city council seat, I'd switched to running for mayor, the other candidates had announced, and clearly I was going to be the underdog. It was time to act.

The Democratic Committee was set to meet on the evening of May 19 and was probably going to endorse Dan Royle, so I needed something to shake things up. We decided I'd announce my candidacy for mayor at noon in downtown Elmira's Wisner Park the same day as the committee meeting. The shady park along Main Street, with American flags waving and flapping from tall poles, provided what I thought was the perfect backdrop. I'd sent out a media advisory to the *Star-Gazette* and the two local television stations, WETM-TV and WENY, that said I'd be holding a press conference regarding a political announcement. I gave the time and place and encouraged reporters to attend. Many make the mistake of including the full story in such a news advisory, which usually means reporters don't need to attend. I kept the advisory purposely vague but enticing enough to draw them out.

The television news directors and reporters called to try to get a better idea of what was happening, and in the case of WETM-TV, the local NBC affiliate, the news director decided to do a live hit, meaning the station would send a reporter, camera operator, and its special remote van to go live during its noon newscast. This was the best-case scenario and underscored why I wanted to announce at midday. A morning announcement would likely make the noon news, which was good, but not as good as the five o'clock or six o'clock newscasts, which have many more viewers. With WETM-TV going live at noon, I'd likely get coverage on four of the station's daily news broadcasts: noon, five, six, and eleven. Both local television stations and the *Star-Gazette*'s online edition also would likely have me all over the news just hours before the city Democrats were set to meet.

About fifteen of my supporters gathered with me at Wisner Park around eleven-thirty that morning. We set up a podium, and I spent a few moments looking over my speech and talking with folks. I had press releases to hand out afterward, again not wanting to reveal the news before it happened. I wore a suit and tie and tried my best to appear calm and collected. I was glad that my supporters included both Democrats and Republicans and some party committee members who were on my side, including Sharon. My neighbor Chrissy Brown was there, too, along with my mom. With them all lined up behind me on that sunny and mild day, I couldn't have asked for a better backdrop.

Before I began my formal announcement, WETM-TV reporter Catherine Varnum asked if I would appear with her for a live interview a few minutes into the noon newscast. I agreed, feeling strange being the subject of the interview, not the reporter. Since this was live television, I was happy to accommodate her and did the interview before my speech. When the moment arrived, the light on the camera turned red, Varnum gave a short lead-in, and then turned to ask me, "Why do you want to be mayor?"

I smiled and immediately thought, "Oh, man. Why do I?" I felt nervous and my mind went blank. But after a moment's delay, I remembered our plan and our talking points and told her, "Well, people tell me they're looking for a new face, new energy, and new ideas . . ."

I don't remember much after that, but when I watched myself on television later I was happy with the interview and everything I'd said. However, I was absolutely horrified to see that my head and upper body were moving ever so slightly back and forth throughout my on-air appearance. Most watching probably didn't notice, but I sure did. Why the hell was my head moving like that? Was that how I always looked when I talked? Or was this something my nerves conjured up just for television? Regardless of the reason, from that day forward, I made a conscious effort to stand still whenever I was on camera.

A contentious committee meeting

The news coverage had the desired effect. Anyone watching or reading the news ahead of the city committee meeting that evening saw that I was running. Any hopes committee members had of a routine meeting went out the window.

The meeting itself was held at the Hibernian Center on Kinyon Street on Elmira's south side. It was a private club of mostly Irish men and women who did good works in the community, hosted an annual Irish festival and Lenten fish fries, and accommodated many Democratic meetings. I'd never been there before, but when I arrived, the large, open interior had a large crowd of Democrats, including Jim, who was moving easily among the tables and talking with people. I said a few hellos, greeted Dan Royle, who made an effort to come say a friendly hello, and sat with Sharon and Andy at a table in the middle of the room. I caught both smiles and looks of disappointment from the others crowded into the hall. I tried hard to project confidence, but this meeting—and what I'd done by announcing hours before—was the very definition of confrontation. My being there and pushing to run was seen by many as a major breach of party loyalty.

I'd come armed with copies of my speech, the same one I'd delivered at my press conference, but I kept the pages in a folder to hand out after I spoke. Again, handing out remarks beforehand is a good way to get people to tune out. They'll read, not listen.

City Committee Chairman Steve McNamara and Dan approached me and asked if I'd be willing to go first when it was time to give our speeches. I quickly contemplated that going first might be a good move strategically and agreed. I think they thought going second was the better position, but I wanted to go on offense. I wanted Dan to have to react to what I said, not the other way around. As it happened, Dan also decided to hand out copies of his remarks before either of us spoke. I thought to myself, "Mistake."

When it finally came time to stand before the crowd, I was struck by how far I'd come in so short a time. I was focused, but I didn't want to appear cocky, so I gave my speech in a calm, even voice:

When my family moved to the Southern Tier 25 years ago, my
earliest memories of Elmira were of seeing movies at the Elmira
1-2-3 on College Avenue, joining big crowds for Pioneers baseball

games at Dunn Field, and watching Elmira Little Theatre productions in the Clemens Center's huge Powers Theater.

As a kid, Elmira always struck me as a busy, vibrant place that people loved. People still tell me stories about outings to Eldridge Park, dancing all night along the river at Rorick's Glen, and grabbing a bite to eat at the Iszards Department Store Tea Room.

All these things are reminders of what Elmira was, reminders of boom times, and times before Hurricane Agnes and the Flood. Times of growth and opportunity. It was a time when Elmira was full of energy and hope.

Today, the Tea Room is gone and the theater and baseball crowds aren't what they used to be, but a heart still beats in Elmira. I can feel it. People I talk to say they want to experience that sense of hope again—not by traveling back in time, but by moving forward to the future. They want to reconnect Elmira to its historic roots, to the founding families that built it, and to the children that hold its promise.

Since moving back to this area 10 years ago, I have come to love this city more than ever. I love the people I've met here. So when people tell me Elmira has lost sight of its future, lost its sense of purpose and its vision, my instinct is to try and help—despite the obstacles.

I want to make this city better. I want to be a driving force for all those who believe in Elmira's resurgence.

That's why I am running for mayor.

People tell me they want a business-savvy mayor with a can-do attitude who can forge alliances and not only envision growth, but make it happen. I believe I have the meaningful experience to do just that.

I've spent more than eight years in management positions for such Fortune 1000 companies as Corning Inc., Accenture, Gannett Co.; and for Cornell and Syracuse universities.

I have 18 years of combined experience as a journalist and communications professional.

I've spent the last 10 years implementing technology innovations for universities, and large and small businesses, including World Kitchen and the *Wall Street Journal.*

I have a bachelor's degree from Syracuse University, and began an MBA at RIT.

Some may say I should have city council experience, too. But I believe a fresh eye brings its own great value. Regardless, I'm no stranger to city government. When I was a newspaper reporter, I covered city and county government for more than four years. I always believed the role of the press made me an active member of the Fourth Estate, charged not with making the laws, but with scrutinizing and explaining the actions of the elected officials who made them. I know how government works and it was my job to make sure others understood, too. Most importantly, I'm not afraid to ask for help.

A big part of the mayor's job is helping to manage Elmira's $26 million budget and working with city employees and the public. I've managed multi-million dollar projects for Dow Jones and Accenture, and I've helped Corning Inc. and Cornell implement business-process solutions that saved money and improved service. In just six months at Cornell, I saved the Graduate School more than $250,000 doing just that. I've managed professional staffs and led business task groups that drew together people with diverse expertise to solve problems. As a communications professional, I'm especially good at talking with—and listening to—the public.

Most importantly, I have a vision I'm willing to act upon. I envision a bustling downtown where business is welcomed and encouraged. I envision storefronts and city streets brought back to life through steady investment. I envision graceful Victorian homes returning to their former glory through the care of committed newcomers of all ages and means. I envision neighborhoods where police and residents work together to solve problems through new community partnerships.

I'm a proud Democrat, and I'm proud of the strong record of the city leaders who have come before me and brought us this far. I have no intention of tearing them down. Jim Hare brought me into this committee, and there's no one who's been more willing to show me what it takes to succeed in public office. All the Democrats on the city council—Steve Hughes, Shirley Williams, Terry McLaughlin, Bill Hopkins and Dan Royle—have worked hard for their neighbors and the city. I respect their work, and I respect their long record of success. It's that very record that will keep Democrats in control of City Hall for many years to come.

It's also a record I will defend. The Trinity site, the modest 3.5 percent tax increase, and the South Main Street revitalization project are just a few strong examples.

The job of the next mayor will be to build on those successes. This race is about taking Elmira and the party into the future. I'm sure Dan and I will have some ideas in common. Where we differ is in vision and approach. To me, this race is about the future. It's about bringing new energy to the city and the party. I want us to grow so that we're no longer content to hold controlling seats in the city alone. I believe we all want more Democrats to join Ted Bennett, Kevin McInerny, and Paul Seidel in the county legislature, too. We want to draw strong candidates, people hungry for change like Bill Knapp and Brent Stermer, two of our newest council candidates. We want one day to take the DA's office, the Senate, the Assembly and beyond. To do that, we must draw youth and energy to our party and our cause. This race is about the Democrat Party embracing a new generation of passionate leaders.

That's why I pledge tonight not to split the party. Yes, Democrats citywide will decide which candidate should lead the ticket. But come September, I will support the winner of the primary. I will not run on a third party line.

I believe in Elmira, as I know you do. Together, we believe in the Democratic Party. I hope you will join me and support me in my bid for mayor.

Thank you.

After delivering my speech, I took questions. Some asked what sort of guarantee there would be that, if I lost the primary, I wouldn't run on a third-party line, such as the Working Families Party, and create a three-way race in November. This, they said, was a sure way to ensure a Republican victory.

I reiterated that I would not seek a third-party line. "I want to run as a Democrat and win as a Democrat," I said. "If I lose the primary, I won't run in November."

I'm not sure everyone believed this, but it was truly how I felt. Yes, I'd been toying with getting another party's line on the ballot, but in that moment, I knew I wanted to run and win as a Democrat. That was the platform I wanted, not just to capture the mayor's office.

The next question came from Bill Hopkins, the sitting First Ward councilman, who by now was quite upset with me for pushing him to exit the council race and then changing my mind. I could understand that, but he'd made the decision not to run, not me. Still, he was angry, and asked me how I could force a primary that he said would end up costing the city about $15,000. That would be the cost of having to pay election workers, print ballots, and stage the election. I took this as a specious argument and said so, and did some quick math in my head.

"It we can't afford to spend the equivalent of fifty cents for each of the 30,000 residents of Elmira to ensure voters can express their opinions in a primary," I said, "we haven't just lowered the bar, we've dropped it on the ground."

It also occurred to me that there were going to be Republican primaries for sheriff and the Fourth Ward city council seat, so the city would have to stage a primary regardless. I understood Bill's anger toward me, but saying no to a primary because of its cost really pissed me off. This struck me as voter suppression, not a core democratic principle.

Before I returned to my seat, my team handed out copies of my remarks. Dan then took the floor. He started to read from his prepared remarks—the same ones he'd handed out earlier—but almost immediately veered off script. We could tell because we had his script in our hands and were following along. The things I'd said in my speech and during the question-and-answer period had apparently stuck in his craw. He continued his remarks, mostly off-the-cuff, telling the committee members he deserved the recognition of the party and the opportunity to run for mayor.

Of course, we found this obnoxious. "No one deserves nothin'!" Andy told me. Once again, we were seeing how the local party operated. A sense of order based on longevity, not ideas. Before the vote to endorse, Jim Hare stood up and said I was creating a monster by forcing a primary, arguing that party division was the worst thing possible.

When it came time to vote, several committee members wanted to make a motion calling on the committee not to endorse either mayoral candidate. Mary O'Dell, the Democratic commissioner, who worked in the Board of Elections office and helped candidates with all things related to elections, had previously told me she supported the idea of no endorsement. She'd been a great help to me in the weeks leading up to the committee meeting by offering guidance on getting on the ballot and other election details. She also provided me with the number of weighted votes that would be in play for any committee endorsement. Each committee member had not one, but many votes, which added up to 1,559. That meant Dan or I needed 780 votes to secure the party nod.

Dan and Jim knew this too, and before the meeting, Jim had collected hundreds of proxy votes from committee members unable to attend in person. That meant he personally held hundreds of votes, not just his own. Smart. I didn't even know such a thing was possible.

When the talking ended, Bill Knapp made a motion for the City Democratic Committee to not endorse either candidate. After some discussion, the roll was taken, and the motion failed. Longtime members of the committee who believed in the status quo clearly outnumbered those who saw a primary as the better option. We were zero to one on the night.

Next came the vote to endorse: Royle or Tonello? The weighted voting took some time to tally, but Jim appeared confident and relaxed. He knew how to work the party levers, and he was pulling them hard. When the votes were in, I lost badly. Dan received 1,275 votes to my 284. He got more than 80 percent, an overwhelming showing. I was zero to two on the night.

As others stood to get beers from the Hibernian Center bar, my team and I sat chatting, feeling disappointed but undeterred. This was by no means the end of the road, and I felt energized when Sharon turned to me and quietly told me, "That's the last vote you're going to lose."

5

# Getting on the Ballot

### First forays into door-to-door

We'd emerged from the May 19 committee meeting a little battered and bruised, but we'd known going in that it wasn't going to be our night. After all, this was the party's night, organized and operated by folks like Jim, not our supporters. Still, we'd been able to convince almost 20 percent of the committee to support my bid for mayor, and that was promising.

Before the meeting had ended, another countywide Democratic Committee meeting was announced for June 6, when Deputy Election Commissioner Mary O'Dell would hand out nominating petitions for Dan, me, and the rest of that year's Democratic candidates. This gave committee members the chance to carry petitions for either one of us facing off in the mayoral primary. New York lection law allowed registered party members to sign a petition for only one of the candidates seeking the same office. That meant we needed to beat Dan to Democratic doors.

We had no way of knowing how many committee members would carry for us or how many signatures we'd get as a result. We needed at least 286 valid signatures to get on the ballot, which meant we needed more than the minimum in case some were deemed invalid and were tossed. With that number in mind, we counted on getting exactly zero signatures from the vast majority of committee members who'd decided they weren't on our side.

This was the first time many of us had carried nominating petitions, and we went out of our way to make sure they were legally sound and that everyone carrying them on my behalf knew the rules. One sheet typically held twenty signatures. A technical mistake could invalidate some or all of them.

Unlike more general canvassing to promote a political candidate, the nominating petition process in New York State required each paper sheet to carry a specific header detailing the office, the candidate, and other information. Since I was seeking the Democratic line on the ballot, anyone carrying a petition—also known as a witness—would have to be a registered Democrat. Those signing had to be Democrats too. So, unlike some political awareness tasks that might be conducted, say, outside a grocery store, the petition process required we knew for sure that those signing our forms were active registered Democrats.

Fortunately, the Chemung County Board of Elections maintains voter registration data for all political parties. Mary O'Dell and her colleagues at the Board of Elections actually printed out the lists for committee members to carry. Since each person represented a specific city election district, she would give petition carriers the pages for their districts. For mayoral candidates, she gave us the entire citywide list, printed on 8½ by 11 inch pages and organized by district. This was a big help because it told us where every registered Democrat in the city lived. The lists were generally organized by street, but using them to go door-to-door was a cumbersome process that required anyone carrying designating petitions to head to a particular street, constantly check the sheets, and do it all as quickly as possible. With just five-and-a-half weeks to gather the more than 300 signatures we wanted, we would have to get about half a sheetful each day. That seemed doable.

To get started, I found an open canvas bag I could carry over my shoulder and fill with campaign literature and the voter lists. I'd made up hand cards (short-but-sweet campaign literature), the campaign stickers, and my campaign business cards. After work on Tuesday, June 7, I headed out to first collect signatures from my own neighborhood. I figured this was the lowest-hanging fruit: close by, some familiar faces, and no need to drive anywhere. It was an unusually hot, dry spring day with temperatures in the mid-eighties.

It took us some time to figure out, but we soon learned that gathering signatures was best done between about five and seven-thirty in the evening, a window of time when people were home from work, maybe puttering in their yards, and not yet settled in for the night. We'd also tried weekend mornings and afternoons, but success at those times was too hit-and-miss. People were out shopping or with their kids or whatever, so we settled on the evening hours as the best time to make the rounds.

We'd come up with a little script with talking points that included the fact that this was the first primary election for Elmira's mayor in more than twenty years, that Elmira needed strong leadership and new ideas, that we needed young people in leadership positions, and more. We also had a script for the first words out of our mouths when someone answered the door:

"I'm carrying petitions for Democratic Party candidate for mayor John Tonello. In order for John Tonello to get on the ballot, we must collect hundreds of signatures. You are listed as a registered Democrat. Will you sign my petition for John Tonello?"

It wasn't an accident that we mentioned my name three times. I had almost no name recognition, though I'd so far appeared a couple time in the newspaper and on television, so we decided we needed to hammer home the point of who the hell I was. If someone didn't want to sign, we'd thank them and move on. If they did, we'd ask if they had any interest in volunteering to be part of the campaign. We even had information on how to politely end a conversation that was keeping us from our rounds. We'd simply ask for a phone number or email and be sure to get back to them later. If someone wasn't home, we'd leave a door hanger that included my website address.

Sharon was a great help in putting these instructions together, and I leaned into her experience. Having been something of introvert all my life—at least until I'd gotten bitten by the political bug—I was a little hesitant to knock on strangers' doors and talk with them, but her advice helped a lot. And once I got started, it got a lot easier.

## Hitting the other guy where he lives

While I was making the rounds those first few days, it occurred to me that Dan Royle was probably doing the same thing—hitting up his own neighborhood to gather the low-hanging fruit. I didn't know for sure, but it occurred to me that he or members of his campaign might swoop into my neighborhood and beat me to the punch on signature gathering. These sorts of paranoid thoughts would not be my last; my brain was working in strategic overdrive and led me to my next thought, which was, "Hey, perhaps I could swoop in on *his* neighborhood."

So I did.

After covering the blocks around my West Gray Street home, where I'd been able to get about ten signatures on my first day, I decided to go to Dan's neighborhood to collect signatures. That would prevent anyone who signed my petitions from signing his and, perhaps, get in his head a little bit. He lived in a nice residential neighborhood that included Maple Avenue, Riverside Avenue, and Robinson Street, and I saw from the voter list that the area included plenty of Democrats.

Though my strategy made me feel like a bit of a heel, I'd decided all's fair in love and war, so I hopped in my car, parked near Brand Park, and started knocking on doors. The first few houses where people were actually home gave me a mixed result. Two people had no hesitation and signed. Then I got to a house where the person knew Dan.

"Oh, no, I can't sign," an older gentleman told me. "I sign for Royle."

I shouldn't have been surprised. Dan had run and been elected three times from this neighborhood. He'd lived there a long time too and was bound to have friends, and I found plenty of them going blindly from door to door. I didn't know anything about Dan, really, and I knew even less about his political supporters. Still, I pressed on, determined to pick up a few signatures and leave a trail of Democrats who could report back to Dan and his team that I'd been there.

I have no idea if this scheme of mine had any real impact, but because I didn't have the Democratic Committee behind me like he did, I was willing to take some risks and blow through some norms. After all, it had been twenty years since a Democratic primary for mayor, and party regulars were probably not thinking much about having to get unique signatures. In fact, I'd learned that most committeemen carried their petitions to the same people year after year, people they knew or, at least, knew they could count on for signatures. I was just going randomly from one door to the next, hopefully attracting some attention and drawing in Democrats who hadn't been included in the process.

Many people told me no one had knocked on their doors in years, which was how I hit on the core idea for what would later become my television commercial, but for now I was just feeling my way along from house to house. At one point while visiting Dan's neighborhood, the enticing smells of Italian food wafted from a small ranch house near Brand Park. It wasn't quite dinnertime, but the aromas made my mouth water. When I knocked, an older Italian woman answered the door and greeted me with a big smile and welcomed me inside. I smiled back, but I really didn't want to go inside because I was pressed for time. She insisted, and I soon found myself in her kitchen with what had to be her sisters or friends, also Italians, who were tremendously warm and kind.

I gave them my pitch, and they smiled and asked if I was Italian. When I told them I was, they gave me approving smiles and started to ask me even more questions. Was I married? Was I seeing someone? What part of Italy were my parents from? I couldn't help but laugh. This was by far the friendliest welcome I'd had. These ladies made me feel there was no way I could hem or haw my way out of their questions. It was like being at a beloved aunt's house. I managed to compliment the wonderful cooking aromas, though I declined an offer to stay to eat and eventually got on my way. The whole experience made me happy, and I thought that whether I won or lost the primary, I'd have met some really terrific people.

## Grassroots and first-timers

A book I used to learn all I could about running for office, the *Campaign Manager* by Catherine Shaw, was chock-full of ideas, including a suggestion to engage people in a campaign who shared similar backgrounds, such as having graduated from the same college or university. As fellow alumni, this could provide a common point of interest or at least an ice-breaker. I thought it was a good idea, so I decided to see if I could put together a list of fellow Syracuse University graduates who were now living in the Elmira area.

At the time, Syracuse University had an alumni website that helped graduates reach out to former classmates to meet up, plan booster events, follow basketball and football, and more. When I logged onto the site, I found I was able to find exactly what I was looking for. The alumni portal listed 345 alumni living in or near Elmira, offering their names and the years they had graduated. Of course, not all of them would be registered Democrats or city residents, but I figured I could look up and cross-reference the names with the voter lists I had. When I did, I found twenty-one matches.

One of the first I went to visit was Margaret Weidemann, who lived just a few blocks from my house on West Gray Street. Margaret happened to be outside when I walked up, and we had a nice conversation in her driveway. She was supportive of my efforts, signed my nominating petition sheet, and even agreed to take one of my yard signs (when I had them).

I called on other Syracuse alumni I'd discovered, including Eileen Ameigh, who graduated the same year I did and lived on Elmira's north side. She had a small bungalow she shared with her husband, and I knocked on their door and got into a nice conversation. Like Margaret, Eileen had never really been involved in local politics, but they were exactly the type of people I wanted to meet. They were smart, successful women, Democratic voters, and—not unlike me—mostly relegated to the sidelines.

My experience of randomly meeting people on their doorsteps and talking about the city was eye-opening. Just knocking and talking without preconceived notions, no hard pitch. It allowed me to hear their concerns about crime, roads, downtown business, and more and helped me refine my campaign message. These conversations also confirmed many of the feelings I'd had about discontent with city government and revealed how many people felt disengaged. The more doors I knocked on, the more I heard from people that it had been years since a candidate for mayor—or any local office—had knocked on their doors. They hadn't been on anyone's go-to list for signatures, so they'd been ignored. I found that troubling and sad. I wanted people to feel engaged or at least able to weigh in on things, and the support I found was energizing.

This part of the campaign experience led me to meet and encourage all sorts of newcomers, some of whom would become part of my campaign. To further that goal, I also put out word about an informal meeting at my house, and I encouraged people with any interest to come by. As you might imagine, this was well-intentioned, but not my best idea. The few folks who turned up were folks I might best describe as "fringe." They were nice and well-meaning but, well, a little odd. I welcomed them and their efforts, but the blind invite didn't have the result I'd expected. Note to self: There's open and inclusive, and there's open and inclusive. I needed to be a little more discerning in the future.


## Crossing the city on foot

After spending more than a week going to door-to-door to collect signatures, I began to grow frustrated with the Board of Elections voter lists. They provided the information we needed to locate Democrats, but they were cumbersome. They didn't make it easy to zero in on streets or neighborhoods with high numbers of registered voters, and they didn't tell me much about the men and women I was asking for signatures. The sheets had voters' dates of birth and their addresses, but I didn't know much else about them. For example, I didn't know if they were regular voters or just showed up during presidential election years. To me, voters who showed up every single year—for local, state, and national elections—were the most engaged voters. The sheets from the Board of Election didn't offer any hint of that.

I decided to address the problem with technology.

In my work at Cornell University and earlier, I'd done a lot to develop databases and web interfaces to make it easy to search for information. At the time, I'd just completed converting the Cornell University Graduate School's "Fields, Subjects and Concentrations" catalog into a searchable database available on the school's website. I felt as comfortable creating database-driven web applications as I did with communications, and figured I could come up with something better than the sheets we were using to gather signatures. For example, I wanted to be able to figure out which city streets and blocks had the highest concentration of registered Democrats. That way, I could go to the most fertile ground possible and more quickly gather the nearly 300 signatures I needed to get on the ballot.

The result was a software tool I created from scratch that enabled my campaign to not only target the most regular voters, but also locate the heaviest concentrations of voters anywhere in Elmira. I built it so I could call up information on my phone via a web browser and no longer have to worry about flipping paper pages while going door-to-door. I'd done a lot of work with MySQL, freely available open-source relational database software, and with PHP code for web development, and figured I could develop an application that suited my needs. All it would cost would be my time.

To populate the data in my software application, I asked Mary O'Dell at the Board of Elections office for the raw voter registration data, which was publicly available in a large text file. Each row in the file included voters' names, addresses, phone numbers, street addresses, party registration, date of birth, and more. It also included their election districts and voting histories. In other words, I could mine the data to find streets with high numbers of Democrats and identify the most active voters, people who hadn't just voted in high-turnout presidential election years, but in every local election. I figured these were the people who were most likely to turn out to vote in a primary and, later, in a general election, if it came to that.

In addition to the raw data, Mary also sent me the data-mapping file, which provided detailed information about each column listed in the large voter registration dataset. That file—listing about 55,000 registered voters in Chemung County—didn't use tabs, spaces, or other delimiters. Instead, it used columns with specific character widths that the mapping file unlocked. Armed with this format information, I wrote a script to convert the large file into Structured Query Language, also known as SQL, so I could pour all the data easily into the MySQL database powering my software application. After some trial and error, I was able to accurately parse the information and make it easy to search.

To make it simple for members of my campaign team and me to access the date, I built a web interface that worked on any computer or cellphone browser. The output would appear onscreen in neat rows, and I made it easy to print the output in case I wanted to hand out detail-rich sheets to others working on my campaign. Finally, I added a feature to make it easy to produce mailing labels, particularly for homes where more than one Democrat lived. I built it so I could send a single piece of mail to, say, the Smith Family, instead of separate letters or postcards to each family member at any address, the software application doing the hard work. This feature alone saved my campaign hundreds of dollars in postage costs.

After some fine-tuning, I had the interface and database built and connected, and I put it to work. In addition to the main database of voters, I added additional data tables to hold voting districts and other information so I could confine my searches to only those voters who lived in the city, not everyone in Chemung County, and tailor the output for that day's canvassing. When I began running database queries, I quickly found all the Democrats who voted all the time and where they lived. I also was able to find households with more than one Democratic voter—husbands, wives, and their children, usually—which helped accelerate signature gathering because we could gather many signatures at once—if every family member was home.

I called my bespoke web application voterBase and immediately used it to create new-and-improved canvassing lists. Andy was doing a lot to help me get signatures, so I was able to provide him with voter lists he could use in the south side Elmira neighborhoods closest to where he lived and elsewhere. I kicked out lists for my own canvassing and added fields in the software to show us which houses we'd visited. This feature also made it easy to track who had signed my nominating petitions so we could reach out to them later to plant yard signs, send mailings, or visit again when we went canvassing later that summer. We figured those who signed my petitions were the most likely to vote for me, so this information was pure campaign gold.

By engineering this solution, we could ditch the cumbersome Board of Election sheets and really start to quickly gather signatures in the numbers we needed. I was excited about the prospect of using technology to help my campaign, and voterBase did just that. It made me feel like we had a real shot at getting the necessary signatures in the short time allowed by election law. Many in the city Democratic Committee thought such a feat impossible, and I heard people at the June meeting say things like, "He'll never get on the ballot." After all, I didn't have the bodies the committee had to gather signatures for Dan. By using voterBase, we were able to close the gap and make it possible for just a few of us do what dozens of committee members could to—and to better effect.

Armed with my voterBase lists, I continued to crisscross the city. I'd get home from work, immediately change into jeans and sneakers, and start knocking on doors. I'd never really explored the city on foot this way, and it was eye-opening. Some neighborhoods were clean and neat, others shabby and neglected. The problems my neighbors and I had dealt with on West Gray Street were not unlike the challenges others in the city were facing. Slumlord apartments abounded, roadways were often cracked and in need of paving, and more. By going door-to-door, I was seeing the city and its people close-up.

That insight was incredibly valuable, particularly when I heard that Dan had turned over much of the job of signature gathering to his family and city committee members. He wasn't showing up at doors in person at the rate I was. By doing much of the work myself, I was able to put my face out there and hear firsthand from fellow Elmirans, and what they told me more often than not reinforced my own perceptions. If Dan was delegating this process to others, I thought he was missing out on a great opportunity. I didn't blame him for delegating—canvassing is a lot of work—but it was clearly another example of how the long-standing committee system was letting him down.


## The "Thank you" cards

By the first week of July, I'd personally walked miles and miles around the city, knocking on doors, talking to people, and collecting signatures. On some evenings I managed to get as many as fourteen signatures before darkness came and I was forced to head home. I personally had gathered about 180 signatures since June 7, more than half of the 286 I'd need to get on the primary ballot. Andy collected a lot too, and he told me some of the committee members who backed me had collected dozens more signatures to add to our tally. Bill Knapp, a committeeman who was running for the First District council seat, which I'd abandoned to run for mayor, personally collected more than thirty signatures. When we added them all up, we felt pretty good about surpassing the minimum threshold to qualify for the primary and having enough extra to counter any petition challenges.

By July 11, we had collected a grand total that was nearly 35 percent more than the legal requirement, but instead of waiting until the Friday deadline to gather still more, I decided to bring my nominating petitions to the Board of Elections a few days early. Before I did that, though, I took the stack to Leo Krolak, a former chairman of the Chemung County Democratic Committee and an expert on local politics. When I met him, he was eighty-four years old and still as fiery and outspoken as ever. I went to his home and he welcomed me into his office, a made-over detached garage behind his house filled with the ephemera of his political past.

Leo looked over my nominating petitions and had just told me everything looked good when I got a call on my cellphone from my ex-wife, Nicola. It was late afternoon and I hadn't been expecting a call, so I excused myself and took the call. Nicola told me she'd just come from the doctor, who'd told her she had breast cancer. I was flabbergasted and felt the blood drain from my face. Though we were divorced, Nicola and I had remained friends, and I was upset to learn her news. I offered to help her in any way I could, and in that moment, somehow, the campaign didn't seem as all-important as it had.

I suddenly felt very tired. In addition to Nicola's news, I'd been running flat-out in what had just been one of the hottest Junes on record, with temperatures reaching into the nineties on several days. The pace and Nicola's cancer diagnosis were wearing on me. Over the course of the campaign, I had literally been sweating it out, often coming home after door-knocking with my shirt soaked with perspiration. On more than one occasion, my Tonello for Mayor campaign sticker simply peeled itself off my shirts because of all the sweat. I decided I needed a rest, and called a halt to signature gathering so I could take a breather. We'd been running flat out, and we needed a break.

But this was just the beginning. Filing the petitions would only be the first step. We'd next have to deal with any petition challenges, a process that allowed any member of the public to come to the Board of Elections to review our nominating petitions and look for flaws or errors. We figured Dan or Jim—or one of their allies—would do just that, but we felt good about having nearly 100 more signatures than we needed. Certainly some might be challenged, but the hardest part was done, and we'd just have to wait out the three-day challenge period to find out if I'd make it onto the ballot. We also didn't have the campaign experience to know what last-minute bumps would knock us off course.

Before the filing deadline, the city Democratic Committee met at Chairman Steve McNamara's home on Fairway Place so all the candidates could collect their nominating petitions committee members had gathered over the past six weeks.

When I arrived a little after seven o'clock, McNamara was there with Mary O'Dell, Bill Knapp, and Dawn Royle, Dan's wife. They were poring over pages of petitions at a card table set up in Steve's living room, where the faces on china figurines stared at us from a curio cabinet and a grandfather clock marked the quiet passing of time every fifteen minutes.

The card table was filled mostly with Dan's petitions and others for Knapp, Terry McLaughlin, and the candidates for city constable. McNamara got me a chair from the kitchen, and I sat down to look over signatures gathered for the other candidates, checking dates and witnesses. That's how it went. Everyone was looking for mistakes.

Not long into the meeting, Mary turned to me with a nominating petition and said, "Here are some for you, John." There were two petition sheets. One from Brent Stermer that had one signature, and one sheet from another committee member who'd manage to get me seven signatures. None of the other committee members had turned in any signatures for me. Though some in the party had been willing to carry my petition, few actually did. I'd known from early on that I couldn't rely on the committee to gather for me, but I was a little nonplussed. Eight signatures! Did I have such little committee support? I didn't condemn Brent's effort because he barely got enough signatures to get himself on the ballot, but some thirty members of the committee hadn't bothered at all. Of the eleven who did carry my petitions—members of my team whom I personally met with back on June 9—most, in the interests of fairness, had carried petitions for both Dan and me.

I watched as Mary two-hole punched and bound the petitions for Bill Knapp and Dan Royle. I'd left the nominating petitions my team had gathered at home because I didn't trust these folks enough to show them off *and* because I wanted my count to remain a mystery. I watched Dawn Royle count her husband's signatures and peeked at the calculator total as she entered numbers. Dan had more than 700 signatures—twice my overall total. There would be no doubt about *him* getting on the ballot.

I returned home and had a beer and a cigarette with Chrissy on her back deck. As much as I didn't want to feel it, I was disappointed. It was yet another reminder of the steady battle I was facing. There certainly would be no letup.

Andy came by later that evening and we vented about the measly eight signatures. That outcome wasn't unexpected, but it wouldn't slow us down. It only reaffirmed for us that we didn't owe the committee a thing. From now on, I'd try to be far less inclined to protect the record of the Democratic incumbents, and I'd certainly not do things "for the party's sake" after the party hadn't done anything for me.

Before leaving McNamara's house, I'd purposefully put on a forlorn face. I knew I had enough signatures to get on the ballot even without those eight Mary had handed me, but I didn't want anyone there to know. I played possum, wanting them to leave thinking we'd failed and that my political career was over before it even began.

In the week before the filing deadline, Dan had put out a campaign postcard carrying the Democratic Committee's postal frank, an ink stamp used instead of actual stamps. I cried foul. After all, state law prohibited political parties from providing financial support to primary candidates, and here the committee had clearly given Dan financial support because using the frank costs less than regular postal rates. I asked an election attorney to weigh in, but he told me what Dan and the Democratic Committee had done was legal because Dan's mailing had gone out before the filing deadline. Again, the political veterans knew what they were doing and had followed the letter of the law, if not the spirit.

Despite this hiccup, early the next week O'Dell called to tell me that I had, indeed, qualified for the ballot. I was ecstatic. All that hard work had paid off. If there had been any challenges, there hadn't been enough to disqualify me.

Within a few days, I'd receive a formal letter from the Board of Elections confirming I was on the ballot. The next step was for a lottery to be held to determine if Dan or I would appear on the top line. They literally put our names in a hat and drew, and luck was on my side. I won the top line of the September primary ballot. It was a small thing, but I figured it was better to be listed on the first row when voters entered the booth, and it made up for a little of the lingering disdain I felt about Dan's mailing.

To keep the flow of communication going, I put out a press release on July 18 announcing the fact that not just I, but all three mayoral candidates, had met the filing deadline with the required number of signatures.

In all, more than 1,600 Democrats and Republicans had signed nominating petitions, and I wanted to highlight that fact. The process had worked, not just for me but for all the candidates. I wanted to highlight citizen participation in the process.

"This is a great day for the democratic process," I said in the release. "The more candidates for mayor—and all public offices—the better. Elmirans who go to the polls September 13 and November 8 will have unprecedented choice this year. That's what democracy is all about."

I also explained how I'd personally met hundreds of voters over the past six weeks and argued that Elmirans were eager to be involved in positive change. "People have told me from the beginning that they want new energy and new ideas," I said. "The first step toward that goal is a citywide mayoral primary that engages the public. It's the first in at least a generation here."

I went on to commend my opponents' efforts to gather signatures, aiming to take the high road. "I congratulate Dan Royle and Dan Mandell on their efforts to engage voters," I said. "I look forward to a positive and spirited debate of the issues this summer and fall."

We also decided to send a postcard to all the Democrats who'd signed nominating petitions, not just the one who'd signed mine. I again wanted to thank registered voters for participating in the process, but when the postcard hit mailboxes, city committee members were up in arms. "It sounded like everyone signed *your* petitions when they didn't!" some claimed. I shrugged it off. I hadn't intended to misrepresent my campaign. I'd merely wanted to engage and thank people.

This sort of "high road" tactic was something everyone on my campaign believed in, at least in the beginning. Our strategy was all about engagement and positive energy. I think political insiders saw it as foolhardy. Why spend money to congratulate your opponents? I thought of it differently. I wanted the city to see us as turning politics as usual on its head, and, at least in the case of getting on the ballot, the end result was positive. People appreciated the follow-up too. We'd asked for signatures, and Democrats had stepped up to help. I didn't want to be seen as getting what I wanted from voters and never acknowledging their contributions. I wanted the nominating petition process to be the first contact with voters, not the last, and the postcard helped underscore that approach.

With a line on the ballot won, it was now time to take a breath and really dive into the campaign. Until this point, running in a primary had been purely speculation. But we'd done the work, followed the rules, and I was now a truly legitimate candidate. Now the real work would begin.

6

# Campaign Materials and Creating a Brand

New face. New energy. New ideas.

With the ballot line secured, it was now time to really step up our campaign efforts. The process of getting on the ballot—and all that door knocking—had been part of it, of course, but it didn't make sense to produce and pay for much campaign material before that happened. Now that I was really in the race, we needed to think about campaign literature, yard signs, mailings, television advertising, and more.

So far, I'd self-financed the few items we'd been using, namely my campaign stickers and the business cards. I'd used VistaPrint.com, which was relatively new at the time, because I could design my own materials, upload my designs to the vendor's website, and get everything delivered in relatively short order. This was a novel approach. Typically, local politicians used Elmira's main print shops, Quicker Printer, CopyExpress, and others to print their materials. These were locally owned and operated at the time, but I didn't really know the owners or their political leanings. I felt that using these local shops might lead to word getting out about what I was up to and how much I was spending. Instead, I used VistaPrint and the Cornell University print shop, the latter offering low-cost, one-color printing services for things like postcards.

The business cards I printed up and used early on were effective, as was the slogan "New face. New energy. New ideas." We knew we wanted to keep using that phrase everywhere we went and in everything we put out. Yes, we would grow tired of repeating the same phrase again and again, but for most people—and potential voters—it would be new each time we said it. If we wanted to build what would ultimately become my brand, we needed to stay consistent with both the message and the underlying premise, regardless of how repetitive it seemed to *us*.

During the run-up to the July 14 filing deadline, I'd put out two press releases. The first announced Elmira's first "e-campaign" for mayor. Since I had built a website and launched it (and included the domain name on my business cards), I thought it would be good to highlight my use of the web.

"The web is a truly democratic medium that empowers people, and that's what my campaign is all about," I said, and I promised to use the internet, email and technology "like no other mayoral candidate in city history."

It didn't hurt that Elmira was the birthplace of high-speed home internet, which began in 1995, when what was then Time Warner Cable used Elmira to experiment with using coax cable to deliver always-on internet. Up to that time, most people were still getting online with dial-up modems, but Time Warner had chosen Elmira as a test bed because so many homes already had cable, which was really the only way to get television in the Chemung River valley. I touted how Elmira's technical infrastructure was a major asset that set the city apart and gave it a competitive advantage against other communities vying for new businesses. Nearly four weeks later, Dan Royle would announce his own website.

The second press release I issued had to do with a fairly esoteric effort to encourage then-Governor George Pataki to renew New York Power Authority contracts that would help preserve jobs at Anchor Glass, a nearby bottle manufacturer that used a lot of electricity. I figured such an announcement would show I was up on some key local issues, particularly helping Elmira and Chemung County remain affordable places to do business.

I posted these items in the Newsroom section of my website, and both were picked up by the *Star-Gazette*, appearing in their election briefs columns a couple weeks apart. While we were now concentrating on mostly internal campaign operations, I wanted to keep my name out there, and these releases seemed to help. They weren't front-page news like my initial May announcement, but these and future releases provided something of a steady publicity drumbeat.

We had about six weeks until the September 13 primary election, and I decided to make some changes inside my committee. Sharon was still advocating for me, but I felt her approach was a little heavy-handed when it came to the city and county committees. I didn't agree with many things the Democratic Committees did, but I also didn't want to sow bad blood with folks I might need to rely on during the general election, if I got that far. Grousing privately with Andy was one thing. Doing it with veteran committee members was another. Yes, Jim and others were working against me, but I didn't want to get into a back-and-forth with him or other committee members. Sharon had done some of that with county Democratic Committee Chairwoman Cindy Emmer so, despite her earlier help, I decided to make Andy my lieutenant. He and I were in lockstep on everything, and though we would often complain among ourselves about party actions, we kept it to ourselves. We wanted to stay positive at every level, and Andy and I had a strong, almost brotherly bond. I never needed to second-guess him, and his wealth of community knowledge was invaluable.

Sharon continued to be an important part of my team, and the rest of my sounding board remained in place, including my neighbors Chrissy Brown and Bonnie Gestwicki, my stepbrother, and my mother. I'd made my mother treasurer, which I thought was a good way to get her involved and played to her organizational strengths. I don't think she much liked having to do the official campaign filings—which could be obtuse—but she was diligent and responsible and took care of the financials without any hiccups.


## Website launch

Although I'd already announced and promoted my website, I thought I needed a better domain name for my campaign. I'd had my eponymous domain for years but wanted something more specific, so I registered TonelloforMayor. com. It pointed to the same website I'd been using, but we started to use this domain instead on all our literature. We even jazzed it up a little by using a small star instead of the dot to give it a political campaign feel.

It seems like a small thing, but I felt the updated domain offered better branding, and branding was really what it was all about. I had to market myself as a serious, legitimate, and non-crazy candidate. Something as simple as a domain name helped do that.

At the same time, I spent a lot of time honing the messages on my website. In addition to posting all my press releases there on the Newsroom page, I also had an Issues page. There I outlined my vision and my experience. I highlighted the fact that I'd held management positions at Corning Inc., Accenture, Gannett Co., Cornell University, and elsewhere. I also talked up my communications and technology experience, essentially putting my resume out there for all the world to see.

On the Issues page, I thought it was a good idea to tell visitors why I wanted to be mayor:

> I thought long and hard about my decision to run for mayor of Elmira, and decided I really had just two choices: I could sit on the sidelines and let things continue as they are or I could step in, share my ideas, and try to bring about positive change right now. I talked with many people, and they told me they don't want to wait for more people to move away, more businesses to pull up stakes or overlook us, or more urban blight and crime to stain and obscure our city. I share their feelings and I'm willing to challenge the status quo to give all Elmirans a choice. Elmira has a strong, proud history, and I'm not willing to let its decline pass as a foregone conclusion. I want to make Elmira better, I want to help the city grow, and I want to be a driving force in Elmira's resurgence.

It was pretty lofty and idealistic stuff, but it's truly how I felt. I expressed similar thoughts in sections I wrote on vision, optimism, neighbors helping neighbors, quality of life, accountability, innovation, and risk-taking. I summed it up this way:

- Vision—Focus on the future and where we want to be as a city

- Optimism—Change our philosophy from "we can't" to "we can"

- Neighbors helping neighbors—Bring together disparate, disenfranchised groups to solve problems

- Quality of life—Focus on those things that make living in the city better and more appealing

- Accountability—Make city government more transparent, accessible, and open

- Innovation—Seek, find, and employ new solutions

- Risk-taking—Encourage those with courage to try new ideas

I also highlighted my intention to fully fund the police department, support community policing efforts, and make Elmira a place where people wanted to live. The whole section of the website was set up as a series of

Q&As. For example, one question asked, "Isn't the city improving already?," and I answered with this:

> Yes, but I think we're still missing the big picture. For example, in 1993, Elmira's Common Council passed a law requiring top city managers to live within the city. As of February 2005, many still did not. I'm not out to blame these individuals or reprimand them. Nor am I talking about enforcing the law or repealing it. To me, that's not the issue. The big picture issue is why do we need a law to force city employees and managers to live here? Why don't these people say, "Hey, this is a great place to live. I want to buy a house here. I want to live here." That's what we must overcome, not piecemeal, but with a broad vision.

Again, it was pretty lofty, but Elmira had a higher crime rate and higher taxes than neighboring communities. These were real reasons why people opted not to live in the city. If people thought crime was bad, we needed to show we were tackling it. If people thought the taxes were high, we needed to do our best not to increase them *and* highlight the value of the services the city provided to its residents. People often think of taxes as a one-sided thing: something they pay reluctantly. But I thought we also needed to promote the upside: a paid professional fire department, great parks, good infrastructure, and more services than any community around.

I'm not sure how many people visited my campaign website and took time to read it all, but if they did, I wanted it to all be out there, plain as day. I wanted people to know I was running out of a personal sense of civic duty and service, not ego. If I misread the public sentiment, so be it. I'd lose, and things could go on as they had. If I was right—and I could convince voters I was the right guy for the moment by being open and honest—we'd have a good shot at winning. I often visited the site just to remind myself of these core beliefs and, if nothing else, to keep myself true to our vision.

## Business cards

One tip from former Mayor Steve Hughes I put into practice was the use of business cards as a form of campaign literature. He'd given me the suggestion way back when I visited him at his home before the campaign season, and I came up with my own simple card design that included my campaign slogan, my picture, and my website address. These cards were easy to stick into screen doors or even behind front-porch mailboxes, and they were inexpensive to produce. It's against the law to place anything inside people's mailboxes (that isn't sent by the postal service), so having business cards was a good choice for simple leave-behinds.

After securing my place on the ballot, I put in a new, much larger order for business cards with VistaPrint, and during checkout, the website offered business card–sized magnets to match. These magnets looked just like the paper cards but were instead printed with a soft magnetic backing. These proved to be especially effective because they could be stuck onto the outside of metal mailboxes and some doors. They also made great refrigerator magnets that people could keep around, which they did. Many people told me my face looked out at them each time they went to the fridge. When I canvassed and was invited into people's homes, I'd sometimes even see my magnets on refrigerators, and I figured that wasn't a bad thing at all. For a few cents, I was able to keep my face and message visible in countless homes.

I ordered nearly 5,000 cards and magnets for about $400, and I still find them popping up in drawers to this day. We had a *lot* of them. I gave them away every chance I got, including at parades, meet-and-greets, and pop-ins, which were times when I went to into bars and restaurants to say hello and casually introduce myself to patrons.

One such pop-in was a visit to the Hi Bar, a great place for wings and beer on Elmira's south side. It was what's known as a *townie bar*, a place where locals hung out. It had a long wooden bar, booths for dining in the pub area, and a casual feel. When I walked in, an older couple was sitting in the first booth awaiting their meal, so I approached with my business cards in hand and casually introduced myself.

"Hi, I'm John Tonello and I'm running for mayor," I said, putting forward a business card for one of them to take.

The woman looked nervous but didn't say anything. She left that to her husband, who asked, "What's your party?"

"I'm a Democrat," I said, not entirely sure where this was going.

"Oh, so you're an abortionist," the man said. Of all the possible responses, I was *not* expecting that, and it caught me a little flat-footed. I could see his face flushing and his whole body beginning to radiate clear agitation.

Instead of arguing or getting agitated myself, I told the man issues like abortion weren't among the things local governments dealt with. That was the purview of the state and federal governments, I told him. I tried to shift the conversation to local issues like streets and crime, but to no avail. The man was clearly a staunch conservative and kept on badgering me about abortion and killing babies until his wife, growing more agitated with her husband, blurted out to him, "Stop! Just stop! Stop it!"

I took that opportunity to thank them for their time and quickly move on to other booths. I didn't leave them a card. Nor did I do many such pop-ins afterward. I had just been trying to be friendly and nonchalant, but there were clearly people out there with strong political feelings. Better, I thought, to do my campaigning in places I really knew.

Lesson learned.

## Yard signs

With just six weeks to the primary election, I needed to order campaign signs and formulate a plan for getting them in front of as many houses as possible. July was still too early to plant them in supporters' yards, but we needed time to have them printed and delivered. We also needed time to get them distributed and planted, which became a huge effort Andy would lead.

As with other campaign materials, I started with local print shops to see what they charged for campaign signs, but, as before with my literature, I was hesitant. I didn't want anyone local to know how many signs I'd be printing or what I was spending. Instead, I looked on the web and found that I could get cardboard signs from online vendors for far less money than what the locals offered. Since we were being as frugal as possible, that seemed like the best option.

The hardest part was choosing from among the dozens of off-the-shelf designs the online vendors offered. Some were fancy, some straightforward, some single-color, some two-color. I knew I didn't want anything too frilly or hard to read, just straightforward signs that could be comprehended quickly and easily when potential voters walked or drove by. I thumbed through one vendor's catalog and literally flipped the pages really fast, using this unscientific technique to see which design just jumped out at me. In the end, it was an easy choice: a sign with three wide horizontal stripes—red, white, and blue. In the top stripe, we had the word "ELECT" printed in reverse bold (white) type on a red background, under which was "TON-ELLO" in bold blue letters on white, and under that "MAYOR" in reverse bold letters on a blue background. The whole thing was bold and simple and, most importantly, easy to read.

To this day, I still marvel at candidates' choices in yard signs. Many are very hard to read or too cutesy, with some sort of script writing or shamrocks or other icons. My communications background told me such choices were mistakes because anything that took away from the message and didn't simply convey the actionable information well enough for passing eyes wasn't going to be effective.

My signs stood out, and that was all we wanted. And because I'd found an online vendor, I was able to get my two-color signs—and the metal frames to hang them on—for less than $4 each. Today's bag-style signs—essentially signs printed on thin polyethylene—are much cheaper than the cardboard ones we used, but they weren't yet widely available. Still, we got the signs cheap and ordered 100 of them. If I won the Democratic primary, I figured we could reuse the ones we already had in the general election and get an even better bang for our buck.

Even before the signs were delivered, we set about coming up with lists of lawns where we could plant them. Andy and others made sure to take note of folks who wanted a sign when we were carrying the nominating petitions and, later, canvassing neighborhoods for votes. But Andy was even more dogged. He'd end up talking to hundreds of people, even cold-calling Democrats from our lists, to ask if they would be willing to place Elect Tonello Mayor signs in their yards.

Andy put together a list for his cold-calling and follow-up calls to people who'd signed my petitions and came up with a script he shared with others on my campaign team:

> Hello, Mr/Mrs . . . I'm calling for the John Tonello mayoral campaign for the City of Elmira. We want to thank you for signing John's petition that allowed him to get on the ballot for the mayoral election. We do appreciate your support. We're also hoping we can place a yard sign in front of your home in further support of John.

If someone on such cold-calls said no, we would thanked them for their time and remind them that we'd still appreciate their vote at the polls for the September 13 Democratic primary. This effort had the two-for-one effect of finding places for signs *and* encouraging people to vote. It was a big effort, and Andy and I exchanged dozens of emails during the process. Over the next few weeks, the sign list continued to grow.

In New York State, local municipalities establish rules that determine when campaign signs can go up and when they must come down. In Elmira, the rules said signs could go up thirty days before an election day, which meant mid-August for the September primary. Until we could lawfully put them up, Andy continued to make calls, and during canvassing, we asked voters for permission to plant signs. As a result of these efforts, we were able to put up dozens of signs on the very first day they were allowed, and we grew from there.

Of course, just as in real estate, location was everything. We sought out supporters on some of Elmira's busiest streets, such as Hoffman and Church Streets, South Avenue, Broadway, Maple Avenue, and others. This remains a common campaign tactic, which gives candidates—or at least their signs—maximum visibility. We even got a supporter who lived across the street from Dan Royle to plant a sign in his yard, which forced Dan and his family to see it every day. When it got stolen, Andy went right back over and planted a new one.

As August went on, we couldn't help but start visually comparing our sign counts with Dan's. He'd opted for one-color medium blue signs with slanted text, which were popping up across the city. Our eyeball counts were totally unscientific, of course, but it seemed to us that we were not just holding our own, but pulling ahead. I credit Andy with making it happen.


## Stickers

Anyone who's ever followed a political candidate knows that the traditional approach is to wear a button of support. We definitely thought about it, but buttons aren't cheap—at least, not as cheap as stickers. Much as I wanted historic-style buttons, I let go of the ideas and instead opted for three-inch round stickers that looked a lot like my yard signs. We wore them on our shirts—and later on our jackets when the weather turned colder—everywhere we went.

As with my signs and other campaign material, I ordered the stickers online. A roll of hundreds cost us about $130, a bargain. At the very least, they were good conversation starters. Later, my barber made up baseball hats with the same logo and gifted them to the campaign. Unfortunately, it was such a hot summer, I didn't end up wearing those hats much, but they were a good addition. The stickers, hats, and signs were all coordinated—on-brand and easy to read.

When I first started campaigning, wearing such branding didn't come naturally to me. Whether it's a sticker, T-shirt, hat, or whatever, you essentially become a walking billboard, which is kind of in-your-face. That's sort of the point, but my long-instilled shyness made such obvious advertising hard to get used to. Still, we knew it had to be done. I was a complete unknown, and I needed to go from zero to elected in just a few months. Unlike Dan Royle, I didn't have biweekly city council meetings or other built-in platforms to make the news or spread the word. I had to be everywhere and anywhere—the Grove Street RiverFest, the VFW Italian Fest, the Juneteenth Festival, and many other community events—and wearing my campaign on my body was the best way I knew to help erase my anonymity.

## Letters to the editor

Another way to get some attention was letters to the editor, which would appear regularly on the *Star-Gazette* opinion page. The newspaper would accept letters well into the election season, so the more letters we could get, the better. Andy kicked it off with a June 18 letter, and in it, he highlighted my work experience and my bipartisan, inclusive approach.

"Residents of Elmira will have an opportunity to elect a new mayor in November," Patros wrote. "John Tonello, a Democrat, is one of the candidates. I've known John for nine years. He is an intelligent young man with enthusiasm, wisdom, and fresh ideas, but his most notable characteristic is his ability to communicate with people."

Patros hit all the key points in his letter, the first of several he wrote and had published in the *Star-Gazette*. My neighbor Chrissy, Sharon, and even Mom wrote letters. It was a simple, zero-cost way to keep my name out there. Andy solicited letters from others, too, and each one was written in their own words. After all, the writers were mostly people who knew me, but not all. There would also be letters from people like Eric Massa, who would run and win a seat in Congress the next year, and William and Jacqueline Kiser, whose house I'd visited while canvassing.

"One day this last summer, someone rang our doorbell," they wrote in the *Star-Gazette*. "Upon opening the door, we were greeted by a very friendly young man who introduced himself as John Tonello. He informed us he was seeking the position of mayor of Elmira and that he would appreciate our support. What? A politician actually making a house call. He asked us if we approved of the way Elmira was being run, and what if any changes we would like to see. The visit lasted about 30 to 35 minutes. He was in no hurry to leave until he heard us out. For the first time as an

Elmira resident, someone had treated us like people whose opinions really mattered. Needless to say, he has our votes."

I was very proud when I read the Kisers' letter. In just a few words, they embodied my entire approach to running for office and serving as mayor. I never just knocked on doors, dropped literature, and ran. I truly wanted to talk with people and hear their ideas. I think the Kisers were open with me because I was open with them. I wasn't seeking to become just another politician; I wanted to become a public servant. That meant taking time to listen and understand. That's why I tried never to appear to voters that I was in a hurry.

Letters from others I didn't really know had similar good things to say about me, the issues I raised, and my approach. Each helped bring confidence to my campaign and the strategy we'd locked in: Don't shove things down people's throats, we thought. Listen to their ideas. Take the time to truly engage. Have a sense of humor. Repeat.

Altogether, our campaign materials helped market me as a candidate, keeping the core message front and center. Social media was new, and the only option at the time was Facebook, but it hadn't become the advertising juggernaut it's become today. Of course, today, social media is a big part of political campaigns and can, and should, be used widely to get out the word, but there's a caveat: Most social media posts target small groups of like-minded users. Unless candidates pay to reach certain audiences—or their posts go viral—social media can give a false sense of support where there is none or little.

Other than the web, we didn't do much with Facebook, but everything else would require money—thousands of dollars—and I knew I couldn't self-fund it all. We would need to raise money to pay for the signs, cards, and other materials, and for television and radio commercials that would air right before the primary election. Now, as our campaign efforts geared up, we needed to think about cold, hard cash.

7

# Making Friends and Raising Cash

## Asking for money

It's no secret that political campaigns require money. Not just state and national races, but local ones, too. Since the Supreme Court's 2010 Citizens United decision literally opened the floodgates to the influx of campaign cash, state and national races are swamped with millions and millions of dollars. Fortunately, we didn't need millions. Not even close. But I did the math on what things were costing—and would cost—and figured we'd need about $7,000 to pay for the primary campaign. If we won, we'd need still more for the general election.

Asking for money is *not* my favorite thing, but I knew it was a necessary part of a political campaign. Instead of thinking purely in terms of dollars and cents, though, we thought of each donated dollar as a sort of vote. Those who contributed would definitely vote for me (if they lived in the city) and would probably encourage their friends to do the same. So the more people we could talk to about money, the greater the chance of garnering supporters and votes.

We also decided early on not to just ask for blind donations to the campaign. When we asked for money, we told potential donors what it would be used for: signs, advertising, literature. That way, we could say things like, "Your $20 contribution will buy us five signs." By connecting donations to real things, it was easier to convince people to give. They could see—in real terms—how their money was being spent and helping me win votes. Contributions didn't need to be large. In fact, we wanted to grow the number of contributors as much as we wanted to grow our campaign bank account.

I started my fundraising where many do: with my family. Right out of the gate, my mom and stepfather, my father, and my siblings contributed to my campaign, ultimately accounting for a couple thousand dollars. Aunts and uncles, neighbors, my former boss at Corning Inc., and even my ex-wife contributed to our efforts. To each, we sent a letter of thanks on the campaign letterhead, another touchpoint to keep the race top of mind.

For broader fundraising, we knew we'd have to host some events specifically for the purpose. First, though, we held much more informal meetings so I could personally get in front of voters now that I'd succeeded in getting on the ballot.

## Meet and greets

The term "meet and greet" is campaign shorthand for opportunities for me, the candidate, to talk directly with voters. They were generally held at public places, like the library, but also at people's homes. I needed to get myself out there, and we figured these events offered a low-cost way to do that. At the same time, announcing these events via press releases that would appear in the *Star-Gazette* would offer the secondary benefit of keeping my name out there.

I sent such a release to the paper in early July for our first meet and greet, which was to be held at Elmira's Steele Memorial Library. A brief appeared in the local section of the *Star-Gazette* on July 8 for an event we'd planned for the evening of July 12.

On that night, Andy, Mom, and I met at the library, unsure how many people would show, even though Andy had sent email to about sixty supporters and the piece had appeared in the paper the previous Friday.

Mom brought a friend from church, who was quite full of ideas. In fact, we couldn't really get her to stop talking. She talked about the Housing Coalition, an organization that aims to help people find affordable housing, and she had opinions on lots of issues. Fifteen minutes into the conversation, Juan Jones came with his brother Miguel, so I tore myself away from Mom's church friend and talked with Jones, who I discovered was not registered with any political party but was curious about the political process. A bit later, an actor from Elmira Little Theatre, whom I'd met when my ex-wife acted with him in the local company's shows, popped his head in. He was picking up some DVDs at the library, happened to see my campaign flier on the door, and decided to join us. One other gentleman came in but took literature without saying anything. He just sort of smiled and backed out of the room.

By the end of the night, I'd spoken to five people between six-thirty and eight-thirty that evening—none of whom was eligible to vote in the September 13 primary. The night was a bust but turned out to be a good learning experience. Mom suggested we should host another library night with more notice, but I vetoed the idea right away. "We need to go to where people already are," I said. "Coming to the library for a meeting is just one more unscheduled meeting in people's lives. Like tonight, no one will come."

Though I'd briefed myself on the issues before the meet and greet, I hadn't really needed to. There'd been no voters there at all. By the end of the night, mostly what I needed was to sit down. As sometimes happens when I'm under stress, my ulcerative colitis had reasserted itself by manifesting arthritis-like pain in my joints. Tonight it was in my knee, which was swollen. After standing for nearly three hours, I could barely bend it. This and the low turnout left me in a foul, dejected mood.

The next meet and greet we did was at a supporter's home, a friend of my parents who had a beautiful place filled with antiques and historic charm. Many of the people there were unknown to me, but I took time to meet everyone, shake hands, and make my pitch to be Elmira's next mayor. The hostess offered soft drinks, cookies, and other food to nibble on, and it was a casual, friendly affair. At least twenty people showed up this time, thanks to the efforts of the hostess and others to recruit their friends. After my one-on-ones, I took the opportunity to address the entire gathering, asking folks at the end to please consider contributing money to my campaign. Several did, but this wasn't truly a fundraiser. However, the good turnout lifted my spirits and told us these kinds of events were far more effective than the one we'd tried at the library.

Later, we'd take advantage of gatherings hosted by local unions and others, which drew in their members during regularly scheduled meetings and events. These were great opportunities to meet fellow Democrats and likeminded men and women without having to do any of the logistics. Oh, and they were free!


## A fundraiser at Horigan's

As July melted into August—it continued to be an exceptionally hot summer—we started to plan what we hoped would be our biggest fundraiser.

Horigan's pub on Davis Street was my neighborhood bar and restaurant, a place where I'd hatched many of my political ambitions with friends over a glass of scotch, so it seemed like the ideal place to gather supporters and drum up some much-needed funds.

Unlike the more informal house event, the fundraiser at Horigan's would feature food, an open bar, raffles, and music by guitarist and singer John Manfredi. We asked for donations of $20 per person or $30 per couple. Mom worked hard to make this happen, talking with Horigan's owners to provide an inexpensive meal of penne and grilled chicken, and desserts mostly in the form of cookies. Initially Mom wanted her friends to make the food, but bringing prepared food to an active restaurant is something the Health Department frowns on, so that was nixed.

We asked guests to RSVP, and we had a great turnout. Dozens of friends, supporters, and family members came, including several of my Cornell University coworkers. We held the event on a Tuesday night, so the turnout was particularly positive for both Horigan's and the campaign. Tuesday was generally the restaurant's slowest night, but we managed to fill the place. I took time to mingle and talk with folks, offered my campaign pitch to people I didn't know, helped announce the winners of the raffle, and, of course, gave a speech. By now, I'd become quite comfortable standing before crowds and making my pitch, and it was well received by the friendly crowd. By the end of the night we'd managed to gross more than $1,000, less than we hoped, but definitely a boost.

A couple weeks later, we held another fundraiser at the home of Martha Horton, a former weekly newspaper editor and supporter. She'd invited her like-minded friends and hosted about twenty people in her historic home on West Second Street. Again, I didn't know most of the people there, but took time to chat with them all, give a speech, and ask for their support—both financially and at the polls. By the time the two-hour event wrapped up around seven o'clock, we'd collected more than $300 in contributions.

With these events and individual contributions, we were well on our way to meeting our $7,000 goal. In keeping with our ambition to focus on our race, not the other guy's, we felt pretty good about the state of our fundraising. We had no idea how Dan Royle was doing on that score. In New York State, campaign filing deadlines are staggered throughout the political calendar, so that publicly available campaign finance information wouldn't be available until early October, after the primary election.

Just days before the vote, though, the newspaper ran a story about campaign spending so far, and we learned that Dan had taken a $5,000 personal loan from his sister and brother-in-law to fund his efforts. He told the newspaper the loan was financing most of his campaign and had to be paid back.

"The primary didn't leave me much time to raise money," Royle told the newspaper.

We were stunned. My campaign would end up raising raising just over $7,000 from donors during primary season, but Dan would raise just $2,800, plus his loan.

## Building a war chest

On the spending side, by the end of August we'd spent just $2,600, with another $2,500 to be spent in the run-up to the election for television and radio advertising. At the same point in the campaign, Royle had spent $4,700 with no television. That told me our frugal efforts to find the best deals on signs, literature, and other expenses was already paying off.

At the same time, the Republicans running for county sheriff also were raising and spending cash on their campaigns. Christopher Moss had spent about $14,000 on that countywide race so far. His primary opponent, William Mayhew, had spent about $12,000. They had significantly more ground to cover, of course. Signs alone to cover the county's 407 square miles would cost a lot more than the seven square miles of the city.

When the newspaper asked Royle if he thought he'd spent enough to win the mayoral primary, he said, "I'll find out Tuesday. I would hope so, but who knows?"

News of Royle taking a loan really surprised me. Of course, I'd "loaned" my own funds to the campaign, but I never considered asking for a loan from anyone else. To me, campaign contributions represented a concrete way to garner support from actual voters. If we couldn't get people to give us their hard-earned money, we figured it would be even harder for them to give us their votes.

That same approach is widely used in modern campaigns, in which candidates tout the numbers of small-dollar donors. In many national elections, it's common to see candidates dip into their own cash and contribute millions of their own money, which is why some are asked to run in the first place. Some of these folks have deep pockets and can often plow through the campaign process on their own money. To me, this has led to too many wealthy candidates for public office and too few "average" citizens, who, like me, weren't bursting with cash to splurge on a political race. We needed financial support, and soliciting money was hard work, but so was soliciting votes. We needed the two to go hand in hand and underscore the broad appeal of my candidacy. To us, few contributions meant little support.

In soliciting campaign donations, I was mindful that I wanted neither too much nor too little money. We'd set a budget, and that's what we aimed for. The goal wasn't to have anything left over, no excess to pad our campaign account. The latter is often common in modern campaigns, in which strong fund-raisers amass large campaign war chests and then share the funds with other like-minded candidates. In state and national races, that's typical. In local races like mine, not so much. But with Republicans holding the region's state senate and assembly seats, those incumbents had plenty of cash to spread around to other Republican candidates. On the Democratic side, we had none. Once the primaries were over, we figured the Republicans would have much more money available, but we kept to our plan and reminded ourselves that money doesn't always win elections.

## Hitting the streets night after night

Running a citywide campaign meant my team and I had to juggle a lot of moving parts in a relatively short amount of time. Most of it we were learning as we went, not having run a campaign before, and we felt the press of time.

In the weeks between when I'd secured the ballot line and the primary election were short, and we needed to knock on as many doors and meet as many people as possible. Putting out press releases, writing copy for postcards, tracking community calendars for events to attend, and raising money were all important, but going door-to-door remained my primary focus.

Fortunately, I had my voterBase application to help. Since this was a primary, only Democratic votes mattered. Later, if we made it onto the November ballot, we'd reach out to Republicans, independents, and people of all political stripes, but right now it was a Democrats-only affair.

Although I'd done what I could to get noticed on television and in the newspaper, not many people were thinking about politics in the middle of the summer. Most were busy taking vacations, heading off to summer camp, or relaxing by their pools. They were not thinking, "Oh, I gotta go vote!" So, in going door-to-door, we weren't just campaigning for me, but informing people about the September primary, which was critical. History told us that voter turnout during primaries would be low, usually just a fraction of the number who might vote in November. New York State has since moved primaries even earlier in the year, making the problem of voter turnout even worse. The result is too few people making the choice of who will ultimately be on the ballot, and those are usually the diehard political types, not your average voters. This reality meant we needed to find all the likely voters we could—and fast.

By using my voterBase software, I was able to do that in minutes. I searched for Democratic voters who voted in *every* election as far back as the Board of Elections data went, and we focused our attention on people who were most likely to turn out in the late-summer primary.

Using data this way provided us with an incredible advantage. We could cover more ground more quickly, though it also meant skipping a lot of Democratic houses. We simply did not have the time to knock on every door.

As with the nominating petitions, Andy and I fanned out across the city. Since I was single and had no family obligations, I could go out every night after work, and I did. We'd avoid actual dinnertimes as best we could, but there was a built-in hard stop: sunset. People are generally reluctant nowadays to answer knocks on their doors, let alone those that come after sundown.

I wanted to visit as many houses as I could, but I also didn't want to appear hurried. This approach paid off on more than one occasion, including when I was canvassing on First Street, a tree-lined street on the city's north side featuring a mix of modest homes. Before knocking, I glanced toward the horizon and figured I had maybe another forty-five minutes before the sun set, and knocked on the next door on my list, a house with a long frontage just off the sidewalk.

When the homeowner answered, he immediately invited me in to chat. Inside, we sat in the cozy living room, where I spent well over a half-hour talking with the man, answering his questions, asking him what was important to him, and generally getting to know him. I also noticed the room darkening as the last of the summer day's sun disappeared.

It was well past dusk when I left, and I reluctantly decided this had to be my last stop of the day. Despite the long conversation, I felt it was worth it because I had left feeling the man would cast his vote for me, and that's all I really wanted. As I went out the front door and walked down the sidewalk toward my home, I saw the man I'd just spoken with walk down a hallway to his kitchen, essentially a parallel inside his home to my path outside his home. With his windows open to catch some of the cooler evening air, I heard the man get on the phone to make a call, and I could hear his side of the conversation, which began, "Hey, you know that guy who's running for mayor? He just left and we had a great conversation. . . ."

I smiled to myself in the dark as I walked on. Taking time to talk and listen—despite the setting sun and the press of time—had paid off. The man was filled with positive energy and was spreading his experience by word of mouth. Nothing was more valuable. I'd managed to leave a positive impression he wanted to immediately share. It told me we were on the right track and that, despite the lateness of the day, remaining unhurried and truly listening was an effective way to campaign. It's harder than it may sound because lots of campaign logistics were always roiling my brain and making me feel like I needed to move on to the next thing. But perception was everything, and if someone wanted to talk, I'd listen.

## Learning that pace is important

Going out every night after work and on weekends kept me busy, and as August wore on and the days grew shorter, I found myself looking forward to rainy days. Canvassing is difficult in the rain, particularly while wearing a satchel of campaign literature, and I did some while juggling an umbrella and my hand cards, but I soon found it wasn't really worth it. If it was raining out, I'd skip canvassing and remain home to work on other aspects of the campaign.

This wasn't by any means a formal tactic for pacing myself, but Andy and I both learned that setting a slow, steady pace was important. I might find myself getting short-tempered or just physically tired, and that told me I needed to take care of myself as much as the campaign. I would run a couple miles several times a week to keep in shape, which helped settle my frame of mind, but so would simply sitting out back on my deck smoking a cigarette and having a glass of scotch.

Though I wanted to be all-campaign all the time, it just wasn't practical or healthy. I needed to find ways to decompress, just think, and still have some fun. Not that I didn't have fun campaigning, but it was mostly work, and I also had a day job that paid my bills, which required me to leave the house around seven each morning and make the forty-five-minute drive to my office at Cornell University in Ithaca. If I immediately went out canvassing when I got home, that would quickly add up to a thirteen-hour day. It just wasn't sustainable. That sort of pace would leave me lying in bed and finding it hard to shut down and sleep, and a lack of sleep would just make everything even harder.

Fortunately, Andy and the rest of my campaign team understood. They didn't badger me into going out every day, and they didn't need to. I was plenty motivated already. But Andy and I would take an evening off to grab some Buffalo wings, drink a few beers, and talk about the other things going on in our lives. Andy had a full-time day job too, and though his wife, Julie, understood his need to work on my campaign, her patience wasn't infinite. Nor should it have been. She and Andy would go out, stay home and watch television, or just enjoy each other's company. I tried to do the same.

As it happened, in the heart of the campaign I was dating a smart, pretty, brown-haired woman named Sarah Hilsman. We both worked in Cornell University's Caldwell Hall, she in the basement for the International Students and Scholars Office, and I on the third floor for the Graduate School. We'd met around the time of the summer solstice and enjoyed each other's company, so we'd occasionally get meals together (often after work in Ithaca, where she lived) and sometimes in Elmira when she came to visit. She had a fifteen-year-old daughter and I had three cats, which complicated things, but we managed to find downtime together that helped me keep my head on straight.

As it turned out, Sarah was no stranger to Democratic politics. Her father, Roger Hilsman, had been an aide and advisor to Presidents John F. Kennedy and Lyndon B. Johnson, and he'd been assistant secretary of state for Far Eastern affairs in 1963 and 1964. He left government in the mid-1960s to teach at Columbia University in New York City and wrote several books. In 1972, he ran for a seat in the House of Representatives but lost the race.

Though Sarah was no longer close to her father when we were dating, she was familiar with high-level politics and proved to be a great sounding board. She, too, was a hard-core Democrat, but she was mostly content to sit on the sidelines and support my efforts.

Spending time with Sarah, Andy, Mom and my stepfather, and other friends helped me balance the fast pace of the campaign with just, well, living. What I hadn't truly known from the outset was how different running for public office was from other jobs, and it would take its toll if I let it. As a candidate, I was literally out in front of people all the time, always "on," always campaigning. There's always something that can be done, and with the clock ticking, the pressure was real. Still, without taking breaks, it would've been all too easy to lose patience and focus. Rest was just as important as the work, which wouldn't end until election day—and depending on how things turned out in September—beyond.

Figure 1. A group of my earliest supporters join me in downtown Elmira's Wisner Park for my mayoral announcement on May 19, 2005, including my mom, front right, and Sharon Mitchell, third from the left. I'd planned the press conference for noon to maximize news coverage, and clips from my live interview aired just hours before the City Democratic Committee met—and endorsed—my opponent. *Source:* Provided by the author.

Figure 2. My campaign business card, which I handed out every chance I got. We ended up printing thousands of these cards and hundreds of matching magnets. *Source:* Provided by the author.

Figure 3. The sticker I created and wore everywhere during the campaign. These were much cheaper than pin-on campaign buttons. *Source:* Provided by the author.

Figure 4. The postcard I sent to likely Democratic voters ahead of the September 13, 2005, primary election. Postcards were cheaper and easier to send than letters. *Source:* Provided by the author.

Figure 5. My first meet-and-greet event at Elmira's Steele Memorial Library, where a few interested men and women showed up, but no city voters. We decided events like this were a waste of time and instead started going to existing events where the people were. *Source:* Provided by the author.

Figure 6. Meeting voters while manning the Democrats' table during an event at Elmira College. I went to dozens of events during the campaign to listen to voters and show my face. *Source:* Provided by the author.

Figure 7. Dan Royle, left, and me at a summer gathering of Democrats at Grove Street Park. Despite the primary competition between us, we got along well. Behind Dan is his son, who would later mount a write-in campaign for his dad. *Source:* Provided by the author.

Figure 8. My campaign yard sign pictured outside my West Gray Street home in Elmira during the summer of 2005. By the end of the campaign, we'd plant nearly 400 signs across the city. *Source:* Provided by the author.

Figure 9. Mom and me during my August fundraiser at Horigan's Tavern. We'd gross about $1,000 that night and went on to raise more than $7,000 for the primary campaign. *Source:* Provided by the author.

Figure 10. Moments after I emerged from one of the old mechanical voting booths for the Democratic primary, September 13, 2005. I literally got to pull a lever under my name, but these big blue machines would soon be retired and replaced with computerized ballot scanners. *Source:* Provided by the author.

Figure 11. Then–Attorney General Eliot Spitzer, right, made an appearance in Elmira to endorse me for mayor, October 2005. Spitzer would go on to be elected governor by a wide margin the following year, but scandal led to his resignation the year after that. I'd end up working with four different governors in my first five years in office. *Source:* Provided by the author.

Figure 12. Awaiting the general election returns at Horigan's with about 100 other supporters, including Mom, right, and incumbent Councilman Terry McLaughlin, left. *Source:* Provided by the author.

Figure 13. Horigan's was packed with Democrats and other supporters on election night, November 8, 2005. Interim Mayor Bill O'Brien, center, is wearing the big smile. *Source:* Provided by the author.

Figure 14. Andy Patros, right, gives me a two-handed thumbs-up as I give my victory speech on November 8, 2005. Andy did yeoman's work throughout the campaign and was key to my success. *Source:* Provided by the author.

Figure 15. The final election night results of the general election on a board at Horigan's Tavern. I won with 56 percent of the vote and defeated Dan Mandell in twenty-two of the city's thirty-one election districts. *Source:* Provided by the author.

Figure 16. Giving my inaugural speech after being sworn in as mayor, January 1, 2006, at the Clemens Center. I reiterated my goal to engage average citizens in city government. Returning Councilman Jim Hare, second from left, and new Councilwoman Carol Mechalke, right, had just been sworn in too. *Source:* Provided by the author.

Figure 17. Presenting my mom, Rosalie Krajci, with the flowers used to decorate the council meeting table during the inaugural, January 1, 2006. My stepfather, Tom Krajci, is at center. Both provided lots of support during the campaign, but when I first told them about my plans to run for mayor, mom later told me, "You could've knocked me over with a feather." *Source:* Provided by the author.

Figure 18. My father, Francis Tonello, lived in San Diego and had been a big supporter of my campaign from afar. When he died in early 2007, I placed his funeral flag in the mayor's office. Above me on the walls are two paintings by Tess Danaher, whose artwork had adorned City Hall's third floor for my Mayor's Art Project. I bought both paintings, and they still hang in my home. *Source:* Provided by the author.

Figure 19. Speaking at Woodlawn National Cemetery after walking in Elmira's annual Memorial Day Parade, May 29, 2006. I regularly spoke at local events across the city, and this was always one of the most moving. Jim Hare, an army veteran, is seated at right. *Source:* Provided by the author.

Figure 20. Among the famous people I'd meet during my tenure was former New York City Democratic Mayor Ed Koch. We sat next to each other when Lt. Gov. David Paterson was sworn in to replace Eliot Spitzer as New York governor, March 17, 2008. *Source:* Provided by the author.

Figure 21. The yard sign I used for the primary and general election campaigns. I picked it out of a catalog because it really stood out. *Source:* Provided by the author.

Figure 22. John Corsi, right, being interviewed by a WETM-TV reporter following a council meeting. John loved Elmira and after serving years as head of the Mark Twain Golf Course was elected to the city council. As the ranking Republican, I appointed him Deputy Mayor. *Source:* Courtesy of Dan Corsi.

8

# Lead-up to the Primary

## Hitting our stride

By late August, we were in a groove. Primary election day was one of the latest possible on the election calendar, September 13, which afforded us a little more time than what was typical, but the daylight was getting short and we still had a lot of work to do.

In the last two weeks of the election season, timing would be everything. We knew we wanted to send out postcards, encourage letters to the editor, air television and radio spots, plant signs, and more. I'd decided early on that we wouldn't do any newspaper advertising, which was expensive and too narrow an audience for the price. Even then, newspaper readership wasn't what it used to be, and though I'd worked in the newspaper business, I couldn't justify the expense. I thought it would be better to use the airwaves to reach voters and budgeted about $2,500 for the effort.

## Direct mail

On the mailing side, we had postcards printed up that would be sent out in time to arrive in mailboxes in the days immediately before the election. We wanted our message to be top of mind, so we didn't send them out willy-nilly. Too early would lessen the impact and be a waste of expensive postage.

Throughout the campaign, we opted for postcards over letters for a couple reasons. For one, postcards would be far cheaper and easier to produce than letters, which needed to be stuffed into envelopes and cost more to mail. Postage rates for postcards were cheaper, an important consideration. Mostly, though, we knew from Andy's postal experience that such campaign literature—like any other direct mail—should arrive ready to read and read quickly. Too many people who find political letters in their mail along with other "junk" toss them without ever opening the envelopes. Andy knew from experience that it was better to send mail that could be looked at and read between the mailbox and the kitchen table, no letter opener required. That meant keeping the message short and sweet.

I came up with a simple one-color design (black type, white card stock) that described my background and experience that would serve me as mayor, including my work at Cornell and Corning Inc., my experience in both communications and technology, and my record of innovation, leadership, and results. The card also included a personalized note from me:

Dear voter . . . I believe our city is poised for a resurgence, and together we can make that happen. It'll take hard work, new energy, new ideas, and a new vision. That's what I offer. That's why I want to be mayor. In this year's Democratic primary, cast your vote for positive change and practical solutions. Please cast your vote for me, John Tonello. Thank you! See you at the polls September 13!

The postcard included a large "Please vote September 13!" at the bottom, a small headshot of me, the tonelloformayor.com website address, and the campaign phrase. When it came time to produce labels, I went back to my voterBase software and searched for the Democratic voters who regularly turned out. At the time, there were more than 5,700 registered Democrats in Elmira, but I wanted to make sure we targeted those most likely to vote in a local, non-presidential election. The result was well over 1,000 households, but many had the same postal address. For those with multiple Democrats, instead of sending multiple cards to each voter at a single address, I had voterBase convert the multiple cohabitating addressees to "Family," as in the "Smith Family" rather than Sue Smith, Fred Smith, and Johnny Smith. This saved us print and postage costs and the time it would take for us to label everything.

For this mailing, Mom went to the post office and got us all the post-card stamps we needed, and we manually went about the task of applying them and the address labels to each postcard. Modern technology allows both addresses and postage to be applied with technology, but it costs money. Instead, we stacked everything on my dining room table and did some old-fashioned peeling and sticking. It wasn't hard work and didn't take us long, and we passed the time chitchatting about names we came across and other campaign gossip, riding the buzz of those final days of the campaign. Unspoken was our hope that all our work wouldn't be for naught.

## Cutting a TV commercial

As election day drew nearer, I continued to write and edit the copy I would use for my television commercial, which would air on WETM-TV, WENY, local cable channels, and also on AM and FM radio stations. The idea was to have WETM-TV's production team create the spot—with the help of my ex-wife, who worked there—and then share the finished product with the other local television station, WENY. We'd extract the audio for use on radio.

Creating an effective thirty-second television spot is no small feat because I felt it needed to quickly summarize my candidacy and compel people to vote. The words needed to underscore my campaign themes, and the video needed to be straightforward and professional looking. After several drafts, I finally came up with a ninety-one-word script, and the production team helped turn it into something great. I drew from my experience on the campaign trail, which highlighted how unique the primary for mayor was and how unusual it was for political candidates to knock on doors. This is what I came up with:

> People on Thurston Street, Baty, here on West Gray and across Elmira tell me it's been years since a candidate for mayor knocked on their doors and asked for their ideas. Well, I'm knocking, and I'm asking. I'm John Tonello. As mayor, I'll involve all Elmirans in the city's future because it will take all of us to strengthen our neighborhoods, create jobs, and spur growth. I have the right experience. I can get things done. We can change Elmira. Vote for me in the Democratic primary, September 13th. I'll listen.

For the video, the production team recorded me saying the words right into the camera as I walked down a Near Westside sidewalk. I'd committed the whole thing to memory (and it's still in my brain) so I would appear conversational and relaxed. I didn't want images of me with some anonymous voice-over, or me in a hard hat shaking workers' hands, or any of that. If I had just thirty seconds, I wanted people to see and hear from me directly.

In addition to filming me speaking directly to the camera, WETM-TV's Kevin Ackley and his production team shot video of me shaking hands with a voter opening his front door to me (Sharon Mitchell's father) and images of me chatting with voters at Wisner Park. They also recorded video of the street signs I mentioned and used those to transition from a view of a typical city neighborhood to me. They did a great job, and perhaps best of all, it didn't cost a thing. When you advertised on WETM-TV, they would do the production for free. In all, we spent just over $3,000 on television and radio—nearly half the campaign budget.

It was a good investment, which I'd soon learn firsthand. When the commercial started airing in the waning days of the primary campaign, I was still going door-to-door and talking with voters. Before the television ads aired, I remained largely unknown, but after they aired, people recognized me *immediately*. At one door, a voter actually said, "Hey! You're that guy!"

If I'd been anonymous before, I sure wasn't anymore. In terms of branding, I *was* the brand, but now people I couldn't possibly have met in person were seeing and hearing me. I knew television was powerful, but this overnight transformation amazed me. Almost overnight, I'd become real to thousands of viewers, no longer merely a name in the paper. I'd done WETM-TV's Sunday local interview show earlier in the summer, but that appearance had nothing like the impact of my commercial. And because we wanted viewers to see the ad at least five times—impressions, as they're known—we had strategically placed ads in the evening news and on a smattering of cable channels, including CNBC, CNN, and MSNBC. We also bought time on the local morning news programs, the *Today Show*, *Meet the Press*, and more. On radio, we bought spots that would run during morning drive time.

If we'd had more money, we probably would've spent even more, but I felt the spread we bought was enough for our purpose. We'd done our research early on and knew what our total ad buy—some forty airings across television and radio—would cost and the number of impressions we could expect. Because we'd saved so much by not hiring an agency to write copy or design campaign literature, we had enough cash on hand to make this happen. We looked for similar ads to air for Dan Royle, but we didn't see any, though one of my supporters had heard the radio ad he was airing. We figured Dan either didn't have the money for television or didn't see the value in it. As a result, my television commercial was the only one running in those final days leading up to September 13.

## A bite heard 'round the neighborhood, then the city

In the waning days of the campaign, I continued to knock on doors and reach as many voters as I possibly could. I had visited hundreds of homes already, but with low turnout expected in the primary, every knock mattered.

On a Wednesday evening, I headed over to Magee Street to canvass, and the third house I visited had a wide front porch with an outdoor couch positioned to one side. The door off the porch seemed like the best one to knock on—it was always hard to tell if people used front or side doors—so I climbed the wooden steps and knocked on the aluminum storm door. Almost immediately, I heard loud barking from inside and performed one of the tricks Andy had taught me: I put the toe of my shoe against the door to prevent it from suddenly swinging open from the force of an aggressive dog. Inside, the homeowner was clearly struggling to get the door open, maybe even moving some furniture out of the way. Outside, the sun was setting behind me, casting my face in shadow while beaming harsh light on anyone—or any animal—coming out of the house.

By the time the homeowner got the door open, his dog was barking madly. With the sun behind me, the dog—a large German shepherd—probably couldn't see who or what was standing outside and leapt immediately at the screen door. Fortunately, the latch held, but he wasn't done. The dog barked louder, and the man tugged hard at its leash to pull it away, but the dog leapt again. This time he was successful, crashing through the screen door and onto me.

I flinched and turned aside, presenting my right arm and shoulder to the attacking animal, thinking it had been a good thing I'd worn a blazer over my T-shirt that day. A split second later, I felt the dog's fangs pierce the skin and the muscles in my right forearm, his jaw holding tight. Seeing what was happening, the dog owner yanked the leash to pull the German shepherd away, but the dog responded by biting *him* before making a second crash through the screen door and closing his big, strong jaw on my right shoulder.

Clearly, I'd chosen the wrong door.

After a bit of a struggle, the homeowner managed to get the dog safely inside and closed the inner door, stepping out to the porch. He sat on the couch and I joined him, both of us panting, our adrenaline flowing, the dog still barking like mad.

"Sorry about that," the man said between breaths. "I don't know what got into him."

When we'd settled for a moment, he told me his dog was current on his shots, so I introduced myself and told him I was running for mayor. We talked for about fifteen minutes, mostly about drugs in the neighborhood and crime in general. He turned out to be a nice guy, thoughtful and sincerely sorry about his German shepherd's behavior. Before I left, I asked if I could put a sign in his yard, and he agreed. I had to smile. The worst encounter of the summer had resulted in a nice outcome, though my arm was now aching badly.

I managed to get to another dozen or so houses, but the pain in my arm was really starting to worry me. At what would be the last house I visited that day, the homeowner saw my ashen face and swollen arm and asked if I was all right. When I told him a dog had bitten me a short time earlier, he graciously invited me inside for some water. I thanked him, and while he was fetching a glass, I gingerly removed my sport coat and took a look at my arm. It had an inch-high knot on it where the dog had bitten me, and there were holes in my skin where the dog's fangs had dug in.

The homeowner was a complete stranger to me, but when he came back with the glass of water and saw the welt on my arm, he immediately offered to drive me to the emergency room. At first I demurred but soon saw the wisdom in his idea and agreed to let him take me. We drove the few blocks to the Arnot-Ogden Medical Center emergency room, and he sat with me in the waiting room and continued to wait while the nurse practitioner gave me a Tetanus shot, wrapped a gauze bandage around my punctured arm, and gave me a prescription for an antibiotic. When I was released, the man drove me back to my car, where I thanked him for his kindness and wished him a good night. Before heading home, though, I drove back to the house where the guy with the dog lived and planted a sign in his front yard.

When I got back to my house, I emailed Andy to tell him about the encounter. He replied quickly.

"Shit, man! Damn!" he wrote. "Keep an eye on it, and definitely keep the wounds clean and use Neosporin ointment. When doing canvassing, that is the one thing I do worry about."

We'd had encounters with dogs before, but nothing like this. I admit I was a bit shellshocked by it all and did *not* want to go back out. Something inside me told me, though, that I needed to get back up on that horse and keep on going. After waiting a few days, I returned to the same neighborhood where I'd left off to continue my door knocking.

The funny thing was, I was almost immediately asked by more than one homeowner in the neighborhood, "Are you the guy who got bit by the dog?" I smiled and admitted I was, but I was mostly surprised by how the news had spread. Apparently, word of mouth had permeated the neighborhood. Now I wasn't just the guy running for mayor, but the guy bit by a dog while running for mayor.

A few days later, I sat down with *Star-Gazette* reporter Brooke Sherman for a story she was writing ahead of the primary election. She was actually writing two stories, one about Dan and one about me, about what we candidates were doing to reach voters in the final days of the primary campaign. I still had gauze wrapped around my arm during the interview, and the reporter asked me about it. I told her the story, and when the story came out in the newspaper, she'd used the dog encounter in her lead.

"Not even a dog bite has stopped John Tonello from knocking on doors in Elmira to get the vote out for the upcoming Sept. 13 primary," she wrote. "Although a large German shepherd took a bite out of his arm last week while he was campaigning, Tonello didn't miss a step and still took the time to chat with the owner about his hopes and goals for the city."

The reporter even included the bit about me going to the emergency room for treatment and a Tetanus shot. So, once again, something bad had turned into something good. We thought the story painted me as a hardworking guy willing to listen, no matter what happened. Ironically, Dan Royle was also among the campaign walking wounded in those late days of the campaign. He came to his interview with the reporter with a cast on his foot. It had turned out that he'd injured his tendon playing softball and was managing to hobble his own way around the city to knock on doors.


## Working the media

When reporters were working on their stories ahead of the primary election, I was always happy to make myself available to them, whether for full stories or merely to get a quote from me on an issue or in response to what another candidate had done or said.

I'd also pushed out another press release to make my own news, this time proposing a Great City, Great Schools collaborative. To me, better links between City Hall and the Elmira City School District could only be helpful. Unlike some cities, where the mayor also has authority over schools, in

Elmira the city and school district were separate entities. Though I had no intention of changing that, I did want to improve the relationship between the city and the school district and become an advocate for local education.

I ended up reaching out to Superintendent Raymond Bryant, and we appeared together for a press conference. I touted the fact that Elmira's schools were better than people perceived them to be and echoed Dr. Bryant's talking points on the benefits of collaboration.

"I agree when Dr. Bryant says Elmira schools are better than their reputation," I said. "The state's School Report Card confirms that. We must work together to improve our schools and our city, and spread that positive message. This is a great place to live. It's a great place to raise children. It's a great place to go to school."

My aim was to link the city and its schools for the benefit of all, including making Elmira an appealing place for businesses to find good, reliable workers. If our schools succeeded, the city would succeed. To me, it was as much about quality education as it was about economic development.

Other media coverage was initiated by the news organizations themselves, including two stories that appeared in the *Star-Gazette* about Dan and me just days before the election, which offered a nice boost before voters went to the polls. We also each had opportunities to write opinion pieces, and in mine I expressed the desire to include more Elmirans in government. I highlighted my key points about improving neighborhoods and downtown, community policing, and more, while Dan took a more personal approach, writing about his upbringing; his twenty-nine-year marriage to his wife, Dawn; and, as a Democrat, standing up for the little guy. It was a good piece, and it also included a line about how former Mayor Stephen Hughes had originally approached Dan to run for the Fifth District council seat. In reading that, I thought that if people liked Hughes, Dan might benefit from that tidbit. If not, it might become a liability.

The night before the primary election, a WENY reporter interviewed me for a news story showing me campaigning at Barb's Soup's On restaurant during the lunchtime rush. The piece aired on the station's six o'clock news. Again, the more coverage we could get, the better, and it was all coming to a head.

Our op-eds and the news stories were a welcome bit of coverage in the lead-up to the election because anything that explained our candidacies—and the fact that a primary election was about to happen—was good. It helped that county voters would be casting ballots in the sheriff's primary and two other city council races, and that coverage might help turnout too.

## Letter-writing campaign

By this point, it wasn't just news coverage and op-eds we wanted. We also wanted to get as many people as we could to write letters to the editor. Again, Andy reached out to a number of folks and asked them to submit letters to the newspaper, mostly our insiders—Andy, Sharon, Chrissy, Mom, and others. Dan's fans wrote letters too. I figured news junkies and those who regularly read the newspaper would see those, but it would be hard to know what kind of impact they'd have. Still, *some* letters were better than *no* letters. And, unlike a general election, there wasn't much coming from the Democratic Committee or its members. Many had strong feelings, but they weren't expressing those feelings publicly, at least not yet.

I also wondered if the *Star-Gazette* would make an endorsement in the mayor and sheriff primary races. Turns out they wouldn't, but I thought the editorial that appeared Monday, September 12, helped bolster my case. The editorial's headline read "Primary stakes" with a subhead reading, "Battles show that opportunistic leaders see need for change."

In the editorial, the newspaper argued that primaries were a good thing. "Other primaries throughout the Southern Tier show that potential community leaders are not willing to stand by the status quo," they wrote. "That's a benefit for all voters, who now have legitimate choices. Candidates have engaged voters in issues familiar to readers, such as economic development and downtown revitalization. The distinction this year is that the discussions have taken place openly and not just within the confines of party committees."

That bit was music to my ears. I'd been preaching that from day one. That was the whole idea. Win or lose, I wanted voters to have a real choice. So far, both the Democratic and Republican Committees had endorsed their insiders. Christopher Moss and I were the outsiders and the candidates who were very specifically not interested in the status quo. I thought the tone of the editorial expressed that well, and it helped raise our spirits, which needed all the help they could get.

## Campaign committee anxiety

With just days to go until voters went to the polls, I started to feel a little frantic. We'd set the goal to accomplish everything on our plate, not wanting to wake up on September 14 thinking, "If only we'd done . . ."

We were running flat-out, attending union events and other goings-on, and much of the feedback was positive, but it was hard to get any real feel for what voters were thinking. In local races like this there were no phone polls or pre-vote surveys. Polls would simply be an expensive way to satisfy a candidate's curiosity, and otherwise useless. There's just *one* poll, and it's on Election Day.

Andy, other supporters, and I exchanged hundreds of emails in the last couple weeks of the campaign. In addition to knocking on doors and planting signs, we'd taken time to talk with television and radio account executives about our ads and done a few interviews, and I was trying my best to coordinate all the moving parts. Fortunately, Andy was executing like a champ. We'd alternate between commiseration and elation as various things happened in those closing days of the primary race, but we had no real idea about how the race would turn out. Could we actually defeat a three-term incumbent city councilman? Could we turn the tables on the Democratic Committee endorsement? Were voters listening?

We had no idea, and the stress was real. We wanted to win, of course, but we also wanted this sprint to be over—one way or another.


## Personal get-out-the-vote calls

When it comes to political campaigns at any level, nothing is more important that getting out the vote. That would be especially true for this local primary. People just weren't used to showing up in September or June or March to vote. When people think about voting, they usually think, "November." We knew this, and Andy and I put together a list of about a dozen supporters who could help us turn all our campaigning into lever pulls.

We'd again used voterBase to generate lists of Democrats who were most likely to head to the polls, but we expanded the database queries to include even more potential voters. As a result, we would need to make more than a 1,000 calls in just a few days, and the more people we had to help, the better.

Among those willing to make calls were my former Corning Inc. boss, Anne Kenlon; my girlfriend, Sarah Hilsman; my barber, Tim Nicolo; and other friends. Most got a list of 100 names and numbers, with more to come if they were willing.

Anne, who was an outgoing communications professional, offered some good feedback on the calls she'd made.

"I was able to reach the majority of the folks on the call list yesterday and got some very good response," she wrote. "Most folks just said thanks for the reminder, but nobody seemed particularly annoyed by the call. Several asked specifically about John because they said they didn't know much about either candidate. And they all seemed very encouraged by the 'new face, new ideas' approach, and especially the platform about drawing more people into the process, the schools collaborative, communication, etc. Short conversations, but I think they found out what they wanted to know!"

Of her list of 100 names, Anne told me six or seven said they had heard or learned about me at some point, and expressed support. Of course I couldn't help doing the math. Fewer than 10 percent of the potential voters we'd reached had said they'd heard of me. It was better than zero, but it made me wonder what sort of turnout we'd have and how many would pull the lever for me.

My friend Amy Wilson, who served as executive director of a local museum, also made calls. She had less luck, finding nearly half of her calls going to voicemail or simply unanswered. Catching people at home—even when people still had landline phones—was difficult. Evenings worked best for most calls, and we wanted to make sure each one was short and sweet. We needed to thread the line between garnering support and, as Anne suggested, annoying people.

Like Amy, I had a similar experience of having many calls go to voicemail. Despite that, I'd take the opportunity to leave an upbeat message and ask for support. Surprisingly, it always felt a little odd to ask people for their votes. Before running for office, I wasn't in the habit of asking people for such a personal favor. Yes, I'd asked people for money and help on the campaign, but it was all part of my underdog thought process, which made it feel uncomfortable to ask for, well, anything. Over the past months, I'd asked people for a lot, but it was one of those things I had to learn to get comfortable with. It didn't come naturally.


## The final day

I spent part of the final day talking with voters, having lunch at Charlie's Cafe in my neighborhood, and making get-out-the-vote calls. Back home that evening, the eve of the election, I took some time to reflect on how far we'd come and where we were. We'd made it onto the ballot, raised more than $7,000, put up signs across the city, sent postcards to likely voters, made calls to get out the vote, issued press releases, and done media interviews. Had we done enough? Had we garnered enough attention for a decent turnout? Could we win this thing?

Late that night, I got an email from Andy with the simple subject line "Ready?"

"Are you ready?" he wrote. "I'm feeling very confident and so should you. Here's to the next phase of the campaign starting tomorrow night!"

Voting would start the next day at noon and run until nine o'clock in the evening, a shorter voting window than in general elections, when polls were open from six o'clock in the morning to nine o'clock at night. It would be a long day of waiting, so I decided I'd walk over to my polling station, Grace Episcopal Church, around noon; use some time to make final get-out-the-vote calls; and then head over to Horigan's at around eight o'clock to await the results.

As a former reporter, I knew from experience that election days are odd. Yes, there's still work to be done, a few appearance to be made, but mostly the day would be spent waiting for the returns. Now I was on the other side. I went to bed that night with my mind swirling, but I truly felt that we'd done everything we could. No regrets. Tomorrow the die would be cast.

9

# Primary Day

## A surprising sense of calm

September 13 finally arrived, and it felt a bit surreal. After more than four months of campaigning, mulling strategy, raising money, and knocking on doors, this particular Tuesday had a different feel than any other.

I'd decided to take a few vacation days away from my Cornell University job so I didn't have to think about anything other than the day's election, but working probably would've helped keep my mind occupied. I'd been balancing the campaign with my work at the Graduate School for months, and I began to wonder what I might do if I eventually won not just the primary, but the general election. I wondered how exactly I would manage to serve as mayor—technically a part-time job—while working my full-time job in Ithaca. The drive up and down Route 13 took a good forty-five minutes each way and might very well limit the time I'd be able to spend in Elmira.

In the end, I decided to just cross that bridge when I came to it, and for now I'd just take things day-to-day. If I lost the primary, the issue would become moot. If I won, there would be plenty of time to figure it out later.

On election day, I woke early to feed Tucker, Edgar, and Arthur and let them into the backyard to frolic. For my rescued cats, it was just another summer morning, and watching them helped ground me. So did scooping their litter boxes. That daily morning routine felt pretty normal, so I tried to keep my mind in that space. According to the cats, it was just another day. I tried hard to replicate their feline nonchalance. After all, *they* didn't care if I won or lost that day.

The day started with temperatures in the sixties, but it would warm into the low eighties despite intermittent clouds. The front of the *Star-Gazette*'s local section that morning featured an election story with the headline "Party faithful head to the polls today in N.Y." On Sunday, the newspaper had run an article about the mayoral and sheriff's candidates rallying in the final run-up to the Tuesday election, and I'd been glad to see a quote from me in the second paragraph that said, "There are two very public races in Chemung County this year—the mayoral race and the sheriff's race—and it's great to see people having a choice."

Like Dan, I'd counted on money from my family too, but none of that was in the form of a repayable loan. According to the September 2 campaign filing, I'd raised nearly $4,000, most of it from local donors. "To us, it was critical to get a broad base of donors," I told the newspaper. "I was committed to running in the black. If we couldn't get money for our message, then we weren't sending the right message."

That goal stood in stark contrast to Dan's approach. He told the newspaper he was holding back some money for a possible general election race, while I had raised a specific amount of money for the primary and planned to spend every dime. If I was able to defeat Dan, our plan would be to raise more money for the general election, most of which would pay for mailings and another television and radio ad blitz closer to the November 8 election. Election signs were mostly bought and paid for already and could be easily reused.

The primary election day *Star-Gazette* story also highlighted two Elmira City Council primaries on the ballot, one with two Democrats squaring off, the other with two Republicans. I believed this was for the good. The variety of primaries would draw attention and hopefully turn out voters, and all the primaries were giving voters choices they hadn't had in some time. Publicly, that was what I'd been hoping for. Privately, I wanted a good turnout *and* a win.

Andy and I had talked regularly about arriving at primary day with no regrets, nothing left undone. My entire team had put together a plan, executed it, and carefully timed our mailings and television and radio advertising, and it was now in the voters' hands. The only thing left to do was await their decision.

Though nearly every story in the newspaper (and on TV) referred to me as a "political newcomer," which I was, we wondered what voters would ultimately decide. If Elmira Democrats were ready for a newcomer, I had a chance, but only time would tell.

Throughout the campaign, I'd worked hard to stay on message and avoid making the race about me. For that matter, I didn't want the race to be about Dan Royle either. I wanted voters to embrace what I was saying and what I stood for: a whole new approach to running City Hall and, perhaps, a breath of fresh air. We'd wanted the race to be about the city's future, not me, though the candidate *me* and the personal *me* were tightly linked, and I'd become a walking and talking *brand.* But we figured a losing battle would be more about what Elmirans really wanted to see in city government, not a referendum on how much they liked me personally. If they thought the status quo and the typical way of running things was fine, I'd lose. If they felt it was time for a change, I'd win. To us, it was that simple.

That's not to say our nerves weren't a little frayed. I wasn't *nervous,* exactly, but the anticipation was real. Calling voters was a good distraction, but that work wouldn't last all day. I needed to find ways to remain upbeat and relaxed throughout the afternoon and allow fate to do its thing. We'd arrived at this day with no regrets, and we also weren't preoccupied with any would'ves or could'ves, which helped temper any doubts we held.

Turnout would be a factor too, which was why we'd focused so much time in the lead-up to the primary on identifying the most likely voters. On each stoop and front porch, we'd heard good feedback, but would folks the data told us voted frequently feel motivated enough—by either Dan or me—to take time in the middle of September to vote? And without the option to vote in the morning, would voters remember to go after work or step out into the evening to vote before the polls closed at nine o'clock? If they read the newspaper or watched local news, they'd probably see the stories reminding them to vote, but we could only hope it would be enough.

Weather could impact turnout numbers too, and I was glad it wasn't raining or bitterly cold outside, which could keep people home. However, Hurricane Katrina had hit southern Louisiana and New Orleans just days earlier, and the Bush administration's response—which he would later acknowledge was less than ideal—was making big headlines. People were focused on the death toll, displaced people crowding into shelters, and more disarray following the Category 3 hurricane. The fallout from the storm, not our late-summer local primary, was top of mind for many.

Though none of this was in our control, I found it hard not to dwell on what *might* happen in the quiet hours before the polls closed. Win or lose, we were hoping for validation of the simple idea that people wanted change and would be willing to vote for it. If that happened, we'd be able to stand proud—even with a loss.

## Voting for myself

After eating a quiet breakfast, I spent some of the morning with the kitties before getting dressed to go vote. I put on black jeans, a red knit T-shirt, and a black blazer. This sort of look had been my thing all summer long, casual but professional. I don't think I pulled off any fashion coup, but I'd lost weight over the course of the campaign, so the jacket fit more loosely than I remembered and helped me look more confident than I felt.

Shortly after noon, I made the short walk from my West Gray Street home to my polling place a few blocks away. I hadn't expected a crowd, exactly, but other than the election workers manning the tables, I was pretty much the only one there. Fortunately a WETM-TV reporter was on hand to capture the moments I'd step into and out of the voting booth and to interview me afterward. Hopefully when the station aired the story later in the day it would help remind Democrats to vote.

Voting in those days took only moments and didn't require a photo ID or driver's license, which some states now require. In New York State, all voters signed an election-district book, essentially a district-wide list of registered voters and their signatures, which the Board of Election had on file. If an election worker was satisfied the voter's signature on the day of the election matched the signature in the book, you were good to go.

After signing the book, I smiled and stepped into the voting booth, one of the old blue mechanical machines I'd seen used since I was a kid. On election days past, my parents had sometimes brought me into similar refrigerator-sized booths with the same cloth curtains that swung closed when they stepped inside and pulled the large lever from left to right. There were no individual bubble forms to fill out with a pen, and no computers. Instead, these old machines allowed voters to step inside and face dozens of manual levers and pull the ones they wanted. In a general election, each row of levers represented a different political party; the columns the individual races. Paper ballots with all the candidates' names hung behind all the levers so the machines could be set up to show voters only the choices in their election districts.

Since this was a primary, my election district ballot offered just two rows for the countywide sheriff's race and two rows for the mayoral race, with my name appearing above Dan Royle's. It was odd to see my name there, and I took a moment to recall all the work we'd put in to get my name listed. As a voter, names on the ballot had always seemed like such a simple thing, but as a candidate, it had become much more meaningful to me. It had been no simple thing to get on a New York State election ballot, and it made me appreciate all the more the efforts put in by Andy, Sharon, Mom, and many others.

When it came time to vote, I pressed the lever under my name, confirmed I'd voted for myself and not Dan, pulled the large lever from right to left to record my vote, and stepped out through the curtains with a big smile on my face. An election worker stood nearby to ensure the machine had clicked in my vote, and I stepped over to talk to the television reporter and her camera operator, who had set up his shot with the voting machine in the background. I'd seen video of candidates voting countless times, but this was the first time I'd been one of those candidates doing it.

After the brief television interview, I left the building and felt pretty good walking the few blocks back to my home. Now I just had ten hours or so to wait it out.

## Gathering the faithful at Horigan's

As agreed, Andy, Sarah, Mom, and several of my supporters met at Horigan's to have something to eat and sip a few drinks. Personally, I limited my drinking that evening. I wanted to be as clear-eyed as possible—and completely sober when reporters called for comments. To calm my nerves, I stepped out for a cigarette or two instead.

During general elections, it's typical for political parties to host election-night gatherings at one central location where all the candidates, committee members, and supporters can await the returns. The fact that this was a primary changed all that.

Most members of the Democratic Committee met at the Elks Lodge on Baldwin Street in downtown Elmira, so the separate gathering of my supporters at Horigan's was much smaller. We'd invited Bonnie and Ralph Gestwicki, Chrissy and her boyfriend, my barber, my former Corning Inc. boss and her husband, and others to join us. We ended up with about a dozen people, with many of us sitting around a large round table talking and laughing and retelling campaign stories. In a few hours, we'd know the outcome of the vote, but right now we tried our best to remain upbeat, hopeful, and relaxed.

By previous arrangement, Andy had one of my supporters stationed at the Board of Elections to collect the tallies as they came in from Elmira's various election districts. Since there was also a countywide Republican primary for sheriff that day, we knew Mary O'Dell and the other election workers gathering the results would be pretty busy, so we wanted our own person on hand to give us the latest.

As nine o'clock came and went, we all looked at each other and pretty much shared the same thought: That's it. All the votes have been cast. Now there *really* was nothing left to do.

Over the next hour, results trickled in, and Andy wrote the totals on a grease board that hung on one of the restaurant's walls. Closer to ten o'clock, Andy took the last call from our ally at the Board of Elections and stayed on his phone for quite a while, so long, in fact, that I had to impatiently shout, "Well? Come on!"

Andy ended the call and looked at his notes. "515 to 400, Tonello!"

We all let out a whoop and a collective sigh of relief. I was all smiles and felt much of the strain I'd been holding inside drain away. We'd actually done it! We'd started from nothing, took on the Democratic Committee and the three-term city councilman it had endorsed, and won convincingly, taking 56 percent of the vote. It was a stunning victory. Our strategy had worked. We'd done what no one in the party thought we could. I'd dared to challenge the status quo and take them all on—and we'd won.

In addition to feeling a sense of glee, I also thought about the voter-Base tool I'd created to target likely voters. I was certain it had become a difference maker, allowing us to pour our efforts into knocking on doors of those most likely to turn out in a primary. If we'd not had that technological edge, I believed the race would've been much closer.

We also knew that all the door knocking I'd done had paid off. All the time I'd taken over the past three months to personally listen to hundreds of voters had been effective. We'd been confident in the approach, but that confidence was reinforced when we read the election-result story in the next morning's *Star-Gazette*. The first paragraph read, "When John Tonello knocked on Vicki Painter's door on Balsam Street on Elmira's Southside, he took the time to listen to her concerns. In turn, Painter voted for Tonello Tuesday night."

"It was a tough choice because I really like both candidates," Vicki Painter told the newspaper. "I think Dan Royle is great, too, but I think Tonello brings something new. He's been door-to-door. He talked to us. He was interested. I think a new face might be the right choice now."

Her sentiments were exactly what we'd hoped for. Another voter quoted in the same story said I represented a new approach. "He's got a lot of good values and it's new blood," the woman told the newspaper. "Maybe that's what we need."

For my part, I told the reporter I was pleased with the outcome of the race. "The message definitely resounded with the people," I told the *Star-Gazette*. "The people wanted to be listened to. They wanted to have their message heard."

Dan Royle had fewer good things to say in his quotes. "It is almost an embarrassment to the city—that kind of turnout," he said, noting he was shocked and upset only 84 of the 906 voters in his own Fifth District had cast votes. "I went through the hot summer and trudged through the city streets and now I wonder why I bothered," Royle told the paper. "And what's going to happen to the city when so few people care to show up? Maybe it's that some people just don't care."

Dan had a point about turnout, but I was shocked by his blunt assessment. I had highlighted engaging voters. He was blaming them. That was something I wouldn't do. True, it was the first time in more than twenty years since the last mayoral primary—and primaries in New York State are often at odd times—but to me, the low turnout was mostly the result of how the local Democratic Party had closed itself off from most voting Democrats—and to new blood. Much of their canvassing had been done at familiar doors. Ours wasn't. We didn't know what we didn't know about the party faithful. We'd used data to find them, listen to them, and earn their votes.

I had also personally out-canvassed Dan. While he'd delegated, I'd gathered most of my signatures in person, giving me a head start during signature gathering that paid off later and had helped turn my campaign into an upset victory. It wasn't chance that made it happen, it was hard work, and I was grateful.

"It showed that people identified with my message," I told the *Star-Gazette*. "I was hoping for a decisive win that showed Elmira is looking for new ideas. I am excited. It is really exactly what I was hoping for."

At Horigan's, most of my supporters went home to get some sleep after the final results were in, but Andy, Sarah, and I stuck around well into the night. With the media interviews over, I could now kick back and savor the victory with a few glasses of scotch. We went over details of the campaign—again—discussed the highs and lows, and just frankly marveled at what we'd managed to pull off. I'd battled Jim Hare, the party, and Dan

Royle with a certain mix of chutzpah and stubbornness, but I'd also committed myself to a message we felt was not ours alone. We'd beaten them all, and it was a satisfying moment—with much more to come.

The vote total was the only sour note. Of the 5,746 registered city Democrats, just under 16 percent showed up at the polls. In the county-wide Republican primary for sheriff, turnout was about 27 percent, with Christopher Moss defeating William Mayhew 3,818 to 2,408 to capture the Republican line. That outcome told me a couple things. First, that Republicans were much more engaged and eager to vote, which could spell disaster for Democrats in the November 8 general election. Second, it told me that Moss's grassroots campaign, which had been in many ways similar to mine, had resonated. He too had no career politicians working on his campaign, and, like us, he'd run a clean campaign with no public mudslinging and no naysaying. We'd each successfully tapped into a broader voter sentiment that suggested people wanted something new, something different, and something that wasn't politics-as-usual.

After a few days' rest, we'd get back out there and start thinking about the race against Republican Dan Mandell, which would prove to be an even tougher challenge. But for now, we relished the primary win and the experience we'd gained. We knew, too, that we'd been campaigning all summer while Mandell and his team had to mostly sit on the sidelines and wait for the Democratic primary to play out. We saw that as an advantage. Despite all those who said a primary would be bad for the party, I now knew otherwise. The primary didn't dampen enthusiasm for my campaign. It had given it muscle and a head start. It was like being shot out of a canon, and we could ride that arc into the autumn campaign.

10

## Getting the Party On Board

The city chair is not set to endorse

The morning after the primary election, I received several emails of congratulations, most with the theme "now the real work begins." In the early hours of the morning—not long after I got home from Horigan's—I'd sent off an email to Andy, again thanking him for all his hard work.

"Andy, you are simply awesome," I wrote. "Your hard work made this win possible. Let's savor it. Let's love it. And know that yours is a rare talent. Great work, dude."

Early the next morning, he replied, "Thanks, it is a pleasure, and I want to thank you for letting me help and get involved. Your final win in November will be the first step to re-building this party in Chemung County. With your leadership in the city, we'll make it happen."

I also received emails from my Aunt Dolores in Rochester; my sister, Maria; my former Corning Inc. boss, Anne Kenlon; my neighbor Chrissy; and new friend and Democratic supporter Lynn Brewer, who wrote, "What a win! Isn't it amazing what a little listening will do!"

I also started to receive emails from folks concerned about specific city issues affecting their neighborhoods. Maureen Beschler wrote to me about the city's plan to acquire some property, which she was concerned would become another city-owned island with no future. She said the city needed to stop spending tax dollars on things that *might* be and avoid ending up in possession of a parcel of land that would come off the tax rolls and sit there forever.

125

If I hadn't known it before, I knew now that I had become not only the face of a political campaign but a potential city leader. Emails like the one from Maureen wouldn't be the last.

Despite winning the Democratic primary, I was well aware that we would need to do some fence mending in the lead-up to the general election. Those who'd backed Dan Royle weren't waking up happy, and we needed to address that.

Yes, our goal had been to unabashedly take on the local Democratic Party, energize it, and show voters we could take on tough challenges and win, but unfortunately, few of the long-standing committee members offered their congratulations or support. I'm sure many held a bitter taste in their mouths, but at least one of them had decided to pitch in to help.

Dan Royle, just a few days after the election, wrote to tell me he'd be happy to publicly endorse me—either through a press release or at a press conference—and that he wanted one of my signs in his yard. He also offered financial support and advice on helping me become better known around the city. He also suggested I use the time I was spending attending city council meetings to campaign instead. Few political veterans reached out like he did, and none was as supportive. It showed a lot of character and his determination to keep the mayor's seat in Democratic hands.

We welcomed Dan's grace and willingness to help, and we believed his support would help bolster my standing with the rest of the city committee. I'd avoided publicly bashing the committee, but its chairman, Steve McNamara, would certainly need some convincing. He was not a fan and kept a low profile after the election. I tried reaching out to him several times, but my calls went unanswered. I really knew we were in trouble when the city committee met at Steele Memorial Library for an election-planning session and he made his position clear.

I sat across a table from McNamara, and from the start I could tell by his body language and frequent frowns that he wasn't supportive of my bid for mayor. When someone suggested the committee put out an official endorsement for me, he balked.

"Well," he began, "We don't even know his platform."

Fellow committee member and Fourth District incumbent Councilman Terry McLaughlin immediately spoke up. "Steve, he has the line. He is the Democratic candidate!"

Terry was a former Elmira Correctional Facility guard who wasn't shy about speaking up. He was pretty vocal on the city council and had made a name for himself when he'd chained himself to a tree in his district to protest the tractor-trailer trucks that unlawfully used those streets. I was grateful he was speaking up now. Terry was a pragmatist and wanted Democrats to hold onto their council majority. He got along fine with Dan Royle, but he'd already put the primary behind him.

It was clear, though, that McNamara would be unlikely to help my campaign, and I privately wondered if he'd even vote for me in November. Other committee members weren't nearly as hostile, and many began to warm up to me and express their interest in helping my campaign in the weeks ahead.

Fortunately, at its late September meeting, the Chemung County Democratic Committee officially endorsed me and Tom Petro, who'd won the Democratic primary to run for Dan Royle's Fifth District city council seat.

"We are very pleased with the quality of this year's candidates and know we will see victory in November," Chairwoman Cindy Emmer told the *Star-Gazette*.

The small blurb—and what we thought was a tepid announcement—appeared in the paper next to an article about a "Democrats for Lewis" committee taking shape in nearby Corning that sought the reelection of Republican incumbent Alan Lewis. He was running against Democrat Frank Coccho, a veteran city councilman and a longtime union guy with a deep, gravelly voice who, as a former Corning Inc. pipe fitter, had served as president of Local 1000 of the American Flint Glass Workers Union and never hesitated to poke at his city's largest employer. Frank had a big personality and long ties with people throughout Corning, but some saw him as too outspoken, so it wasn't surprising that some Democrats had decided to support the Republican in that mayoral race. Still, I was glad I didn't have Frank's problems.


## Some key endorsements

With Dan Royle willing to endorse me, we arranged a press conference in downtown Wisner Park. We gathered a small group in the early afternoon, and the theme was not just collaboration, but an urgency to engage voters.

"I want people to get involved," I told the gathered reporters. "I want people to vote. With less than 1,000 votes cast last week, we must do all we can to get voters excited."

Dan echoed my comments. "This election is far too valuable to risk staying on the sidelines," he said, noting that the city council's Democratic majority was in jeopardy.

Unlike him, I cared less about the Democratic majority remaining intact and more about changing the status quo. Yes, I wanted Democratic ideas to dominate, but more than that, I wanted the city to be much more responsive to citizens of all stripes. To my mind, the six-to-one Democratic majority hadn't done that successfully, and now Democratic dominance was in doubt. With the election that had just passed, Dan's council seat would be open and contested. Shirley Williams, the Second District councillor, had decided not to run again, so that seat would be contested too. Jim Hare and Terry McLaughlin were running again for their seats, and John Corsi, the sole Republican who called himself the "Lone Ranger," was running unopposed. There was little guarantee that the Democrats would retake the majority, and with so many new players, the political balance after November would be anybody's guess.

Individual and organization political endorsements would offer some visibility and votes, and that season was now ramping up. Most November candidates would soon be invited to attend a public Meet the Candidates night hosted by the Sheetmetal Workers Local 112 headquarters on Clemens Center Parkway. The evening would allow candidates to mingle with union workers, give speeches, and make their pitches for votes. I always enjoyed these meetings held by the "tin-knockers," as they called themselves. The men and women the union represented were down-to-earth, often Democratic leaning, and definitely not shy. Though the Sheetmetal Workers Local didn't endorse candidates, the informal gathering would be a great chance to meet voters and spread the word.

Other unions did endorse, such as the local United Auto Workers and the Civil Service Employees Union, or CSEA, which represented about 1,200 public employees in Chemung County. In early October, I was invited to speak to the Chemung-Schuyler County Labor Assembly and made an impassioned plea for support, centering my comments on job creation to stem the flow of young people leaving the area, rejecting the idea of privatizing civil service jobs and supporting union labor for local development projects. I also made a pitch to the individuals, not just the collective.

"Tonight, as you decide which candidates to endorse," I told them, "I hope you'll consider these issues and these solutions, and consider what's important to you personally. The next mayor of Elmira must be someone who can bring people together, someone who listens, and someone who welcomes open discussion. To me, the Next Great Idea can be born far from City Hall. If you've followed this race, I think you've seen that I'm a fighter who's not afraid of hard work or challenges. Mine is an independent, fair-minded voice. That's what I bring to the table. That's what I want to bring to the mayor's office. I ask for your support."

I completed a questionnaire for the CSEA, but given Dan Mandell's ties to the sheriff's department as a civil servant, I didn't think I stood much of a chance to pick up the endorsement. Not unlike the Democratic and Republican Committees, many local union folks had strong political and personal loyalties. I was unknown to most of them, so I wasn't surprised when the United Auto Workers and CSEA eventually endorsed Mandell for mayor. However, the CSEA did end up endorsing Democrats Jim Hare, Terry McLaughlin, and two other Erin Town Board candidates.

Andy and I privately expressed our disappointment with the lack of union support, but we saw the writing on the wall. We would press on regardless and focus on voters who felt disenfranchised and unheard. That had been our strategy all along, and we weren't going to fret long about union endorsements even though, as Democrats, we were strong believers in union efforts to empower workers.

In late September, I received word from Jim Hare that New York State Attorney General Eliot Spitzer was making a swing through the Southern Tier and offering endorsements. Jim was the local coordinator for Spitzer, who was planning to run for governor the next year. Jim asked if I would like to appear with him, and I jumped at the chance. Personally, I was eager to meet Spitzer, whose ideas and work I admired. It helped that Eliot Spitzer, as attorney general, had become popular with both Democrats and Republicans, so his endorsement would provide both visibility and, potentially, broad voter approval.

It also was one of the earliest times I began to understand that by winning the primary, I was now playing a much bigger role with some of the biggest names in the Democratic Party.

After some discussion, it was decided to hold the press conference with Spitzer in the main first-floor foyer of Elmira City Hall. I would've preferred a more neutral venue for a political show, but I relented when Jim and Cindy Emmer suggested City Hall for its simplicity. In Corning, Spitzer and Coccho had appeared at Sorge's Restaurant, a popular Italian restaurant located on the city's historic Market Street. A local Elmira restaurant, park pavilion, or other non-government locale would've been my preference, but I knew the Spitzer team's time was limited and agreed to make things easier for everyone.

At midday on October 6, we gathered at City Hall to await Spitzer's arrival. I wore a dark suit and tie, hoping to match Spitzer's buttoned-up look—and to appear as mayoral as possible—and brought along a speech to unveil my public safety priorities for the city. Key to my remarks was a line about bolstering the Elmira City Police. This was long before defunding the police became a thing, but it had become clear to me during the primary campaign that one of the big reasons people didn't want to live in Elmira was the perception of crime. It was more than a perception. Elmira, like other Upstate New York cities, had a drug problem. Much of the crime was related, and the seventy or so members of the police department were hard-pressed to stay on top of it.

Many Democratic Committee members were on hand with us at City Hall, along with television and newspaper reporters, when Spitzer arrived with his campaign team, all looking sharp and professional in suits and ties. Among them was a surprisingly familiar face: Marty Mack, the former Cortland mayor I'd covered as a young reporter for the Syracuse *Post-Standard*. He was now one of Spitzer's deputies and a key member of his campaign team. Mack greeted me warmly, and his presence helped calm my nerves a bit. "Not all these Albany bigwigs are unknowns!" I thought. Mack's appearance alongside Spitzer helped bring it all down to earth because here was a guy I knew who had humble roots and strong Democratic ideals.

When it was finally time for the event, Spitzer stood at the podium with an air of practiced confidence that amazed me. When he spoke, his voice was loud and confident, and without notes he started to speak about me as though he'd known me for years. He told the audience I was creative, hardworking, and nonpartisan and that I understood issues facing both Elmira and New York State, from taxes to health care.

"These are the issues that need to be addressed," Spitzer said in comments that appeared in the next morning's *Star-Gazette*. "We can do it better, and John is that person. Hard work pays off. Hard work is something he believes in."

It was all a bit overwhelming. This popular public servant, who was famous in New York and beyond, was praising my efforts. It was pretty heady stuff. I was so thrilled by his comments and his speaking style that when it came time for me to speak, I used a louder, more fervent tone than I normally used. I somehow felt the need to sound as confident as he did, so I was off and running. I think it sounded okay, but that was the first and last time I did that. I was much more soft-spoken than the future governor, and his style—while impressive—wasn't my style. Still, in the moment, I simply couldn't help myself.

Spitzer's swing through the Southern Tier generated a lot of local media coverage, and I added his endorsement and my speech to my website. Of all the endorsements, this one would prove to be the biggest and most visible. With his presence, Spitzer burnished my Democratic credentials and, for many, validated my candidacy. Since I was still trying to mend fences with local party folks, this was important. If Eliot Spitzer could support me, surely they could find it in themselves to support me too. It also didn't hurt that I got to make a personal connection with one of the biggest players in New York politics.


## A Democrat cross-endorses

Despite Spitzer's endorsement, I still faced a steep uphill battle—not just for votes, but for support of the local Democratic Committee. My relationship with Jim Hare, while strained, warmed a bit with the Spitzer event, and he eventually agreed to place my sign in his yard, but others held onto their dislike for me and my campaign.

Key among them was First District Councilman Bill Hopkins, whom I'd planned on challenging before switching gears and running for mayor. At the Democrats' endorsement meeting in May, he had made it clear he thought a primary was a bad thing, and he wasn't a fan. Perhaps it was because he felt I'd pushed him out of his seat and then done him wrong again by not running for it. Committee member Bill Knapp had gotten on the ballot and would be the Democrat's candidate, but he'd just been unlawfully arrested for soliciting in August, and with the urging of Jim Hare and others, had withdrawn from the race. That left Republican Susan Skidmore and independent Ed Hrasdzira vying for his seat.

Regardless of any First District tumult, Hopkins remained unhappy with my approach and publicly endorsed my opponent, Dan Mandell. "This is not about politics," Hopkins told the *Star-Gazette*. "It's not about Democrats or Republicans. I vow to represent this district's population."

Hopkins had not given me any forewarning about his support for Mandell, but when a newspaper reporter called me to comment for the story, I took aim at the chumminess of the endorsement and said it didn't surprise me.

"It strikes me as politics at its worst," I told the *Star-Gazette*. "I'm not making deals or promises to any select few. My allegiance is to all the people of Elmira."

The same article also made mention of the United Auto Workers union endorsing Mandell. It was clear I couldn't get *everybody* to like me, but I'd done my best to downplay Hopkins' crossover. I was trying to be consistently on the side of average voters and citizens, not a good old boy.

## Continuing to battle the status quo

October became the most tumultuous month of the campaign, not surprisingly since time was short and the pressure was on for all the candidates across the city. I continued to send out the occasional press release, update my website, and hold regular campaign meetings, though a lot of that now happened via email. Andy and I felt like we were moving in a hundred directions at once, and we kept a close eye on the news to see what was happening.

With the October campaign finance filing out, the *Star-Gazette* printed two stories about candidate spending so far. The two sheriff's candidates together had spent more than $54,000. William Mayhew, now running on the Conservative line after losing the Republican primary, had spent the majority of that, some $34,000. On the mayoral side, the newspaper reported that Dan Mandell had raised more than $14,000 so far and had spent nearly $11,000, including nearly $10,000 going to a local marketing firm. Dan Royle, while no longer in the race, reported raising just over $2,800 and spending about $6,500 on the primary. The October filing showed my campaign had raised just over $7,100 so far and spent $6,000, most of which was related to the primary. We'd hold a few more small fundraisers with the goal of raising another $5,000.

The financial numbers were interesting, but what really captured our attention was reporter Brooke Sherman's repeated references to the mayoral race being something of an understated affair. The first paragraph said, "On the Elmira mayoral campaign trail, money talks louder than words. That's been the case so far, anyway."

What?

I'd spent the entire summer making news, and I had seen plenty of coverage of Dan Royle and Dan Mandell. Even the newspaper's pre-primary editorial had said we were all out and about. All the candidates were regularly making the rounds, going door-to-door, appearing at candidate meet and greets, and more. I'd gotten the word out via press releases, my website, and the Spitzer endorsement, too.

"I know that people know who I am now when I go door-to-door," I told the newspaper.

The reporter reached out to a couple voters for comment, too, including A. J. Jordan of Hudson Street on the city's south side, who told the *Star-Gazette* he planned to vote in November and was disappointed no one had stopped at his door. "I thought they'd be going at it with more vigor," he said.

For the hell of it, I looked up A. J. Jordan in my voterBase tool and discovered that he had not voted in the previous city election. As a result, he hadn't shown up in our canvassing lists. Though he was a registered Democrat, we weren't able to hit every door and had prioritized voters who turned out at every election. Unfortunately, he wasn't among them. I decided the best response was to give him what he asked for, so I looked up his address and drove over to Hudson Street to meet him. He was home, and we had a good conversation standing out in his yard. He was a nice guy and definitely appreciated that I'd taken the time to come talk. Not only did he take a yard sign, but his neighbor across the street, Tim Tobin, took a sign, too, and gave me a check for $25. "I really want you to win, man," Tobin told me.

Despite this small victory in battling the idea of the mayoral campaign being quiet so far, the newspaper's spin struck me as extremely odd. I'd met and spoken to the reporter many, many times and didn't have any real hint as to why she thought we were running a low-key campaign. I thought back to the interview I'd done with her at the *Star-Gazette* offices on Baldwin Street during the primary, a move that was similarly odd. As a reporter, I never did interviews at my office. I'd always wanted to talk to people in *their* natural environments. If she'd reported most of the campaign from the newsroom, then, sure, it might appear quiet, but that wasn't reality.

I suspected that the editors might be seeding the idea of a quiet campaign, but neither had I seen them out and about the city at the myriad events and festivals I'd attended. I decided I'd write off the "quiet campaign" as an anomaly—until I saw the following Sunday's newspaper. The headline atop the front of the Local section read, "All's quiet on the campaign trail."

Again?

In this story, Brooke Sherman again talked with two local voters but also interviewed former Mayor Stephen Hughes. "I have found it to be surprisingly quiet, and I don't conclude from that that there are no issues of concern for the voters," Hughes told the *Star-Gazette*. "I have yet to hear any candidate for city office really talking about those things that voters should be informed of. The candidates for mayor this year may have underestimated the complexity of the task at hand and have found themselves engaged in what maybe is an underwhelming proposition."

All this really rankled. Dan Mandell and I had "underestimated the complexity of the task"? What the hell did that mean? Mandell had led the Republicans' political committee, worked years in government as a member of the sheriff's department, and was well-known. Hughes had notoriously thumbed his nose at the local Democratic Party folks and had, admittedly, been something of a darling to the *Star-Gazette* editors, who'd given him pages of coverage when he resigned in March. Yes, I was a newcomer, but I'd done my homework. Mandell was no neophyte either.

What was different, to Hughes and the newspaper editors perhaps, was that we weren't walking around making grand promises. Dan Mandell and I agreed on many issues, but we had different approaches. Neither of our approaches, though, was anything like the status quo the incumbents represented. The whole concept now struck me as the opening salvo of something bigger. Dan Mandell and I were new mayoral candidates in a city where business leaders and the newspaper had helped cultivate the status quo. If they thought everything was peachy keen, they were the ones underestimating things, not us.

A key case in point was the different issues voters talked to me about. When I spoke to white voters, they invariably talked about poorly paved roads, taxes, crime, and deteriorating neighborhoods. Black voters all said the biggest problem was the police. This contrast first surfaced as I wandered the grounds of the Chemung County Fair back in August. It also came up when I attended the Juneteenth Festival in late spring. It continued to be an issue I heard about at the doorsteps of homes owned by black residents. To them, the police were not treating them fairly. They told me racial profiling was real. They also said they were treated poorly by police and had been pulled over in their cars for little cause.

At the time, according to the US Census, blacks or African Americans represented just over 13 percent of Elmira's population. Whites represented 82 percent. Of the seventy members of the Elmira Police Department, no officers or patrolmen—none—were black. By my math and moral measurement, that wasn't right. Across New York State, about 15 percent of the population was black, but made up more than half of the prison population.

Since Elmira was a prison town home to the Elmira Correctional Facility and nearby Southport Correctional Facility, many Elmirans earned their livings in the prisons. According to the Fortune Society, a nonprofit focused on improving successful reentry of inmates into communities, nearly 60 percent of Elmira Correctional Facility inmates were black, but 97 percent of the guards were white.

Did that imbalance influence the larger community? It's hard to know for certain, but as a candidate for mayor I heard about it and knew it was real. The city's poorest neighborhoods, particularly the Second and Fourth Districts, which were close to Elmira's city center, were home to many black residents. Those areas were also rife with crime, slumlords who allowed their rental properties to languish, and little voice in government. Shirley Williams, who'd represented the Second District on city council, wasn't running for reelection that year. She'd been a strong advocate for her constituents and, by not seeking a third term, left the political field—from the mayor on down—to all white candidates.

Again, the status quo was alienating a big chunk of Elmira's population. Solving such problems wouldn't be easy, but recognizing it as a problem was a good first step. A front-page story in the *Star-Gazette* back in February had looked at the racial segregation that dominated local churches, but the paper had done little else to highlight the city's racial divide. Black Elmirans were clearly underrepresented in elected and staffed city government, and I recognized that needed to change.

At the same time, the LGBTQ population in Elmira was growing more visible and getting short shrift too. The Chemung County Gay, Lesbian, Bisexual, Transgender and Intersex Coalition started holding a Pride event at Wisner Park the year before I ran for mayor, and hundreds attended to show their support. So did 150 protesters, who gathered across the street from the downtown event, reading from Bibles and praying aloud. As a result, police were asked to provide protection for the event the following year, when I ran, and protesters were absent.

As with other community festivals, I'd planned to attend the Pride event but got pushback from Jim Hare when I mentioned my plans to him back in June. "You should be careful with that," he told me.

I didn't want to hear that. What was wrong with supporting the LGBTQ community in the city where I wanted to be mayor? I realized Jim didn't have any personal issues with the gay community, but from a political point of view it was an unknown and therefore potentially perilous. The status quo said don't stick out your political neck. I attended anyway and became the first candidate for mayor in the city's history to attend and speak. To me, embarrassment wouldn't come from attending but from the fact that no one in my position ever had.

The annual Elmira Pride event would continue to be a contentious gathering in the years ahead, even though any passersby would likely see it as just another community festival, with balloons, food, musicians, and people just having a good time. For some, though, it wasn't the sort of thing Elmira wanted to be known for, and that saddened me. The status quo was—again—shutting out good, tax-paying citizens and largely ignoring them. That's not what I wanted the city's future to look like.

Throughout the campaign that summer and early fall, my eyes were opened to all the "many Elmiras" that existed within the city. As I thought about it, it had become clear to me that each resident had his or her own perspective of the city. They drove different streets to work and school, went to different churches and synagogues, shopped and ate out in different neighborhoods. For each of the city's 30,000 residents, there were different perceptions of everyday life, and I wanted to win the mayor's race so all of them could be recognized, not just tolerated, and welcomed by their neighbors. Having worked for corporations and universities like Cornell, I knew that diversity was a strength, not a weakness. A mix of perspectives and ideas helped organizations and communities move forward. I wanted that to be true in Elmira too.

My battle against the status quo would never be simple or easy. It would take perseverance and risk, but as we began the campaign against Republican Dan Mandell, I wanted fairness and inclusion to be front and center.

11

# Switching Gears:<br>Facing the Republican

## Reshaping the campaign

Throughout the summer, my campaign for mayor had been focused on beating back my own party, but the fall election would require a different approach, one that distinguished me from my Republican opponent.

That largely meant sticking to our game plan, but unlike the primary, the stakes weren't about securing the Democrat line on the ballot. It was about the mayor's office and all that entailed. Yes, my talking points would remain much the same, but I had to be seen as more than just a new face with new ideas. I needed to show that I had the right experience to lead and get things done.

Shortly after the primary win, I spoke to the Chemung County Sunrise Rotary, a large gathering of local business and community leaders. I'd been invited by member and Democratic supporter Bob Butcher six weeks earlier. Perhaps he'd been prescient. I told the gathering:

When my friend Bob Butcher first called to invite me to speak to you, the Elmira mayoral primary was still more than six weeks away and this meeting was originally set for the day after, September 14.

Of course, as a crowd-hungry campaigner, I immediately agreed to come, but then I thought, "What does Bob know that I don't know?" I mean, what will the underdog have to say on the morning after?

I sent Bob an e-mail and asked him, "Do you have a back-up, too?" He said, "No, just you."

No pressure.

I mean, I know Bob's a bright guy, but clairvoyant? No way. He just doesn't look the part. I've since changed my mind. I'm thinking of asking him to be part of my senior campaign staff.

I'm here this morning to share with you a little about my experience so far in my campaign for mayor. I'm not here to campaign or bore you with my stand on various issues, though, I'm happy to answer any questions you have about issues later. But for now, I want to share with you a little of what we've learned so far.

Just by way of some background, I have never run for public office before. A year ago, I was like most voters—interested in politics, but mostly detached from the political process. I campaigned for Sam Barend for Congress, but for the most part I was an interested observer in most of the races taking place last fall.

What made me get off my couch and into a race like this was a sense of frustration, really. My neighbors and friends and I talked a lot about what we thought was right and wrong about the city, the state, the federal government, and the common theme was frustration.

We didn't set out to blame anyone; we just thought that people were ready for something—and someone—entirely new. Our idea was to focus not on the past, but on the future. To avoid blame, and pursue a positive vision of what-comes-next. On May 19, I announced my plan to run at a press conference in Wisner Park.

I can only speak for myself, of course, but as a newcomer to this sort of thing, in the four months since then, many things struck me as interesting or downright shocking. For example:

Interesting: "Dog bites man" is still front-page news. Yes, a German shepherd bit my arm a couple times while I was going door-to-door, but as one of my journalism professors once told me, it's really only news if the man, not the dog, is doing the biting.

Shocking: It's harder than ever to get people to vote—even when local, state, and national issues are affecting their lives.

For those of you who haven't followed the Elmira mayor's race closely, here are the raw numbers. About 915 Democrats showed up to vote. I received 515 votes to Dan Royle's 400. Combined, we were able to draw out just 16 percent of the city's registered Democrats.

The hotly contested Republican primary for sheriff drew a slightly larger percentage of voters, about 6,200 countywide or about 27 percent of registered Republicans.

The numbers might seem low, but consider this: In the city, 80 percent of eligible voters don't vote in any election in any year because they're not registered. Dan and I split 16 percent of 20 percent. It's incredible, really.

As a former newspaper reporter, numbers like these interest me because they describe people and human behavior. They describe trends and priorities. They paint a picture of American democracy.

It's not pretty.

I knew going into this race that engaging voters would be a challenge. In fact, it's been 22 years since a Democratic primary for mayor in Elmira, so we had no idea how many people would actually turn out. In the end, about 40 percent of the Democrats who voted in the last mayoral election voted last Tuesday. That doesn't sound so bad, but it still stinks.

But I'm not one to blame voters. That's too easy. I believe the problem is more complicated than that.

Part of problem, I believe, is the lack of primaries themselves. Twenty-two years is a generation and, to me, that's way too long since voters had a real choice. That lack of open debate of ideas and different perspectives leads quickly to leaders self-selecting their successors. It also pushes voters further from the process. In the end, it leads to hard feelings because people forget how to disagree without becoming disagreeable.

Ultimately, it leads to low voter turnout because people come to realize that they're really just rubber-stamping party choices. Most people I talk to tell me party doesn't matter in local races, that they vote for the person. Given that, it's little wonder people fail to show up. They've been marginalized and they know it.

That must change. We must learn again to discuss ideas openly, to rely less on nice personalities and more on sound arguments. We must learn to say, "I disagree," and still be able to shake hands or lift a beer.

That's half the reason I took on the challenge of running for office. I truly believe that in order to get things done—to create a business-friendly city, an atmosphere for job growth, safer neighborhoods—we need to engage people again. We need to show that open debate is positive, that participation—real participation—can happen and it has its own rewards.

That means we have to change some fundamental ideas about how government works. And we have to model that change, not just talk about it. I'm very pleased when people tell me that my campaign has shown that change can happen; that energetic people with no campaign experience can win elections and shape the debate.

Time will tell if the approach that led to our success in the primary will translate into success in November—I'll have to ask Bob about that—but I believe at the very least it will start us down the path toward positive, open debate. We all win when that happens.

The thing is, I just don't see any downside to getting people talking again. I see no downside to inviting everyone to join in. Democracy thrives on that.

It does put new demands on our public officials, though, because it demands that our leaders be willing to listen to differing opinions, seek out different points of view, act on that input, and allow citizens to see the successes they help bring about. I hope, in some small way, we've begun that.

My speech was modestly received, meaning no one stood up and cheered, but I saw a lot of nods in the room. I also saw a lot of stoic faces. True, many in attendance weren't Elmira residents, but many had businesses in the city. Whoever became the city's next mayor would matter to them all.

## Staying out in front

With that in mind, we reminded ourselves of the need to stay out in front on the issues and in the news. That meant taking time to keep my name in the newspaper and on television and talking with people. One of the biggest opportunities to get that visibility would come in late October, when I agreed to participate in a live, televised mayoral debate with Dan Mandell in Mandeville Hall at the Clemens Center. The debate would be co-sponsored by the *Star-Gazette* and feature a panel of reporters and a representative from the League of Women Voters. Audience members would also be able to ask questions. After the live hour-long broadcast, WETM-TV would re-air the debate on its sister station, WTTX.

We also knew that my appearance at the debate would highlight my grasp of the issues, something that would, hopefully, stand in sharp contrast to the so-called "quiet campaign." I'd done a lot to learn all I could, and I'd talked with hundreds of people, all average citizens to whom I most wanted to appeal on debate night.

I'd never been a big fan of presidential debates, which always seemed stilted, rule bound, and mostly full of partisan talking points. Now I was about to participate in one of my own, and I didn't want it to be as onerous, but I'd never taken the stage for a debate before, and that worried me.

In high school and college, I hadn't been on any debate teams or anything like that. I knew enough to school myself on the issues—which I'd been talking about for months—and did some debate prep with my campaign team, but mostly I was going to approach the night by being as open and honest as possible. I'd take each question from the panel and say what I thought—for good or ill. I'd listen to what Dan Mandell had to say, and respond if necessary, but I wasn't going to switch tacks and go after him personally. That would be the worst result, I thought, because it would show that I was out for myself and against him. Yes, I wanted to defeat him, but mostly I wanted to paint a picture of a positive city future and my qualifications to become mayor.

While we waited for the debate, Andy pumped up the letter-to-the-editor campaign to help refute the newspaper's theme that Dan Mandell and I hadn't been visible throughout the campaign. On October 22, the *Star-Gazette* published a letter written by Richard Reidy, a Democratic Committee member, that bore the headline, "Tonello has aggressively run mayoral campaign" and said: "I would like to take exception to the Oct. 16 Star-Gazette headlined [story] 'All's quiet on the campaign trail.' John Tonello has been very actively campaigning since he announced his candidacy for mayor last spring. John is the type of forward-thinking person Elmira needs as its next mayor. Check out John's website. You will see one candidate who has not been quiet on the campaign trail."

Others felt as Reidy had and were angry about the newspaper's portrayal of the campaign, but, admittedly, the debate and the news coverage weren't the only things crowding my mind. Three days before the debate, my ex-wife, Nicola, had surgery to address her breast cancer diagnosis. If the lymph nodes they'd removed and analyzed tested positive, she'd need additional surgery in another week. That turned out to be the case.

Despite our divorce, Nicola and I remained friends, and her continued good health was important to me. She'd been staying upbeat, but I knew she was facing a tough road with the surgery and the coming chemotherapy. Despite the campaign, I offered to pick things up for her from the grocery store, take in her garbage cans, feed her cats, and do anything else that could make her life a little easier. She'd moved on and was dating a guy she'd met while working at WETM-TV, but I still wanted to give her support. She was supportive right back.

On the eve of the debate, she sent me an email that said, "You'll be fine tomorrow. Be yourself and have fun. That strategy hasn't failed you yet!"

I told her I'd be lying if I said I wasn't nervous, and she replied, "Of course you're nervous . . . you'll be great."

My entire team was helping me, offering debate advice, and giving me tips. I welcomed them all. Sharon sent me a list of possible questions to help me prepare answers for the night, such as:

- Reminding me to breath, smile, and avoid getting ruffled

- Pointing out that Dan Mandell had only worked for the government and had no experience with economic development or small-business issues

- Keeping in mind the four or five things I wanted people to remember and get them into every answer

- Expecting the unexpected

She also suggested my answers to questions about various city issues—jobs, neighborhood revitalization, bringing downtown back to life, the Arena, taxes, improving communications with the county, and my lack of political experience—and reminded me to be specific.

It was quite the list, and I would need to come up with coherent answers, but my goal had been to be the sort of mayor who welcomed ideas from around the table and across the board. I hadn't been at the table for past decisions, but I felt confident I could lead in a way that encouraged open discourse to arrive at reasonable solutions. Could we lower taxes without laying off staff, the city's biggest single expense? Could we generate new revenue through grants? Could we help fund home renovations in sagging neighborhoods? Good questions, and I had some ideas, but in the end I believed it wouldn't be *me* dictating the solutions to the city council, the city manager, and the city. The answers would be found collaboratively.

Ten days before the debate, the newspaper asked Dan Mandell and me to comment on city issues, namely our opinions on the city's current leadership (a subtle reference to city manager Sam Iraci), our plans for addressing the city's debt, and what we thought were the defining issues of the year's election. These weren't exactly the questions atop most voters' minds, but we answered them without attacking each other. Like me, Dan wanted to see a rebirth of the city and more downtown development. We actually agreed on many issues facing the city, but I emphasized better communication as critical.

A week before the debate, both of us were asked by the *Star-Gazette* to provide our platforms. This struck me as an odd request since I'd laid out my entire platform and approach on my website months earlier. With the recent "quiet campaign" story, I wanted to reiterate my stand on the issues. Dan Mandell provided four main points: public safety, economic development, fiscal responsibility, and maintenance of city infrastructure and neighborhoods. He said he wanted to increase targeted police enforcement through the city and strengthen the drug enforcement unit. On economic development, he said he wanted to hire a grant writer, reduce red tape and parking rates, and market vacant space.

I provided nine points and added more specifics. For example, with public safety I wanted to promote community policing and move resources to the night shifts, when crimes were at their worst. On roads, I said I wanted to shift money from reconstruction to resurfacing. Rather than do one major road project a year, I believed resurfacing offered a way to dramatically improve many city roads. On neighborhoods, I promoted renovation, not demolition, and believed the city should provide tax incentives for converting multi-family houses back to their original single-family origins.

In each of my talking points, I included better communication in my answers. In reality, not all the city had been doing was bad. The communication had been bad—to the public, among city council members, and with city staff. People repeatedly told me it was rarely clear why the city was doing what it was doing, and that had caused mistrust and discontent. My aim was to change that.

For Dan and me, these issues impacted Elmira's quality of life and its future. If we couldn't clamp down on crime, broken streets, and rising taxes, the city would continue to falter. But to me, these were problems the community needed to address together, and the debate would be about which of us could better lead those efforts.

In the debate, we'd need to make some distinctions, and this was one. I planned to continue my rallying cry around what I knew best: communication and my long experience in business. I wasn't planning to go it alone on any solutions to the city's ills, and I believed a calm, thoughtful approach was the right way forward.

## The debate

On the night of the debate, most of the 100 or so seats in Mandeville Hall were filled when Dan Mandell and I greeted each other with a handshake before taking our places behind our respective podiums. To our lefts sat the moderator—WETM-TV anchorman Jeff Stone, who hosted the *Twin Tiers Weekly* local news program on which we'd separately been interviewed—and, across the stage, the panel of questioners. When seven o'clock came, the hall was darkened, the camera lights turned red, and the debate began.

I tried my best to remain calm, but I felt anything but. Fortunately, the debate began with our opening remarks, which we'd prepared beforehand. In my three minutes, I said:

> Good evening. Thank you for this opportunity to come before you. Thanks to the *Star-Gazette*, WETM and WTTX, and the League of Women Voters for hosting this debate.
>
> Ladies and gentleman, Elmira is at a critical point in its history. This mayor's race is about the future and restoring hope. Regardless of what you believe about the path that's brought us here, we all can agree it's time for new energy and new ideas. It's time to begin Elmira's resurgence.
>
> Collaboration is the key to charting that resurgence. When people are asked to help, and their ideas are heard and valued, things change. I believe the right mayor with the right experience can help Elmirans become part of the solution. That's why I'm proposing new ideas like:

Community policing that forges ties between people and the officers who serve them. Efforts to strengthen the ties between the city and its schools so we attract new families and businesses. New efforts that bring City Hall to the people, not just people to City Hall.

The mayor's No. 1 job is to listen. After nearly 20 years in the communications business, I know how to do just that. It's time to elect a mayor who can do that, too. I'm the clear choice.

Listening is just part of the job, though. The next mayor must act. The key is which of us has the better ideas and which of us can better solve problems and lead.

I earned degrees at Corning Community College and Syracuse University. I've held management positions for Fortune 1000 companies and major universities. I have a proven track record of innovation and results.

I've made this area my home for much of the past 25 years. I bought my first home on the Near Westside. I have a great love for this city and its people, and I have a strong desire to see Elmira thrive and grow. Tonight, I ask you to think about Elmira's future—our future—and about who can take us there. I believe I'm the clear choice.

I thanked the audience and the viewers at home and braced for the questions. Dan and I were asked about taxes and other city issues, but the comment the reporter spent the most space on in the next day's *Star-Gazette* was how Dan and I might balance our day jobs with the mayor's duties. Dan worked as the Chemung County Jail supervisor; I worked in Ithaca. Dan said he would be more accessible because he lived and worked in the city. I said I would be able work from home and use technology so I could be "able to attend ribbon cuttings, grand openings, and meetings during the day."

Most of the debate is a blur, and when the hour wrapped up, I felt I hadn't done well *at all*. I felt the questions were mostly about how things *were* in the city, not how they could be. At one point, Dan made multiple mentions to his wife, which Andy later perceived as a way for Dan to underscore the fact that he was married and I wasn't. He never said anything about it directly, but I noticed these comments because they stood out in what was primarily a civil evening. When a panelist asked us to explain a decision the city made that we didn't think was good, I spoke about the decision to increase council and mayor terms from two years to four. "I think that's a big mistake," I said. "These positions are the face of the community."

Despite making a few solid points, I thought Dan did too. But mostly I felt like I hadn't done enough. Maybe it was the cameras or the live audience, but I just felt awkward for the entire hour.

Fortunately, I received an email the next day from a supporter, who said he thought the debate went well.

> Your comparison of the relatively small amount of city tax "burden" compared to school and county taxes was to me the strongest point of the debate. It was a revelation to me, and I am sure it is something that almost nobody else is aware of. I think it blows apart the GOP platform of "cutting the tax burden" on the population as an empty fabrication. I think it bears repeating.
>
> The strategy of using the sale of the Water District to pay down the debt and free up debt service funds for civic improvement was brilliant. It is clear, logical, and easy to understand. It is also a proven economic model, as demonstrated by the unparalleled national economic prosperity of 1992 to 2000. It is a real example that people can grab on to.
>
> I think Mandell got in a cheap shot about you "dividing the city"; a cheap shot because he never said how he would unite the city.

The local ABC affiliate, WENY, also provided a summary of the debate that included feedback from the station's political analyst:

> It's political crunch time with Election Day right around the corner. On Tuesday night, Elmira residents got an up close and personal look at the candidates for one of Chemung County's biggest races. At Mandeville Hall in the Clemens Center, the candidates for Elmira City Mayor outlined their campaigns. It was the first public debate and most likely the last before the general election on November 8th. Both Democrat John Tonello and Republican Dan Mandell are political newcomers

campaigning to be the next mayor. They are concerned with similar issues like economic development, lowering taxes, fighting crime, and bringing business to the city, but their approaches are very different.

Tonello says, "I believe my approach is comprehensive. I've spent a lot of time researching the issues of the city, not just living here but finding out what it is the city needs, and what we can do better or differently in the future." Republican Dan Mandell says, "I have a plan. Public safety. I'm looking at sharing services with our other municipalities to fight crime, bringing in a business recruitment person that's going to recruit business to Elmira, and using our existing resources to help."

According to political analyst Dr. Stephen Coleman, both candidates were civil, polite, and clearly defined their plans for the Queen City. Dr. Coleman thought both candidates were very articulate. He says the residents of Elmira should be proud of both candidates. Both candidates fine-tuned their strategies at the debate and are now concentrating on November 8th. They both will head door-to-door to meet residents and listen to what they have to say.

I felt better about my debate performance after I read and saw these reports, but the *Star-Gazette* was far less generous. The newspaper's editorial two days later bore the headline, "A debate, of sorts" and went on to say the "mayoral showdown in Elmira was polite yet devoid of major defining differences." It went on to say, "Both candidates have pleasant personalities. They'd be welcome at any Elmiran's dinner table on a Sunday afternoon. But the low-key debate made it hard to tell who had the greater leadership potential. If there was an overall impression of the candidates, it was that they are still learning about city government, a process that will continue after one of them is inaugurated on January 1."

We thought the newspaper was a little dismissive and snarky, but that had become par for the course. Something just felt off in the *Star-Gazette's* campaign coverage since I'd won the primary. I certainly hadn't expected any sort of preferential treatment for having once worked for the newspaper, but the tone of the election coverage struck all of us as out of step with the feelings we heard from people across Elmira.

Staying on the streets

Despite the time necessary to prep for the debate, raise money, attend public events, and juggle all aspects of the campaign, I continued to go door-to-door most evenings. We believed this was our ace in the hole: meeting and listening to voters. The newspaper, veteran politicians and others could say what they would, but we'd tamp down any negative feelings we had by canvassing. It was real and helped ground us.

Going door-to-door in late October was much different than those early days in June. Now many people knew who I was when I knocked on their doors. My primary television and radio ads had boosted my visibility quite a bit. The televised debate and other on-air appearances had done the same. So had coverage in the newspaper. That had been the goal, and it was working. When I showed up at people's doors and voters asked me questions, they knew I had a fifty-fifty chance of becoming their next mayor. That encouraged many to be very frank about their concerns.

The other difference was that we were now appealing to *all* registered voters, not just Democrats. I again used my voterBase software to mine data about the most likely Elmira voters, those of all political stripes who consistently cast ballots in off-year, local elections. This had worked for us in the primary, and we felt it would work for us now. A lot of people can *say* they vote, but the data didn't lie. We knew who voted, and we put our energy into meeting as many of them as possible.

With just weeks to go before the election, we were doing our best, but we knew there would be obstacles ahead. We just didn't know what they'd be. This campaign stuff certainly wasn't like any other work I'd done. I'd never had a job where I'd wake up to headlines criticizing me or my work. Turns out, in political campaigns, that's as normal as April rain, and all we could do was brace for what was to come.

12

# The Marathon Takes Its Toll

## A small core team does the heavy lifting

We'd managed to mostly make peace with the local Democratic Party, and by the late stages of the campaign, many on the committee were helping us. Some committee members would go with me to local public events, write letters to the editor, put up yard signs, make calls on our behalf, and more. We were also counting on them to spread a positive word or two about me, and we'd definitely need their help in getting out the vote. Still, Andy and I were at the center of it all, exchanging hundreds of emails and phone calls in the closing weeks.

The pace was definitely taking its toll. I was finding it harder and harder to fall asleep each night, my mind refusing to empty itself of strategy questions, voter sentiment, the media, and all the details tied to putting up signs. Physically, I was fine—actually better than usual because of all the canvassing I did—but my brain was filled up. It's one thing to *say* the public barbs should be brushed aside, but it's another to actually *do* it.

My lack of sleep also started to make me feel more paranoid. My approach had always been idealistic, and if I were to win, I wanted to get there by doing right by the city and its residents. But the distrust I'd harbored since the start of the campaign remained. I trusted Andy and Sharon, but I kept those I didn't know as well on the periphery. Part of me wanted to embrace every single person who supported me, but I held on to a degree of wariness.

As a result, I'd developed a new skill during the campaign: the ability to very quickly size up people. I used to tell Andy I'd know in less than five minutes if someone was with me or against me. I was reading faces, body language, vocal cues, language inflections, and more. This sort of quick vetting was anchored in my gut feelings, and when I trusted my instincts, they were almost always correct—good and bad. After six months of campaigning, this ability was now second nature to me—and Andy—and we sounded each other out when in doubt, rapidly deciding whom to trust—or not.

Though I'd reached something of a detente with Jim Hare, I remained wary of him too. That proved to be the right decision when he and Fourth District councilman Terry McLaughlin held a press conference October 27, ostensibly to chastise Dan Mandell and me for comments we'd made during the mayoral debate two days earlier.

"The record needs to be set straight," Jim told the *Star-Gazette* and local television reporters. "People who are running for office this year have no recognition of what has been accomplished."

The two incumbent councilmen, both of whom were running for reelection, said the city's tax base had grown by $60 million over the previous seven years and that the city was learning to do more with less, including entering into shared services agreements with other municipalities to lower costs.

"It's obvious that there has been, by both candidates, a lack of clear understanding of the issues," McLaughlin told the newspaper.

The reporter called me for comment, and I was a little taken aback. "I am disappointed they wouldn't call me and tell me this is how they felt," I told the *Star-Gazette*. "I couldn't disagree more that I don't understand the issues of the city. I respect [Jim and Terry], but people don't want the status quo. I am the face of a campaign of people that want a different direction in the city. This campaign represents a different approach. I am the outsider here."

Dan Mandell also was quoted in the story, taking exception with how the city tore down a property on Hudson Street without plans to redevelop it. "That's not being fiscally responsible," he said.

The kicker was the last paragraph, which simply read, "At the conclusion of the press conference, Hare and McLaughlin endorsed Tonello in the mayoral race."

I read that last line and laughed out loud. These two veteran local politicians had just spent time tearing me down—but they wanted me to win. Incredible. And why, I thought, didn't they just call me up and tell me—before the debate or after—what they were thinking? I took it as their way of garnering some publicity for their own council races, which, perhaps,

I was making tougher. But if they were facing tough questions from their constituents, that was fine by me. But *they'd* been the ones to complain about airing party laundry in public. Here they were doing just that.

This bit of news—along with Hopkins crossing party lines to endorse Dan Mandell—created a stir among my campaign team.

Sharon had been watching television when she saw a preview of the eleven o'clock news that would feature the story about Jim and Terry criticizing Dan and me. She told me they were afraid of me and my candidacy, and I should be angry enough about it to take the gloves off and criticize the record of the last ten years.

My mother was on the thread, too, and weighed in. "[I] tend to agree with Sharon," Mom wrote. "The media have been sporting for a fight. But the jabs have to be well thought out, delivered with strength and directness, but without the appearance of petulance. The important thing to remember is that the people (voters) are the ones who are responding favorably to John. I just got a call from another person who was very convinced by John's delivery at the debate: articulate, intelligent, etc. No matter what, John has presented himself as a true representative of the people. Hopkins is a lame duck; Hare and McLaughlin have smelled blood and are attempting to capitalize on it. After all, if John wins, it makes them look like dorks because they didn't want him to run."

Ah, the joy of a mother's love. I agreed with Mom that now was *not* the time to take the gloves off or go negative. That hadn't been our approach, and regardless of what my opponents said, it wouldn't become our approach. We had to trust our strategy, particularly the bit about ignoring the naysayers. But as election day neared, that was getting harder to do. More was at stake, and everybody felt it.

Andy and I agreed we needed to stay cool. "I believe your stance in the media came off very well today and last night relative to the [Hare and McLaughlin] situation," Andy wrote. "They ran your 'status quo' statement in the Election section. So overall, okay I think." To the rest of the team, he added, "John has to maintain an even keel. Political posture. As all of us know, the media will *never* get our side of the story right/straight/correct. I mean, look how much time John got tonight for the Hopkins piece. If we haven't learned this yet, we've learned nothing. All this can easily get us unfocused."

We totally understood the calls from inside the team to punch back—we definitely felt it, too—but that was the emotional trap we most wanted to avoid. It had always been important to take a breath, find something else to think about, and *then* assess and respond. Digs and bad press were part of the political game, but the key was to never react quickly or emotionally. We needed to be thick-skinned about these attacks and focus on the goal, which was to build trust and confidence with voters. If we got down in the mud, we'd become the very thing we were railing against. It was never easy—and we did a lot of swearing among ourselves—but we needed to keep telling our story—and showing it.

## Are we missing something?

In early November, the *Star-Gazette* published a story about the October campaign finance filings, which showed that Dan Mandell and Christopher Moss, the sheriff's candidate, were the biggest spenders so far. Mandell, who didn't have a primary to spend money on, was dramatically outspending us. He'd raised $15,000 to my $10,000, which included a nice $1,000 donation from my brother, Joe, who'd included a brief note with his contribution: "Win!"

In the story, Dan Mandell said he'd used $13,000 of his money to hire the local advertising agency Howell, Liberatore & Wickham to create his signs, mailings, and radio ads. "I would have had to take a lot more time off work to campaign if not for Howell," he told the newspaper.

By the end of October, I'd spent $8,400 for both the primary and the general election campaigns, most of it on the costs of mailings, and television and radio ads. In addition to my brother's recent contribution, donations were still coming in, and I'd managed to raise about $1,500 via my website. Of course, we hadn't spent any money on an ad agency like Dan had. We did it all in-house, with WETM-TV providing free production for what would be our second and final campaign television ad. We were saving money on ad buys—where agencies generally take a percentage of the spend for themselves—and by designing our own mailers and literature. All our yard signs were already bought and paid for, and by doing the work ourselves and with volunteers, we'd saved thousands of dollars.

"They key for us was to raise enough money to do all the things we wanted to do and spend every dime," I told the *Star-Gazette*. "That's basically what we've done. It's a great exercise, I think, to show our whole approach being very savvy with money and not blowing it on fees or services that we could do ourselves."

I wasn't surprised that Dan Mandell had hired an agency. That was pretty common. My team and I had some unique skills that helped us avoid hiring professionals. Though the agency Dan had hired had a strong reputation, we all believed they hadn't done him any favors by creating expensive four-color literature and coming up with a yard sign design that was dark blue with a sort of scripted "Dan Mandell"—and hard to read. My stock signs were much bolder and simpler. That was just one small point, but it told us that money wasn't everything.

With Dan's financial advantage, we wondered if he would air television ads, but the newspaper story made it clear he was only planning to use radio. We'd spent about $3,000 on television during the primary and would spend a similar amount in the days before the November 8 election, and we now concluded Dan didn't have the budget for it. That would be to our advantage.

As I'd discovered in September, television was powerful. It's no secret that it's the single best way to be visible, particularly in the final days of a political campaign. We'd always believed voters deserved to see and hear from the candidates, and though we knocked on hundreds of doors, we knew we couldn't physically reach everyone that way. To us, television was the next-best thing. It now appeared that Dan Mandell, like Dan Royle before him, didn't value television advertising nearly as much.

Despite the lateness of the campaign, we were running in the black, and the money difference didn't trouble us too much. However, we did begin to wonder what we might be missing. In particular, we asked ourselves if we were putting up enough yard signs. We believed we were. Andy worked on our master sign list daily, providing regular updates, and we could all see the evidence of his work as we drove around the city. Our signs were easy to spot and appeared across the city. Dan Mandell's signs were everywhere, too, but we had saved a lot of time in getting them up for the general election by having our primary supporters simply replant the signs we'd already distributed.

On appearances, we wondered if we'd been visible enough. I'd been on local news, the local Sunday morning talk shows, and at dozens of community events. The calendar had been full for months, so we felt good that we'd reached far and wide—despite what the newspaper suggested.

Before the final deadline for letters to the editor, we had good support there too. We were keeping pace with letters written in support of Dan, and we had a good sense from the unsolicited letters, like the Kisers', that my personal outreach was paying dividends.

On the get-out-the-vote front, I'd spoken with Jim Hare about coordinating Democratic efforts on election day. This was critical because it meant that many committee members—not just the ten or so who were "true believers"—would be helping to call voters and get them to the polls. This would benefit all the Democrats running, not just me.

It also helped that the election day ballot would include a vote on a proposed new library district, which would set up the county library to operate independently. If it passed, the referendum would give the library its own taxing and operational authority, separate from Chemung County government. The library district effort had started three years earlier, when the county cut $250,000 from the library system that forced it to close two branches and cut staff by 20 percent, but with the issue now on the ballot, we felt the referendum would spur voter turnout countywide and, we hoped, encourage city voters who'd lost libraries to cast ballots.

As we went down the list, we checked all our boxes. As Andy said, we were "rockin' and rollin'" and making an all-out push toward the finish line. We could rest afterward. For now, we were pouring everything we had into the race.

## Oh, yeah, I have a day job

Throughout the campaign, I'd done my best to balance my work-work balance. That is, managing all the moving parts of the race *and* my job at Cornell University. On the Cornell side of things, I was fortunate to work with some truly great people. The dean of the Graduate School at the time was Allison "Sunny" Power, a professor of ecology and evolutionary biology who'd been appointed dean in 2002. During her tenure with Associate Dean J. Ellen Gainor, a professor of performing arts and theater, they introduced several innovations, including helping to make graduate school at Cornell much more accepting of married students.

My boss, Associate Dean Sarah Hale Wicker, who held an MBA from Cornell, was no slouch either. She managed much of the graduate school staff, including Student Services, which helped students navigate their time at Cornell, from the application process and registration to funding and the all-important thesis submission process. She was particularly forward thinking in how she spearheaded efforts to digitize the Graduate School's paper processes, including debuting a new online application.

I'd kept Sarah informed of my side hustle job of running for mayor, and she was supportive—and accommodating. I used vacation days for campaign-related work while keeping up with my work as the Graduate School's communications director. I was responsible for several publications and the school's website, which I transformed to match Sarah's desire to make it easier for students to navigate graduate school. Some of this work I could do remotely, but I hadn't pushed that option during the campaign because, after all, Cornell provided my livelihood. I never wanted to shirk—or be perceived as shirking—my work.

In a way, my daily trips north to Ithaca and Cornell were a welcome relief during the campaign. In Elmira, I'd started to become a minor celebrity, but in Ithaca and on the Cornell campus, I was anonymous. My work with the deans and the rest of the Graduate School kept me grounded, and working on campus was a treat.

The historic ivy-clad buildings—including Caldwell Hall, where we worked—were beautiful, but Cornell was much more than that. The university's mission was to educate *and* create new knowledge. As such, in addition to the big brains that made up the faculty, staff, and student body, the campus welcomed many world-famous men and women to speak and teach. Caldwell Hall was just a few steps from the Space Sciences Building, where renowned astronomer Carl Sagan had once worked, and as a space enthusiast, I often thought of him and his work when I walked past his old offices.

The whole university just dripped with history and intellectual stars. For example, when I crossed campus to go to lunch one summer day, I saw a familiar face walk by. The face belonged to none other than John Cleese, the actor and comedian perhaps best known for his work on the British television programs *Monty Python's Flying Circus* and *Fawlty Towers*. At the time, he was a visiting professor who taught classes about humor, and there he was just strolling along with another professor.

That sort of casual interaction among people from all walks of life was just one reason I loved the university atmosphere, which stood in stark contrast to less progressive Elmira. I wanted to bring some of the Cornell sensibilities I'd come to know—engagement, a thirst for knowledge, diversity, and innovation—to Elmira.

Although Cornell and Elmira were similar in age—Ezra Cornell founded the university in 1865 and Elmira was incorporated in 1864—they had become very different places. Moving between both every day helped remind me of what was possible. Cornell University was by no means perfect, but it was much further ahead on many professional and social issues than the city I called home. I thought if I could infuse even a small part of that university experience into the city, we would all be better off.

As election day neared, I also faced my old, but now more pressing, conundrum. I'd publicly explained how I'd use technology and remote work to balance my day job with being mayor, but we—the deans and I—mostly punted the issue. It would only become something to address if I won in November. Still, I now had to think about it in real terms. The mayor's job was *technically* part-time and paid just $10,350 a year. It couldn't replace my Cornell income. But having juggled the campaign and my work at Caldwell Hall for six months, I believed doing both jobs would be doable, if not time-consuming. If I won, I was determined to make it work.

In the meantime, it would be important to remember to maintain a good balance, not dwell on things we couldn't control, and avoid any temptation to change our strategy in the final days of the campaign.

13

# Lead-up to Election Day

## Cutting a new TV commercial

Raising and spending money on television ads was core to the campaign, and when I sat down to write the script for the General Election commercial, I knew I wanted it to be upbeat, positive, and reflective of what voters had been telling me for months. I also wanted it to be me talking to the camera as much as possible so it was direct and personal.

After a few drafts—and editing to get the words down to thirty seconds—I ended up with this:

> Since May, I've crisscrossed Elmira listening to hundreds of you tell me, "Elmira needs a change." I couldn't agree more. I'm John Tonello. As mayor, I'll lead that positive change with specific ideas and thoughtful solutions, not empty promises. I won't settle for quick fixes. I'll work with you, and I'll work hard to make Elmira safer, stronger, and better. I have the right experience. I can get things done. We can change Elmira. Vote for me on Election Day November 8th. I'll listen.

The spot opened with me walking toward the camera in downtown Elmira's Riverfront Park and then cut to slides that said, "Reduce taxes by growing Elmira," "Cut red tape for a business-friendly Elmira," and "Rethink road repair so more streets get paved." It then transitioned to a shot of me talking to supporters in Wisner Park and, finally, incorporated a clip from the primary ad with me saying, "I have the right experience. I can get things done. We can change Elmira."

That last bit was important because some were grumbling that my lack of political experience was disqualifying. To me, politics wasn't the domain of career politicians, but of average citizens with a willingness to step forward and represent the best interests of the community. Being mayor didn't require a degree in political science or years as a party back-bencher. To me, American democracy was, at its core, citizen democracy. No professionals required.

The team at WETM-TV did a nice job with the commercial, though it was hard to top the one they'd produced for the primary. Still, we thought it effectively showed me as normal, friendly, honest, and approachable—the embodiment of our campaign themes. I thought it was important to reiterate what voters had told us they wanted and acknowledge their discontent. Yes, the ad was intended to convince voters to vote for me, but I also wanted it to convey the fact that I truly identified with city residents and would work for *them*.

We again booked airtime in early November, the final week of the campaign, with most ads set to air over the weekend and into Tuesday evening, including the local election day newscasts. In all, we'd spend more than $4,000 on radio, television, and cable for the spot, again targeting news programs, drive times, and cable networks we thought would be seen by likeminded viewers. It might seem like a pittance in modern terms, but for my campaign it was a lot of money—and a critical part of our strategy.

## Fighting a wave of negative newspaper coverage

In these late stages of the campaign, the newspaper and its editors were beginning to seed doubt in the ability of Dan Mandell or me to serve as mayor. The so-called "quiet campaign" theme was clear in the final weeks of reporting, including a story on November 2 with the headline "Quiet campaign for Elmira mayor coming to a close" and the subhead "Some voters say they still don't know candidates Mandell, Tonello."

This time the story did not seek comment from us candidates but offered the comments of two local voters who said they'd heard little about either of us. Such a lack of visibility was understandable to some degree, but did these two random voters interviewed for the story really represent the city writ large? It was truly disheartening. We'd worked hard to reach as many people as we could, yet the reporter had managed to find two people who'd heard nothing. The journalist in me asked, "Could the newspaper not find any people who *had* heard from us to include in the story for balance?" Apparently not. However, the reporter did give plenty of space in print to Elmira City Manager Sam Iraci Jr.

He told the newspaper that Mandell, other council candidates, and I had misrepresented the city's record and didn't understand the manager-council form of government. "Just following the campaign, I'm not sure to what degree the role of the manager is understood," Iraci told the *Star-Gazette*. He went on to say he was "alarmed" by inaccurate statements from the candidates that put the "rest of City Hall on edge."

Iraci had been with the city for nearly twelve years, had just turned fifty-five, and was eligible to retire. I'd reached out to him earlier in the campaign with the hope that he would answer some of my fundamental questions, and he graciously provided detailed answers. I'd used the information he gave me in many of the conversations I'd had with voters, both publicly and one-on-one. I hadn't spoken to Iraci in these late stages of the election, but the city manager was widely seen by local business leaders, editors, and others as a strong, stable public servant who ran city government efficiently and professionally. However, we'd also heard from people from inside and outside City Hall that he'd overstayed his welcome.

Personally, I was neutral when it came to the discussions of Iraci's possible retirement. It had been speculated for months, but Jim Hare and others had recently campaigned on the promise to renew the veteran city manager's appointment come January. I didn't know Iraci that well, but I'd come to learn he had a close working relationship with former Mayor Stephen Hughes. The *Star-Gazette* also had frequently editorialized in support of Iraci's decisions. In the closing days of the campaign, something told me that the editors of the newspaper were somewhat enchanted with the status quo and saw the combination of Dan Mandell or me and the absence of Iraci and Hughes as a major shift toward the negative.

Again, Andy and I and others on my campaign team did our best to shrug off the latest "quiet campaign" report, but some on the team wanted to punch back. It was just getting so tiring. We had enough to think about without the newspaper slamming not one, but both candidates for mayor. The editors were clearly not fans despite the fact that I'd been accommodating to reporters, and I'd been open and honest from the start. I'd also provided the newspaper with a detailed platform (even though it was on my website and talked about publicly), which the paper would later describe as being "impossibly long." I could only shrug and wonder.

On November 2, the newspaper ran more stories about the mayoral election, which was now less than a week away. Stories about Dan Mandell and me appeared along with a question-and-answer list on topics such as city taxes, police consolidation, First Arena, and the city's master plan as it pertained to economic development.

These reports were relatively balanced, but both stories quoted Jim Hare, who reiterated his concern about us misrepresenting the city's accomplishments. He took on Mandell for a "moral" conflict of interest of working for the county and the city at the same time if he was elected mayor. That had been Jim's old saw and straight-up negative campaigning, which was echoed in his quote in the story about me.

"People who are running for office this year have no recognition of what's been accomplished," Jim told the *Star-Gazette*. "We don't want to take steps backward." He went on to say that I had "rebuked the concept of party unity by not agreeing to a citywide Democratic platform."

I responded as I always had, highlighting the fact that I was "not among the party's chosen for this year's election."

"It goes back to the primary," I told the newspaper. "I wasn't the party choice there. I represent a change just as much to them (Jim and Terry) as to anybody else. I can understand their hesitation and their wariness."

I also explained that my goal was to draw people together. Yes, veteran politicians, businesspeople, and others would—and did—find fault, but they represented the status quo. I did not.


## A write-in effort


With the election just days away, the newspaper began to run its annual candidate endorsements. It had rolled out endorsements for Chemung County sheriff, favoring Christopher Moss over William Mayhew, and favored Proposition 3, which would create a county library district. They then moved on to each Elmira City Council race, endorsing incumbents Jim Hare and Terry McLaughlin and newcomers Susan Skidmore, Brent Stermer, and Robert Bailey. Incumbent Republican John Corsi was running unopposed in the Third District and did not receive an endorsement. Without knowing the newspaper's editorial schedule, we assumed the editorial board would publish its mayoral endorsement on the final Sunday before the election, November 8. We had no inkling which way they'd go: Mandell or me? We just had to wait it out.

In the meantime, on the Friday before the election, the *Star-Gazette* ran a front-page story with the headline "Hughes urged to run for mayor as write-in." Accompanying the story was a large graphic with big, black ballot-style fingers pointing to each of the candidates. In the topmost finger was written "Write-In" and pointed to a picture of Stephen Hughes. Below that were "Republican" and "Democratic" fingers pointing to Dan Mandell and me, respectively. Under that was a picture of Linda Forrest, the Republican deputy commissioner for the Chemung County Board of Elections, demonstrating in an actual voting booth how to write in a candidate.

The accompanying story was difficult to read. After all, Hughes had resigned in March because he'd failed to get a waiver that would allow him to hold elective office while simultaneously working for Catholic Charities, a nonprofit the city helped fund with federal money. Though he still needed a waiver, the paper explained, if he was elected, he would be eligible to serve again as mayor.

Instead of providing an outright "I'm not a candidate" statement, Hughes instead told the newspaper, "Quoting Mario Cuomo, I am not making plans to make plans. I am honored to serve as long as I did, and if someday I am called back, I would do that with great pride."

What the actual hell?

Former City Councilman John Keefe III, a longtime Hughes supporter, told the newspaper he would support the former mayor as a write-in candidate. "I wouldn't even think twice about it," he told the *Star-Gazette*. "All you have to do is tell (voters) to write him in. I'd do it in two minutes. I wouldn't bat an eye."

The newspaper even called on county executive Tom Santulli to weigh in. I'd heard he and Hughes did not have a great working relationship, but, regardless, he said he hadn't heard talk of a potential write-in campaign. "My thought would be that it may be driven by the fact that this has been one of the most quiet mayoral races in the city's history, and maybe that's got some people grumbling," he told the newspaper.

What? Him *too*?

The story quoted me as well. "There's been talk all along, and the coverage of the race has been that there's not much going on and it belies the truth," I told the *Star-Gazette*. "We've been pushing the message and meeting people one-on-one and in groups. People are very engaged and know what I stand for and what Dan Mandell stands for."

For his part, Mandell said he could understand a write-in for Hughes, whom he said had been well liked. "Those are the people who are still supporting him," Dan told the paper.

We pored over this new development among my committee, and we were just simply flabbergasted. What the hell was going on? Was Stephen Hughes going to swoop in at the end and steal the election? I received some comments via my website from voters who were as appalled as we were.

"With friends like Mayor Hughes you have no need for political enemies," wrote one supporter, who lived on the south side. "Hughes does *not* expect to win this year as a write-in candidate. His objective is the election of Mr. Mandell, by stealing several percentage points of the vote from you in this year's close race. It will be far easier for Hughes, two years from now, to oppose Republican Mandell; far easier than it would be for him to oppose an incumbent of his own party."

A former city councilman who had recently and unsuccessfully run for a seat on the south side wrote, "I was not going to email you on this but I must. Why in the world is there really all this ta-do about Steve with the write-in stuff? Don't they realize what a detriment this could be to you in the election? Are they that unconfident [sic] with your ability, or is it leftover sour grapes because Dan [Royle] did not win? Then throw in this baloney about his kids and the write-in vote and it is a heck of a mess."

Unfortunately, the mess continued Saturday, when the *Star-Gazette* ran another story, this time with the headline "Interest grows for Hughes write-in."

It said, in part, "While support seems to exist for the former mayor to return to the seat he resigned from in March to avoid a conflict of interest, Hughes is less than eager to lead a write-in charge."

It amazed me that the newspaper could take the word of a couple people and turn it into this sort of reporting. They had yet to identify any massive outpouring of support for Hughes, who at least told the newspaper, "I'm very flattered by people's good will toward the concept of a write-in, but I don't want to in any way, shape or form encourage it. I am not taking any part in the activities at all," adding that he didn't want to confuse voters. Still, he went on to wax poetic about his time in office.

Well, that was something, anyway. But the story again found a couple of random voters, including one who told the newspaper, "From what I'd heard, I was kind of leaning toward Tonello. This could put a whole new spin on things."

Clearly, the confusion the newspaper had engendered was taking root.

In the same day's newspaper, yet another write-in story was published with the headline "Royle's children want dad's name written on ballot." According to the paper, Dan Royle's oldest son and two of his other children had encouraged friends to write in their father's name. "There are still a lot of people who are undecided, and I am afraid these people aren't going to vote at all," Jeff Royle told the paper. "There is a viable third option. They could write in my dad."

Dan Royle said he appreciated his kids' support and told the paper, "I understand that there's some frustration with this campaign. I think it has been quiet, but let's just let it play out."

This was getting ridiculous. Was the perception that it was a "quiet campaign" due to the fact that Dan Mandell and I hadn't attacked each other? That we hadn't slung mud or tried to drag each other down? I'd lived in the city for seven years, and I didn't recall any grand campaigning in previous elections. Wasn't the fact that the people thought it a quiet campaign at least partially an issue with a lack of news coverage? Wasn't the *Star-Gazette* a part of that? If no one had heard anything, wasn't it because they weren't reading the newspaper?

We really didn't get it, and it felt like something was afoot.

To help blunt the write-in effort for mayor and get some clarity for voters and myself, I called Steve that weekend and asked him to put the rumors to rest. He'd publicly said he wasn't actively supporting the write-in effort, but his other comments clearly had left the door open. He'd been in Elmira government for eighteen years and had plenty of supporters. Without a clear statement, the situation could quickly unravel—for Dan Mandell and me.

During the conversation, Hughes asked me, "Do you believe in God?"

I hesitated and replied, "What does that matter?"

He told me God has a purpose, and I, like him, should trust in that purpose.

Now, I respect people's religious beliefs, but I wasn't going to put much stock in prayer to turn the election one way or another. When the call ended, I hoped Steve would do the right thing and definitively bow out, but I wasn't 100 percent sure he would. These kinds of political vagaries were beyond my understanding. Power was at stake, and it created a strange swirl that was difficult to fathom.

When Sunday morning came, I woke early and went straight to my front porch to grab the paper. I needed to see the *Star-Gazette*'s mayoral endorsement. I flipped to the Opinion page and, sure enough, the lead opinion piece was headlined, "Elmira mayor." But the subhead made my stomach drop. It read, "The only candidate with mayoral potential isn't campaigning, but voters can put him on the ballot—Stephen Hughes."

There it was. The "quiet campaign," the write-in effort, and the repeated mention of our poor mayoral qualifications had been leading up to this.

The editorial, written by Associate Editor David Kubissa—a guy I'd worked with when I was the newspaper's online editor and later metro editor—was biting:

> Democrat John Tonello and Republican Daniel Mandell Jr. have pounded on a lot of doors in the past several weeks, but between their block-by-block efforts and their campaign platform, something has been lost in translation.
>
> Their message has failed to inspire. Yes, they both believe in better public safety, working with business, keeping close tabs on government spending and taxes and improving neighborhoods. In their October 25 televised debate, they seemed to agree on far more than they disagreed.
>
> After the lackluster turnout for the September 13 primaries, we had expected them to turn up the volume and fill the unnerving indifference that had settled over this campaign. A student council race has more vigor than we've seen from this one.

The opinion piece went on to say that Dan and I had failed to see the good the city had done over the past ten years, and we would fail to build on those successes. Kubissa also wrote that we would have "done well to cut [our] teeth as council members. Then [we] would understand the ins and outs of government."

The opinion piece continued, "Tonello and Mandell are on the ballot, but neither one meets the standards Elmirans deserve for their mayor. The one person who does isn't on the ballot, but can be if voters choose. Yes, former Mayor Stephen Hughes is an option, and the one who gets our vote."

Executive Editor Bill Church wrote a separate column on the same page that also endorsed Hughes. He reiterated the points of the main editorial, including, "Campaign rhetoric aside, John Tonello and Daniel J. Mandell Jr. have done little to create that community buzz."

I finally blew my top, probably scaring my cats with my profanity-laced outburst. I quickly got on the phone to Andy, who'd read what I'd read and was equally pissed off, and told him we needed to respond immediately with a rally in downtown Wisner Park. We got on the horn and called as many supporters we could find and met at the park at two o'clock.

Despite the short notice, we got a decent turnout of about fifty people, including *Star-Gazette* reporter Ray Finger, another guy I used to work with during my time at the newspaper. Unlike others at the paper, though, I had a lot of faith in Ray's objectivity. He was a solid, dependable reporter with long experience, so when I saw him there to cover the last-minute rally, I was glad.

When it came time to speak, my voice was filled with emotion and anger. I was mad that a few newspaper editors could do Elmirans such a disservice based more on what they'd read from the coverage in their own paper than what they'd seen in person. I'd been to dozens and dozens of community events and public activities. If they had attended those same activities, I'd never seen them, and now I felt they had overplayed their hand, and I said so:

> The *Star-Gazette* has done all it can in the last few days to confuse voters and try to influence the outcome of the Elmira mayor's race in a way that ignores both readers and voters.
>
> I'm here today to set the record straight.
>
> The *Star-Gazette* editorial board has it wrong. I resent the accusation that I lack the experience or passion to be mayor. Tell that to the voters who supported me in the September Democratic primary. Tell that to the thousands of Elmirans who've urged me to run, and personally asked me to be their voice. How dare anyone say I'm unwilling to fight for the people of this city.
>
> Steve Hughes has confirmed he is not a candidate. This year, there is only one mayoral candidate who is qualified to lead this city forward. Only one mayoral candidate who has listened to voters, not special interests. Only one mayoral candidate who can build on past successes and set a clear vision for the future.
>
> I am that candidate.
>
> I'm willing to make hard choices, even if the *Star-Gazette* isn't. Why? Because we have a lot of work to do to lead Elmira into the future. There are no simple answers. There are no quick fixes. Only together, through collaboration and consensus, can

we keep our neighborhoods safe, retain and attract businesses and jobs, and rebuild our neighborhoods.

Being mayor is about reaching out to people. Not special interests, but interested citizens. I'm supported by Democrats, Republicans, and independents; members of local unions; business people; Attorney General Eliot Spitzer; and thousands of fair-minded, hard-working Elmirans who want a better future.

I believe Elmira has come a long way. I want to build on past successes. My campaign and the campaigns of all the Democratic candidates—Terry McLaughlin, Jim Hare, Brent Stermer, Tom Petro—have been positive and issues-based. Our ticket has experience and vision. We all believe in making Elmira better. And we're all going to fight for that.

The mayor's race is about the future. It's about getting people involved. It's about standing up for the people of this city and doing what they've asked all of us to do: To listen, to work with them, and to help make their lives better.

That's exactly what I intend to do as mayor.

Please turn out in force Tuesday. Join me—join all of us—in setting Elmira on a clear path to the future.

The next morning's newspaper included my comments in a story headlined "Tonello rips newspaper for Hughes endorsement," and it concisely summarized the write-in push of the past week. Unfortunately, there was no story with Hughes formally bowing out. With one day to go to the election, time was running out for him and the newspaper to disperse the confusion.

Despite that, we heard from many people that the *Star-Gazette* had been off-base in endorsing former mayor Hughes. Rather than increasing its credibility with readers, it had tarnished it. The paper's Hughes endorsement had a clear link to the write-in coverage and all the stories about the so-called "quiet campaign," and people saw right through it. In his column on the Opinion page a week later, Kubissa tried his best to mitigate the damage.

"A week ago today on this page, the newspaper's Elmira mayoral endorsement of Stephen Hughes as a write-in candidate drew mixed reviews. Some people thought we were jerks. Others thought we showed guts. Two callers wondered if we—actually I because I wrote the editorial on behalf of our board—had lost it. Two other callers offered congratulations. And that's the nature of newspaper endorsements."

Interestingly, Kubissa wrote that the paper had published 102 reader letters about the year's elections between October 8 and November 8, including the sheriff's race, the proposed library district, and the mayor and city council races. That seemed like a lot to me and hinted at a lot of engagement, not silence. All I could think was that the editors, like many others with long ties to the status quo, weren't ready for change.

## Confusion and clarity

It had been a busy weekend, for sure. My television and radio ads were airing and we were making the final push to reach voters, but all the write-in stuff had become a big distraction. I was gratified that my campaign had pushed back, and I'd show that I wasn't *always* going to take shit and ignore it.

As election day dawned on November 8, I was glad to finally see a front-page story headlined, "Hughes: 'I am not a candidate'" with the subhead, "Former Elmira mayor discourages write-in effort, urges voters to choose from 2 candidates."

Better late than never.

The newspaper story was based on an open letter Hughes had written to the community and also repeated the fact that the newspaper had endorsed him Sunday as a write-in. "For nearly 18 years, I served residents of this community with honor and integrity, and it is in this spirit I ask city voters not to exercise the write-in option," he wrote. "On Tuesday, I will exercise my right to vote for one of the designated candidates for the office of mayor."

The reporter also interviewed Hughes by phone, and he had added, "I thought back to every decision we ever made in city government, and it was always made on the simple principle 'Do the right thing,' That's what it came down to for me—do the right thing."

He added that a write-in would be unfair to Dan Mandell and me and that he didn't want the outcome compromised by a last-minute write-in effort. Though a Democrat, he refused to endorse me or Mandell.

Dan was quoted in the same story, saying, "He's a stand-up guy for making (his decision) clear. I know Steve. I know Steve very well. He's always a great guy, and this speaks more for his character."

I, too, was interviewed and said I was grateful to Hughes for clarifying. "What's important to me is what's important to the people of Elmira. I want what the people want, and this clarifies the issues surrounding this race."

I also offered an olive branch and a small tip of my hat to past city accomplishments. "There are many successes that the past administrations have had, but to me this race is about who's best to build on those successes and lead Elmira forward," I told the reporter.

If you'd asked me at the start of the race if I'd be dealing with these sorts of editorial and write-in shenanigans, I probably would've just laughed. People in power don't *really* pull out these kinds of stops to maintain the status quo, do they? Silly me. This series of events solidified for me that the few always wished to dominate the many, to obfuscate and sway, to create their own false narratives—anything, really, to avoid change. It had made me angry, but no one had ever told me politics would be fair.

## 14

# Election Day

### Making calls and appearances

The day's news had providing a rousing start to my morning, but with election day finally upon us, we needed to keep our focus. I'd taken a vacation day from my job at Cornell and planned to head to my polling place around nine o'clock that morning to vote, head out to breakfast, and make a few local appearances. As usual, I started the day by feeding Tucker, Edgar, and Arthur; scooping their litter boxes; and letting them out into the yard. Their only concern was that the once-warm weather had turned frosty, forcing each of them to perform that typical cat hesitation before stepping outside. I was just happy there was no rain—or snow—to keep voters at home.

Unlike the primary election day, this one didn't feel quite as calm. This was it, and there were a lot of moving parts, including a meeting at a union hall later in the afternoon with fellow Democrats to make calls to voters and a gathering at Horigan's that evening to await the returns.

Our team, including Andy, Sharon, Mom, Amy Wilson, Sarah, and many others, had been making get-out-the-vote calls, which was the last critical element of the campaign. Without people actually pulling levers, all would be for naught.

As before, we prepared a script for callers:

Hello, this is __________.

I'm a volunteer working for John Tonello, the Democratic candidate for mayor of Elmira.

I'm calling to remind you to vote this coming Tuesday, November 8th. Your polling place is _________. Polls open at 6 a.m. and close at 9 p.m.

We're anticipating a close race for mayor and all the city council races, so your vote really matters. John asks for your support, and support for the entire Democratic ticket.

We thought providing specific voting information—such as voters' actual voting places—would be helpful, and we also wanted to give support to the other Democrats running. He hoped it would be enough.

We got some feedback during this process that was encouraging. Andy sent me an email that said, "Maureen Daly shared with me, completely unsolicited, that she's done campaign phone calls before where some voters have appeared angrier and also some have appeared uninterested. She felt this time that many of the people she called were forthright with telling her you had their vote, as opposed to years past. Just a little bit more 'feel good' for you today."

That *did* make me feel good.


## We've done all we can do

In any race for public office, there are moments when everyone working on the campaign wonders if there are any things left undone. We'd implemented our strategy, rested when we had to, and checked everything off our lists. The goal had been to finish everything by election day, and we felt certain we had.

The day's final election day story in the *Star-Gazette* explained how the candidates in the sheriff's and mayor's races had spent their last days of the campaign. Everyone was making big efforts to knock on doors. The paper reported that I'd spent Monday visiting voters, lunching at Charlie's Cafe on Hoffman Street near my home, and making calls to get out the vote.

"We're just clarifying for voters who have questions [about] my qualifications and our plans for a positive future," I told the newspaper. "It's an exciting time."

The reporter asked the inevitable question: Was I nervous?

"I can't say I'm nervous. I'm curious," I told her. "At the beginning of the campaign, we set out to involve the people in the political process, and regardless of the outcome, we have succeeded in that. Now it's just waiting to hear what the voters want for the city."

Dan Mandell told the newspaper he had spent the final Monday before the election at his county job and would spread fliers that evening.

By election day, my nerves were jangling. How would this political experiment turn out? Were we on-target about the sentiments of voters? Were we off? Way off? Again, there would be no pre-election polling to offer any hints. There was just one poll, and it ended at nine o'clock that night.

I received several emails offering good luck, including a short and sweet one from Andy: "Rock on today, dude!" I also received supportive emails from friends, relatives, Cornell coworkers, and others. Lorraine Heasley, a graphic designer I'd worked with at Cornell, simply wrote, "Good luck! Good luck! Good luck! Good luck! Good luck! Good luck! Good luck!"

That gave me a welcome laugh. My girlfriend, Sarah, was supportive, too, and I was glad she would be on hand while we awaited the returns. Sarah had been a great emotional support throughout the campaign, and I'd leaned into her calm and intelligent influence.

In the late afternoon, I joined other Democrats at the union office on Church Street, where party members sat at banks of phones the union folks had made available to us to call voters. Cindy Emmer, chair of the Chemung County Democratic Committee, was there leading the charge, and I overheard her tell someone, "I don't think John knows how hard it is to get elected."

Cindy had a lot of experience with local elections, so I couldn't just dismiss her words, but I also knew that, by now anyway, I had a pretty good inkling of how hard it was. Nothing had been easy or simple, including dealing with the party itself, but I was heartened that so many fellow Democrats had laid aside their differences and were dialing phones on my behalf—and the rest of the Democratic candidates.


## Turnout at Horigan's

Unlike the night of the primary, my favorite local tavern, Horigan's, was the official site for the city and county Democratic election night gathering. By eight o'clock the place was packed and, in Andy's terms, rocking and rolling. One corner of the restaurant was dedicated to gathering and posting the election returns, with Cindy and others in close contact with party contacts stationed at the Board of Elections. When numbers came in, the boards would get updated as quickly as possible.

A few of my yard signs adorned the walls of Horigan's, and many of those on hand wore their Tonello stickers. I dressed in black jeans, a blue button-down shirt, and my favorite dark-blue sport coat, and standing and seated were some of the most prominent local Democrats in Elmira, include interim Mayor Bill O'Brien—captured with a huge grin in one of our election night photos—and current and former council members, county legislators, friends, and supporters. Leo Krolac, the former county party chair, was there too. Anyone looking to have a quiet drink or dinner at Horigan's that night was out of luck.

I walked through the crowd feeling a bit like a bridegroom at a wedding reception. Everyone was in a good mood, feeling confident, and loosened up a bit with alcohol. Though I wasn't drinking, I felt surprisingly calm. Many asked if I was nervous, and I just told them we'd done all we could. There was nothing left to do.

The city had thirty-one polling districts, but the mayoral race wasn't the only one on the ballot. The countywide sheriff's race, library referendum, and individual city council races—and others—would require the Board of Elections to gather returns from hundreds of polling stations across Chemung County, so the prospect of getting a quick result in the mayor's race was nil. When the polls finally closed at nine o'clock, the party mood shifted to one of anticipation, with candidates like me sneaking regular peaks at the tally boards.

We didn't have too long to wait. Just before ten o'clock, all the reports were in and the numbers were on the board. With thirty-one of thirty-one polling places reporting and more than 5,400 voters casting ballots, I had won. The final, unofficial count: Tonello, 2,753. Mandell, 2,201. The margin was 56 percent to 44 percent.

I was floored and a bit numb, feeling simultaneously happy and stunned. Was this really happening? Had I just been elected mayor? Was *this* the final outcome? I knew it was when the crowd at Horigan's erupted into a loud, relieved cheer when the results were announced and written on a large chalkboard. I accepted hugs from Sarah, Mom, Andy, and others, and as I looked around the place, I saw the faces of so many friends and supporters who'd made it all happen. It truly had been a team effort, and I was grateful, but at that climactic moment, it all felt a bit unbelievable.

We'd pulled it off. We had actually pulled it off, I thought. As I accepted smiles and congratulations from everyone, the news wasn't all good for Democrats that night. Incumbents Jim Hare and Terry McLaughlin had won reelection, but the remaining three contested seats were won by Republicans. With incumbent John Corsi to add to their ranks, the Republicans would hold a four-to-three majority on city council come January.

Still, it was the grandest of nights for my campaign and the entire team. We had set out on a mission, tapped into voter discontent, and had come out victorious. I'd gone from a complete unknown to mayor in just six months by knocking on doors, listening to voters, staying positive, and pushing back against the party veterans and negative newspaper coverage.

I felt vindicated, particularly when the Board of Election released the final official results. I ended up with 2,844 votes to Mandell's 2,108. Just forty-six voters had written in Stephen Hughes. So much for "interest growing for a Hughes write-in," as the paper had suggested. The results also revealed that I'd won twenty-two of the city's thirty-one election districts outright. In two others I'd lost by just a handful of votes. Some 279 city voters had cast ballots without choosing anyone for mayor.

It wasn't just a win, but an overwhelming one across the city, with voters crossing over to elect me. Nearly every district in the city had given me broad support, and turnout was nearly 8 percent higher than the mayoral race run two years earlier. I was particularly proud of that number. Not only did it show more voter engagement, but it also contradicted the newspaper's complaints about a "quiet campaign."

We agreed that a couple things helped with the turnout, particularly the open seat for sheriff, won by Republican Christopher Moss with 14,820 votes to Conservative Bill Mayhew's 3,512, and the referendum to create a library district, which passed 9,170 to 4,843.

Before the night at Horigan's ended, I stood on a chair and addressed the crowd, thanking everyone for all their tireless support, particularly Andy, who'd done yeoman's work to help get me elected. When I called him out, he humbly didn't say a word, but gave me a two-handed thumbs-up.

"We did it!" I said, extolling the virtues of listening to voters and repeating my mantra to engage new people in city government. "We kept voters at the top of mind, and they rewarded us today. I believe it will take all of us to make a great future."

I'd written two speeches for election night, one to use if I lost, one if I won. Fortunately, I got to use the latter:

> When we began this race, we had two simple goals: The first was to offer people a new face, new energy and new ideas—a real choice for mayor.

The second was to get people involved in this process again. We especially wanted to involve people who had never been part of a campaign before.

Of course, we had a third ultimate goal: To win the mayor's office!

We have much to be proud of. And I mean we. We did what we said we would. We stuck to our plan. We never made it personal. We never wilted in the face of pressure from critics. Even in the most stressful moments, we kept our heads, respected each other, and kept voters top of mind. They rewarded us today.

I want to thank the voters and the hundreds of people I met going door-to-door who took the time to tell me their ideas and vision for the future. I will do all I can to turn your trust and your ideas into reality, and I will work very, very hard as your mayor.

I'm looking forward to working with all the people of this great city. I'm also looking forward to working with city employees who make our government work. I believe it will take all of us, working together, to build a great future based on past successes.

I want to personally thank the many people who made today possible. Dozens of people who contributed time and money, advice and ideas, shoe leather and moral support. I want to thank Cindy Emmer and members of the Democratic Party, Councilmen Dan Royle, Terry McLaughlin, Jim Hare, and Shirley Williams. Candidates Brent Stermer and Tom Petro. I also want to thank the nearly 400 Elmirans who planted my signs!

Today would not have been possible without the tireless work of the members of my campaign committee—Rosalie Krajci, Sarah Hilsman, Sharon Mitchell, Amy Wilson, Nicola Pytell, and others—who gave their all to make this happen.

I want to thank my parents—my mother Rosalie, my stepfather Tom, and my father Fran—who instilled in me the desire to serve, to give back, and to take on difficult fights. I'm here today because of their example.

Finally, I want to thank my campaign manager, Andy Patros. He was a dynamo from the first moment he joined the campaign, coordinating tasks and people, and putting in long

hours to further our cause. He was selfless and hard-working,
and brought brilliance and humor that have brought us here.
Thank you all. For everything.

I echoed the same comments in an interview moments later with a
WETM-TV reporter. With the microphone and bright camera light in my
face, I reiterated my hope that Elmirans were pulling for me and the vision
we had laid out. As I spoke, I saw my stepbrother Eric Krajci watching me
from a few steps away. It's a memory that remains fresh in my mind. Like
me, I think he was a bit numbed by everything that was happening. We'd
grown up together, but neither of us had really thought such a thing as me
becoming Elmira's mayor was possible. I took his quiet gaze as a message.
The city would be watching.


## The immediate aftermath

The next morning's newspaper featured the city election on the front page,
with the simple headline "Tonello elected" printed in large type across the
top. Next to it was a picture of me smiling and listening to my cell phone
outside Horigan's. I'm pretty sure that picture was taken while I was talking
with my father, Francis, who lived in San Diego with my siblings.

The main focus of the *Star-Gazette* story about the mayor's race was
the new split on city council, with Republicans taking the majority. "To
me, it's really not a Democrat-Republican split," I told the paper. "We have
new faces, and it's important to get those faces to work together." It wasn't
my best quote, but the sentiment was sincere. I didn't believe in fostering
a partisan divide. As I'd said a thousand times, I wanted to engage everyone in solving the city's problems, not drawing lines in the sand based on
party.

One thing was clear: The election outcome showed voters were not
happy with city government as it had been. If I hadn't run, I felt sure that
Dan Mandell would've been elected that November 8 along with the other
four Republicans. Many quoted in the newspaper story didn't think I could
pull off the job of leading from the minority.

Among them was Jim Hare, who told the newspaper that the four-
to-three Republican majority would make my job more challenging. "His
leadership skills are going to be tested," he said.

Quoted in the same story was my primary opponent, Dan Royle, who was much more pragmatic. "It's going to start with challenge No. 1, and that's to decide if they want this city manager to continue," Royle told the newspaper. "You better make a decision on that and make it quick, especially with a young, inexperienced council."

I'd made prior arrangements to meet with the city manager the next day, figuring if I won, we would meet; if I didn't, we wouldn't. I thought a meeting would show my eagerness to get to work, and the newspaper thought it important enough to send a reporter and photographer, who took a picture of me and Sam Iraci sitting in his office going over his proposed budget for the next fiscal year. Dan Royle had been right when he said the city manager issue was the top issue facing the new council and me. The next day's story was mostly about whether or not Iraci would stay on or retire.

"I think the city is best served the sooner that decision is made," Iraci told the *Star-Gazette*.

Other newly elected members of council expressed support for Iraci, though new Second District Councilwoman Carol Mechalke said she was uncertain. "I think we need to decide, Democrats and Republicans, and then sit down with Mr. Iraci and the department heads and talk about what skills they have and how they can help us."

I agreed with her. Iraci had been critical of the mayoral race, and I wasn't fully convinced he would be on board. "The themes of the campaign were change, and that's not me," Iraci told the paper. "I think it might be a better opportunity for a new council to get a fresh start (with someone new)."

Despite that, I told the newspaper that if Iraci did decide to leave, I hoped he would help the city transition to a new city manager. "It's not just a matter of sweeping out the old and sweeping in the new," I said. "It's a matter of doing what's best for the city."

We wouldn't have to wait long. One week after the election, Iraci announced his plans to retire. The story in the November 16 *Star-Gazette* bore the headline "Elmira faces challenges," a large picture of Iraci smiling with arms folded across his chest, and the small headline "It's time, Iraci says." In the story, he said, "It's time to give somebody else a chance to see if they can do it better."

Stephen Hughes was quoted, too, saying, "My concern is that the perception and the confidence the public has will diminish largely because of a leadership vacuum that is happening in city government."

Ah, yet another vote of confidence from the former mayor. Clearly, the naysayers weren't going to stop on election day, but I, not the former mayor, was now in a position to show that the city would be in good hands—with or without him and Iraci in City Hall.

It didn't take long for Iraci to weigh in on who might succeed him. In a story that appeared on the cover of the November 18 *Star-Gazette*, Iraci made it clear he wanted to see Elmira City Assessor John Burin succeed him. "I've got a lot invested here, and I don't want to see it all fall apart," Iraci told the newspaper. "I think John presents the best opportunity to hit the ground running."

To his credit, John Burin declined to comment for the story. The new council members did weigh in, though, suggesting Burin would be a good, qualified choice. "We don't want politics to be a part of this," said Republican incumbent John Corsi.

I set a meeting with the new council for the following Tuesday, when we would start to discuss replacing the city manager and arrange times to meet to discuss the city budget. Though we weren't yet sworn in, we would get a start on our work.

I also took time to meet with John Burin, who, at fifty-two, was a prematurely white-haired guy with an unassuming style and nearly twenty years of experience in city government, the last nine as assessor. In our brief discussion, I found I liked him, and I told the newspaper that hiring a new city manager before Iraci left at the end of December was important.

"It is something that we shouldn't rush, but we shouldn't delay either," I told the paper. "My hope is that this new council comes up with a consensus choice between now and January 1 and that it is someone who can work closely with Sam so we are in good shape going into January."

At the private Tuesday meeting, the council did come to a consensus, recommending that Iraci appoint John Burin deputy city manager. When the rest of us would be sworn in on New Year's Day, Burin would become acting city manager. We'd also recommended the city begin a search to permanently fill the job.

After the closed-door meeting, I held a press conference announcing the decision. "John Burin has the experience and know-how to serve the city of Elmira in this role," I said. "The search in no way suggests otherwise, but makes clear that the incoming council wants to do all it can to conduct an open and rigorous search for the next city manager."

I also told the newspaper that this council decision showed we were not Keystone Cops, but were indeed serious about the business of the city. "This is a step in demonstrating to the public that there is an orderly transition in place," I said.

We would, indeed, conduct a thorough nationwide search for a city manager. I thought this was important for the city and for John. He'd been tapped by Sam Iraci, but I didn't want everyone to think he was some sort of anointed successor. If he was going to get the job permanently, I wanted everyone to know he'd done it on his own merits. I believed he would benefit from that independence and hopefully not be seen—for good or bad—as Iraci 2.0.

"It's a lot of responsibility," Burin told the newspaper. "I honestly don't believe you replace a Sam Iraci with another Sam Iraci."

I'd hoped to show with this council decision that I could lead the newly divided council, communicate what was happening to the public, and tamp down criticism that none of us was up to the task. I'd campaigned on being visible and forthright, and I felt this was a good start. The new faces around the table were good people, and I was glad for John Corsi, who would repeat his election night phrase more than once: "I'm not going to be the Lone Ranger anymore."

In fact, I quickly formed a good relationship with John Corsi and the newly elected Republicans, whom I didn't really see as Republicans but as fellow newcomers. They'd won races of their own and earned the right to sit at the council table. I wasn't going to shut them out. I had long before decided that I would not hold party caucuses to discuss city business and council votes, as my predecessor had. One of the reasons John Corsi referred to himself as the Lone Ranger was that while the mayor and five councilmen would caucus, he'd always been left out. I hated that idea and told the new council I would not convene party caucuses, and I never did. I wanted them to know what I knew when I knew it. I wasn't going to play political games and hold back information. I wanted everyone serving with me to have all the facts all the time so they could make informed decisions.

In reality, the Republicans were much easier to get along with in the beginning than Democrats Jim Hare and Terry McLaughlin. Terry held strong opinions, which was fine by me, but less so when he would verbally attack Jim at our council workshops. But by far, I would have the most difficulty in the months to come with Jim, who seemed to regularly keep working political levers behind the scenes. Despite our recent detente, I was warming up to working with him. It would take him some time to get there.

Never was that made clearer than when John Corsi told me in frank terms, "Hare is not on your side."

John told me he had heard and seen things, and he was letting me know about them. In my earliest days as mayor-elect, I was going to have to navigate a new world, but John Corsi made it clear early on that he wasn't a game player. He was honest and sincere and had endured years of criticism and exclusion from the Democrats on the council, who frequently dismissed him as old and out of touch. Yes, he was the oldest member of the council, but he was not out of touch. He was savvy and resilient, and the fact that he came to me with his concerns showed me he was someone I could trust. That trust would serve us well in the future.

As mayor-elect, I met individually with each member of what was to be the new Elmira City Council. I found that we shared a lot in common. Perhaps none of the newly elected councillors was more excited to land in City Hall than Carol Mechalke, who'd first run for the Second District seat way back in 1977. She'd eked out a win over Democrat Brent Stermer by just twelve votes. Brent was a good candidate, but given Carol's decades-long struggle, I told her I was happy for her.

To Carol and the others, I made it clear that politics wasn't what I was about, and communication was. Though I was nearly twenty years younger than the other council members, I wanted each of them to know—from the earliest moment—that, as mayor, I looked at us as a team with an important charge. We'd been elected to bring change, not just talk about it.

Terry McLaughlin quickly buried any animosity he felt toward me during the campaign and began an early effort to be named deputy mayor. The deputy has two main responsibilities: to sign things on behalf of the city when the mayor is unavailable and to appear in the mayor's place at public events. Terry had held the role before, and things hadn't warmed up enough between Jim Hare and me, and since I'd decided to choose a Democrat for the role, Terry would ultimately get the nod. He would hold the position for less than twelve months, though, because the following year he ran for the Chemung County Legislature and won, leaving city council for good.

As I began switching from campaign mode to mayor-elect mode, I felt we were off to a good start. Everyone agreed to a series of public budget meetings to get an early start on the $26 million city budget, and we had unanimously agreed on having John Burin appointed as deputy city manager. I also scheduled a number of December orientations with all of us and the city department heads. Though all of us had yet to be sworn in, we were getting down to business—and getting along.

## Winding down the campaign

In the days following the election, we all took a deep breath, but there was still some campaign work left to do. Topmost on the agenda: collect all the 400 or so campaign signs we had tirelessly planted around the city. Local municipal law gave candidates just a few days to get rid of them, so we spent some time driving around neighborhoods and collecting them. They'd done their job, but plucking them from yards was bittersweet.

There would also be campaign finance filings to complete, which was mostly on Mom. Of course, she kept close tabs on things, and the accounting was pretty straightforward. When the final spending reports became public in December, the *Star-Gazette* wrote a story about how Christopher Moss and I had both spent less than our opponents but had won. Moss had spent nearly $37,000 to Bill Mayhew's $42,000. In the mayor's race, Dan Mandell had spent more than $16,000. I ended up spending just over $12,000.

"I think your best advertising is yourself," I told the newspaper. "I'm not surprised that more money didn't mean more votes. In the end, at least at this level, I don't think it's about how much money you spend, but how much work you do getting out there and talking to people. When you buy help, it's not as strong as the help you get from volunteers."

It was nice to learn that we'd spent 25 percent less than our opponent, a pretty large difference in a local race. But we'd paid in time and sleepless nights too. We proved, though, that sound financial planning—done early—is critical to a campaign for public office. It didn't hurt that our budget consciousness was another good talking point that showed I knew how to manage and budget money. I'd had professional experience managing budgets, but, like other aspects of campaigning that prepare candidates for success in the seats they seek, our money management efforts had taught me a lot.

November and December also were filled with opportunities for me to thank everyone for their efforts. I sent letters and emails and had a letter published in the *Star-Gazette:*

> Thanks to all those who supported me in my campaign for Elmira mayor. I'm honored by the broad support I received.
>
> I set out to conduct a campaign that was positive and focused on solutions. I intend to conduct the business of the city in the same way.

I'm looking forward to doing that with the new council. Regardless of our party affiliations, all seven of us want to see Elmira thrive and grow.

We face a new challenge now that City Manager Sam Iraci has decided to retire, but it's a challenge we're able to meet. I'm confident the city's department heads and staff, together with the new council, will continue to ably move Elmira forward.

The work already has begun. In the week following the election, I met with the members of the new council, interim Mayor Bill O'Brien, the city's department heads, city employees, county leaders, and others.

We have our work cut out for us, but I'm confident we can and will work together to ease this transition and accomplish great things.

It wasn't an accident that I included the bit about "ably moving Elmira forward." Comments in newspaper stories featuring Hughes and others had jumped on us early as clueless clucks. Even the *Star-Gazette*'s political reporter had asked me how I was going to figure out how to run things, particularly since I was brand-new. I told her there were a lot of great people around to give me help when I needed it and reiterated my mantra that public offices like mine weren't the domain of political scientists or career politicians, but average citizens.

She, like many others, looked at me like I was crazy, but I continued to receive congratulations from happy Elmirans, friends, family, and others, which gave me a sense of optimism. I even got a happy greeting from Linda Schornstheimer, the executive secretary to the mayor and city manager, at the weekly farmer's market in Wisner Park. "We voted for you!" she told me. It was the start of a wonderful working relationship.

I also got a congratulatory call that nearly knocked my socks off.

During my visit to the Elmira Fire Department headquarters to meet the chief, my cell phone rang. I didn't recognize the number, but thought maybe it had a Washington, DC, area code. When I answered, I was surprised to hear, "Hello, John, this is Senator Chuck Schumer."

New York's senior US Senator Chuck Schumer was actually calling to congratulate me on my win. He told me public service was an honorable endeavor, wished me luck, and told me to call him any time if I needed his help.

Wow, I definitely wasn't in Kansas anymore.

15

# Early Days

## Mayor-elect

Though the new council had already started its work on the budget and the city manager transition, we had all yet to be sworn in. That happened on January 1 at Mandeville Hall in the Clemens Center. In addition to the inauguration, the January gathering would also be our first official meeting and would require us to appoint John Burin as deputy city manager and reappoint the city clerk, Angela Williams. We'd also appoint former interim Mayor Bill O'Brien as city attorney to replace his longtime predecessor, John Ryan, who'd left in December to work for the school district.

Democratic City Court Judge Thomas Ramich approached me about doing the actual swearing in, and I agreed. He would join us at the table set up on a stage along with Bill, City Chamberlain Joy Bates, and Carl Hayden, whose ties to then-Senator Hillary Clinton and other Democratic heavyweights were difficult to ignore. I'd asked him to be master of ceremonies, and my stepbrother Eric agreed to do the honors of holding the Bible for me.

Just after two o'clock on New Year's Day, I lifted my right hand, repeated the oath of office, and was officially sworn in. I was now mayor of the City of Elmira. The whirlwind of the past year had, amazingly, brought me to this unique moment. As I looked out at the audience, I saw familiar faces that included my mom and stepfather, my cousin Gae, other extended family members, and many of my friends and supporters. There were also many faces I didn't recognize but would come to know in the months and years ahead. Politicians often say they feel humbled at such moments as these, but I also felt the weight of my new responsibilities, which I touched on in my inaugural speech:

> Council members, honored guests, ladies and gentlemen, I'm truly honored to stand here today as mayor of this great city. It's fitting, I think, to reflect upon what brought us all here: the American democratic process. For more than two centuries, soldiers and civilians alike have defended the right of the people to govern themselves. The principle has endured the strain of wars and natural disasters only to reveal a nearly limitless strength and resiliency. It's truly remarkable.
>
> That principle and a spirit of cooperation are alive here today. It's an exciting time for Elmira. This is a rare moment—in the natural order of change—when we have a chance to build upon all the good that's come before us and set our sights on exploring new opportunities and new ways of working together for the common good.
>
> That's how I see the work of the city. It's by no means a solitary task. Hardly. It's a task shared by the members of this council, the city staff, and all the people who have come to this historic city to live, work, and raise their families.
>
> This is Our City. This is Our Future. This is Our Time.
>
> You'll hear me repeat that theme in one way or another over the next two years because I believe that only by working together can we make great things happen. Only by focusing on solutions can we sustain the optimism and hopefulness each of us brings here today. Only by listening to each other, communicating openly, and working together can we shape our shared future.
>
> I plan to lead by example, and bring the ideas and ideals that shaped me to the mayor's office.
>
> For instance, the former newspaper reporter in me wants to see things laid out clearly for all to see. The geek in me wants to see technology used to its fullest to save money and make government more efficient. The Gen-Xer in me wants young people to have a voice. And the kid in me who was raised as one of seven children wants to find common ground.
>
> I'm happy to say the work already has begun. Since November, the new council and I have met more than a half-

dozen times, begun the search for a new city manager, begun reviewing the 2006 budget, and much more.

I've begun other initiatives, too, initiatives that take a long view to Elmira's future by engaging the public in city government in real ways. My goal is to open new dialogues, break down old barriers, and nurture long-standing relationships. I believe the result will be growth and investment, flourishing neighborhoods, and a strong sense of city pride.

Listening to Elmirans proved invaluable during my campaign, so I have taken steps to maintain that link as mayor.

I've launched a blog—the first ever for an Elmira mayor—that will allow me to communicate directly with citizens via the internet.

I will soon form several Citizen Advisory Teams that will work with the community to draw out the best ideas and help me turn those ideas into policy and law. The first of these teams will focus on Downtown, Neighborhoods, Arts and Tourism, and Diversity.

Additionally, I will use the mayor's convening power to bring together people and policymakers for public forums that encourage public debate on the most pressing issues before us, from jobs to literacy to daycare to crime. These will be gatherings of ideas, not egos.

I will bring the same approach to the city's business.

For example, I believe citizens should have a say in hiring Elmira's next city manager. That's why I will ask for public input and, with council's support, form a diverse Community Advisory Panel, which will offer us honest feedback and advice during—not after—the hiring process.

I will encourage similar openness in all city hiring so we continue to recruit and retain the best and the brightest. Open hiring practices will strengthen and diversify our workforce.

I will encourage open discussion of the city's budget, how we spend taxpayers' money, and why we make the choices we do. It's no secret that this council faces some real challenges. We must commit limited resources to maintaining our roads and city services, and make tough choices about taxes. I won't sugarcoat the reality of it or put off the hard decisions for another day.

By the way, it's no accident that former Chancellor Carl Hayden and Superintendent Ray Bryant are here today. I believe education is integral to Elmira's future and the city's ability to retain and grow its economic core.

That's why Dr. Bryant and I already have begun working together to find ways to share resources. We're working with the county, too, because we see a great potential to save money, eliminate duplication, and improve services. People and businesses considering a move here want strong schools, and we want to show the world that Elmira is a city that places a high value on education and collaboration. We're not going to be shy about that.

Collaboration will not end there, however. This is only the beginning.

I'm fortunate to have this council to work with me as mayor. I'm impressed with the breadth of knowledge and experience these council members bring to the table. All of us are committed to doing what's right for the city. I will work hard to build consensus, and encourage the open exchange of ideas, as democracy intends.

I said earlier that this is not a solitary effort, and I would not be here today if not for the support of many dear friends and family. I want to take this opportunity to publicly thank you all for your support, patience and wisdom. It's because of you that I am here today. Thank you all.

After my speech, I stepped off the stage to present Mom with the bouquet of flowers that had adorned the council table during the meeting. I thanked both her and my stepfather for their support, and I thought it was a nice way to publicly acknowledge my mother's work. The picture of me handing the flowers to Mom appeared in the next morning's newspaper along with coverage of the ceremonies for city council and new Chemung County Sheriff Christopher Moss.

A lot of change was afoot. Of that there was no doubt. The long-familiar faces of Sam Iraci and Stephen Hughes were absent. So, too, were the faces of former council members Dan Royle, Bill Hopkins, and Shirley Williams. The stage was literally set with new blood, and I was looking forward to the challenges ahead. I didn't have to wait long.

# Early challenges

Before the swearing in was over and our first council meeting wound down, Jim Hare made news by criticizing the owner of the Elmira Jackals minor league hockey team that played in the troubled downtown First Arena. He said Mostafa Afr should sell the team and give up his role as managing partner of the arena.

"The writing is on the wall," Jim said in a story that appeared in the *Star-Gazette* on January 3. "This guy is going to go, and sooner is better than later. His whole attitude toward the Jackals this year was one of disinterests and lack of contact. Programming at the arena has never been aggressively pursued. Vendors who provide for the arena have gone with bills not being paid. You can't operate that way."

The new arena manager, Mike Marinaccio, told the newspaper that Jim's comments were unfair, especially given that Afr had worked with the city to broker a deal that brought the minor league hockey team to Elmira and the new arena. "[Afr] was the only guy who came across with a deal five or six years ago," Marinaccio said. "He made it happen and now everyone is trying to run him out of town."

I made it clear that Jim's comments at the council meeting—which I took as an effort to upstage me on the inauguration stage—did not represent my position or the city more generally.

"My approach is let's work together," I told the newspaper. "Let's collaborate and come up with solutions. I don't believe you can get very far by jabbing in the dark. Too often, it's easy to say, 'Here's a problem' without offering a solution. My hope would be reasoned discussion that involved all the interested parties. We can do it openly without trying to intimidate someone into acting."

Unfortunately, I'd soon learn that the city's troubles with the arena extended well beyond the public tiff between Jim and Afr. When the original deal was struck to build the 125,000-square-foot arena, it had cost about $15.5 million. The city planned to fund a portion of that with federal Housing and Urban Development money to the tune of $4 million. This HUD financing was a loan the city would have to repay. Those repayments started small, at $50,000 a year, but the year I took office the payments ballooned tenfold to $500,000.

On an already tight city budget, $500,000 was a big hit. Doubly so when it was seen in the light of how repayments of the HUD money, often intended to help older cities like Elmira restore homes and neighborhoods, would not improve neighborhoods at all. It was a financial sinkhole. The previous administration had planned to use its portion of the arena's profits to help pay off that loan, but the arena had yet to turn a profit. The entire $500,000 would have to come from city taxpayers, diverting money away from what I believed were much worthier projects.

The proposed budget presented by our predecessors initially looked for a tax increase of 4.8 percent, but we whittled that down to 3.9 percent. "No one here is entirely happy," I told the *Star-Gazette*, "and I take that as a good sign because we are going to keep working."

Many wanted us to spend about $23,000 on demolishing the old Brand Park Pool, a sixty-year-old aboveground cement structure that was in disrepair and had seen diminishing use. Some in the community wanted us to spend about $250,000 or more to repair the pool, but I jokingly told people it would be cheaper to buy those who currently used the Brand Park Pool their own backyard pools than invest in the old structure. In the end, we approved closing the pool—and eliminating its operation costs from the budget—but it would ultimately take another twenty years for the city to approve its demolition.


## An end to professional baseball

In just my second week in office, attention turned away from the arena to baseball and the Pioneers, Elmira's professional minor league team. The January 10 morning newspaper bore the front-page headline "No Pios in 2006," explaining that the Pioneers had dropped out of the professional Can-Am League. The subhead read "Elmira, with a long history of minor league baseball, loses its team."

I'd received a call from Pioneers General Manager Tom Sullivan the previous day telling me of this development. I'd come to know Tom, who separately owned the Albany Diamond Dogs minor league team, when I'd covered the Pioneers as a *Star-Gazette* stringer a few years earlier. I also was a Pioneers fan and tried to attend as many games as I could at Dunn Field, which sat along the Chemung River on the city's south side. Professional baseball had been played there since 1939 and had at points been affiliated with the Tigers and the Dodgers. In 1951, Don Zimmer—a player who would go on to become a manager for major league teams—married his wife at home plate on Dunn Field. Baseball was part of Elmira's history, and, sadly, it looked like it would end under my watch.

The *Star-Gazette* Opinion page suggested the city spend money on a study and, perhaps, build a new stadium to replace historic Dunn Field. It also suggested forming a city-county taskforce. That all seemed like a lot to sustain something that had become unsustainable.

According to Tom Sullivan, the Pioneers had lost more than $100,000 the previous season, a sure sign that people weren't attending games in great numbers. The city actually helped to subsidize the team and was poised to commit $57,000 in my first budget to the Pioneers and the costs of operating Dunn Field. But Tom told me the cost of running the professional team, which included about $500,000 just to be part of the league, not to mention player salaries and general operating costs, was no longer sustainable. I asked what we might do, and he told me about the New York Collegiate Baseball League.

The collegiate league ran under the auspices of the NCAA, so instead of having professional players, college players would take the field. In those days, college athletes could not be paid per NCAA rules, so the costs associated with fielding a team would be nominal. Most collegiate players would live with host families and work local jobs while playing for the Pioneers. Running the new franchise would cost about $50,000, far less than the pro team.

In a matter of a few short days, Tom put together a local ownership group, and the rest of the league owners approved adding Elmira. The new city council was supportive, too, so in the span of less than ten days, we had successfully found a way to continue Elmira's baseball tradition.

As Mark Twain might've said, "The reports of baseball's death in Elmira were greatly exaggerated." It had taken some work—and I was fortunate to be close with Tom Sullivan—but I was proud to show baseball fans and the entire city that I was up to the task of solving problems.

In the end, collegiate league baseball was a boon. Yes, it lowered costs, but it was, to my mind anyway, a better brand of baseball. For many of the previous professional minor league players, Elmira and the Cam-Am league represented last-chance ball. I personally had witnessed fights among the Elmira players in the dugout and lackluster games. The collegiate league's college players were on their way up and hungry. The team made the playoffs that first year and won it all the next season with a sweep over Glens Falls.

# The armory collapse

Elmira City Hall, a beautiful Beaux Arts building at the corner of Church and Lake streets, was a classic old municipal building that, like many others, had long since been outgrown by its modern-day staff. To help offset the space crunch, New York State had given the former Armory, completed in 1888, and the accompanying rear drill hall to the city for $1. The red brick building became home to the Elmira City Police and, more recently, the city's IT department. Hallways were added to connect the Armory directly to City Hall's west side.

Because of its age, the floors of the Armory were anything but flat, pitching this way and that from more than 100 years of settling and modern use. Despite its oddities, all was mostly well and good until Friday, March 20, when I got a call from John Burin that the front of the Armory had collapsed onto Church Street. An officer had just passed through the front doors when hundreds of pounds of bricks, windows, and other debris came crashing down.

"It was a horrendous noise!" Elmira Police Department secretary Yolanda Lopez told the *Star-Gazette*. "I *knew* the building was falling down."

Fortunately no one was hurt, but John Burin—whom the council four days earlier had appointed to the permanent city manager job after a two-and-a-half month search that drew thirty-eight candidates from around the country—made the call to have all staff evacuate the building. "It's an old building," he told the newspaper. "Band-Aid (repairs) only last for so long. I'm not leaving people in there."

The city had invested $230,000 in the Armory in 1977 so it could be used for city office space but closed it six years later because heating the nineteenth-century building each year cost upwards of $70,000. Eight years later, the city poured $2.3 million into the Armory, but none of it had been enough. The Armory simply hadn't been built to last as long as it did. Its brick exterior facade was only part of the problem. The main interior walls were made from the same brick—not steel or cinder blocks. The whole thing wasn't safe, and sooner or later it would have to come down.

In the meantime, a portion of the Elmira Police Department was suddenly without a home. Areas of City Hall housed some of the police operations on the first floor and in the basement, but the chief and detectives bureau had no place to go. Fortunately, John Burin was able to secure for them a single-story office building across Lake Street from City Hall. City council and I approved a lease, and we had the building renovated within a few months so police services could continue. It would take another year and a half, though, for us to tear down the old Armory. We simply didn't have the money. John and city attorney Bill O'Brien would manage to get nearly $500,000 from the insurance company, but it was estimated to cost upwards of $1 million to raze the structure because of asbestos and lead abatement and the simple fact that the building abutted City Hall on one side and private buildings on the other. It would have to be a delicate job.

## The deficit

It was clear in my first months as mayor that money was tight—and getting tighter. As acting city manager, John Burin began to notice quite a few irregularities in the city's finances. The financial irregularities came to a head in early summer, when members of the Elmira Police Department went to cash their paychecks—and they bounced.

Though we thought we had plenty of cash on hand, it turned out we didn't. John soon discovered that the city had a $2.1 million deficit, meaning it had spent $2.1 million more than it had. This wasn't debt. This was like drawing money from a checking account with no fund balance. We were in serious trouble. Our predecessors had quietly grown this deficit in the five years before I took office, and now we had inherited it—and would have to fix it.

But why had paychecks bounced without warning? As it turned out, local banks that held city deposits from taxes and other revenues had been floating the city when there hadn't been enough cash on hand. None of this had been a formal policy, but it quietly ended when John and I came to City Hall. We also discovered that when the previous city council had voted to pay city bills at each meeting, the checks were addressed and signed but left sitting in a safe until there was enough money to cover them. That meant city vendors were waiting months to get paid.

We immediately made decisions to dramatically reduce spending, including chopping $427,000 from the year's capital spending, halting all non-emergency overtime, realigning code enforcement and fire department staff, and delaying the purchase of new vehicles.

"[These cuts are] not going to get us home," Burin told the *Star-Gazette*. "It's a $2.1 million deficit. But it's a start. We have to start rethinking about the way we do things here in the city."

A year later, Burin would replace the city chamberlain—essentially the city's chief financial officer—with government newcomer David Vandermark. He had never worked for a municipality before, but he had spent his career in finance, and he had a no-nonsense style that was also fair-minded. In short order, he became lovingly known as "Dr. No" because when department heads came to ask him for money, he more often than not told them, "No!"

The three incumbents on city council—Jim, Terry, and John Corsi—had all been in office when the city ran up the massive deficit, but I decided early on not to point fingers at them—or at the former mayor and city manager. Clearly the problem rested at their feet, and the public knew it, but I did not want to be out there laying blame. I wanted people to know about the problem as soon as possible and keep the public informed about the steps we were taking to fix it.

"A lot of the financial situation that the city is looking at is not new," I told the *Star-Gazette*. "What is new is that you are hearing about it, and we are discussing this frankly and openly."

I wondered what the newspaper's editors now thought of the write-in endorsement of Hughes. The new council and I were pissed off, but we were going to fix the problem. "I'm committed to working our way out of this situation," Burin told the paper. "We all have to understand this did not happen overnight. It's not going to be taken care of overnight. But if everyone works together, we can work our way out of the deficit position and hopefully into a surplus position. It's just going to take a new outlook on the way we do things."

In the interests of transparency, I formed a Blue Ribbon Commission of local business leaders, the county executive, the publisher of the *Star-Gazette*, and others. I wanted the process to be wide open, not hidden away. I wasn't sure what sort of ideas we'd get from commission members, but I thought it was right to engage as many people as possible. Some of the business people suggested things that were perhaps suitable for private-sector businesses but illegal under state law, such as eliminating the paid fire department and replacing it with volunteers. We wouldn't be doing that.

As it was, we already were getting pushback from the police union. I'd set meetings with all city staff at which John and I could tell everyone what was going on and reassure them. They were the first to know of the problem. I'd learned in my earliest days as mayor that staff usually heard about city business when they opened the morning newspaper or tuned into the television news. I'd changed that by requiring a specific sequence of announcements: council first, then staff, then the media and the public. Staff listened to us and asked questions, but we reassured them that we weren't yet planning layoffs. Nor were we contemplating bankruptcy. Still, we couldn't rule out anything yet.

The police union's gripe was that the deficit was a false narrative that just happened to emerge when their contract was up. That wasn't true, and they eventually understood the city's financial problems were real. In fact, with David and John doing more digging, we soon realized the deficit was really more than $3 million. We were in a deep hole, and it was real.

Getting out of it wasn't simple or easy, but the city council members and I were largely unified. We also built a whole new kind of trust with city department heads that all but ended the long-held practice of padding budgets. If something was worthwhile, we'd fund it. If we thought it wasn't, we wouldn't, and David "Dr. No" Vandermark would enforce each decision. We also all agreed that we didn't want to tax our way out of the deficit. Sharply raising taxes to fix the problem was a nonstarter.

Instead, we sharpened our business practices, hired grant writer Jennifer Miller, and kept careful tabs on all our spending. Jennifer did wonders by finding grants to fund equipment for the police—things that normally would've fallen on the city budget—and more. There was state and federal money to be found, and she did.

What ultimately got us out of the precarious financial situation was trust. John and I had worked hard to be transparent with everyone, and that transparency caught on inside City Hall and out, helping us eliminate the deficit and return to a surplus in just eighteen months.

We'd had to raise taxes a whopping 7.5 percent the following year, but the council voted unanimously on the spending plan, and we were able to keep the increase to 3.5 percent the year after that, and 2.85 percent and 1.76 percent in successive years, all of which were below the inflation rate. This feat was particularly rewarding because the 2008 financial crisis centered around predatory home-lending practices had slowed the economy and lowered sales tax revenue.

Raising taxes was a tough pill to swallow, but we'd inherited a financial mess. Laying off police—the city's single biggest expense—would do more harm than good. When people asked about high taxes, I'd ask, "Do you want more police? Yes. More road construction? Yes. More services? Yes. Higher taxes? No." Such was the conundrum of municipal finance. Most everyone wanted services, but no one wanted to pay the price in their property taxes. Fortunately, by getting our financial house in order, we were able to improve our bond rating, streamline day-to-day operations, and make other adjustments that saved the city—and its taxpayers—hundreds of thousands of dollars.

None of this was ideal or what I'd campaigned on, but it underscored the vagaries of government problems over time, which candidates like me could only guess at. When I'd taken office I had no idea about the deficit we'd inherit, the collapse of the Armory, the costs of relocating the police, and more. Unexpected problems arose and needed to be addressed, but I kept true to my word by making all our actions public and communicating regularly with council members, staff, media, and Elmira residents.

## Communication pays off

Throughout my first year in office, we'd face a lot of challenges, both bad and good. The Armory collapse and deficit were bad, but on the plus side was a $1.25 million federal grant we'd received to restore the viaduct the railroad used to run trains through downtown and a $400,000 state grant to renovate the historic downtown Riverside Florist building on Water Street.

Mostly, though, my eagerness to communicate and remain nonpartisan was paying dividends. A year into my term, on January 2, 2007, the *Star-Gazette* ran a story with the headline "Mayor gets praise for juggling" and the subhead "Tonello carefully navigated crises in first year, Elmira officials say." I was happy to read quotes in the story that reflected my approach.

"The mayoral position is a political position. There's no getting around that," John Burin told the newspaper. "But my experience has been that [John] always puts the city first and politics second. He's not your typical politician, that's for sure."

John Burin also told the paper that even though I'd never been in government before, I had a good handle on the issues and had come up to speed quickly. "He truly cares about the city," Burin said. "He does his best to reach out to anyone and everyone. Sometimes I wonder how he does it."

It was true that I was trying to be as engaged as possible, attending almost all the events to which local groups, churches, and others had invited the mayor. And when I went to these events, I didn't just pop in with a proclamation, read it, and depart. I stayed. My secretary, Linda Schornstheimer, would later tell me that I attended far more of these events than any mayor she'd worked for—and she'd been around City Hall for twenty years.

I arranged my schedule so I could get to City Hall each day around four o'clock and used evenings and weekends to attend events or do paperwork. I wasn't married and had no kids, so I didn't have to leave a wife and children at home. I also worked with the Cornell Graduate School deans to reduce my hours—and pay—by 20 percent. I certainly wasn't independently wealthy, but the mayor's salary helped make up the gap a little. By cutting back at Cornell, I could spend full days at City Hall each Thursday, when we held informal public council workshops to go over the agenda. Between my work at Cornell and the city, I was easily putting in sixty-hour workweeks.

Republican Bob Bailey, who'd joined the council at the same time I did by winning Dan Royle's former Fifth District seat, told the newspaper he was supportive of my efforts. "He's a nonpartisan mayor. He works with both sides. He's a people person. I think he's done a terrific job."

Jim, who'd fought me during the campaign, had changed his perception of me as well. I'd worked hard to engage him as I did everyone else, and he, too, complimented my efforts. "He has made a real effort to have all of us work together," Jim told the *Star-Gazette*. "Ideally, you always want the council to be unified in everything that you do, and I think he works to try to do that."

The story went on to highlight my efforts to keep staff and the public informed, and I told the reporter that one of my biggest surprises of the past year was the result of such a simple thing as keeping city workers informed.

"It had a really big impact in helping to dispel rumors and make people feel a little more engaged in some of the decisions that were happening," I told the newspaper. "The last thing I wanted, as we were going through changes such as the Armory or financial things, was for city staff to read about that stuff in the paper first."

The only criticism in the story came from Lawrence Frawley, who was described as a "keen observer of City Hall for many years." He said I was a very active mayor, but perhaps I was trying to do too much.

"I think he's stretching too far," Frawley told the newspaper, adding that he would like to see me focus more time and attention on developing downtown.

Another Elmiran quoted in the story, Nina Oliphant, said I was "very sincere" and brought a breath of fresh air to city government. "I am always very informed when I talk to him, and he's always very interested in talking and explaining things to you," she told the paper. "I think he understands what the problems are, but he's being influenced by some 'old guard,' and that is unavoidable."

True enough. It was simply not possible, I'd found, to bring in a fleet of new ideas without some old ones remaining behind. I'd learned that patience is key. "It always takes a little bit longer to do something than you think," I told the paper. "You have to really be committed to something to make sure it gets done because it does take some time. You have to have that patience."

Things weren't perfect, to be sure, but I'd kept true to my word to communicate and engage everyone. I appointed all-new members to the planning and zoning boards; formed citizen committees to help advise me on historic preservation, the arts, and other issues; and I was showing up. What I didn't know, I hunkered down and learned. I listened to everyone I could, even when I didn't love what I was hearing. But I found that my long campaign for mayor had paid off in spades when I *became* mayor. I'd developed a thick skin, tried never to react emotionally to criticism or crises, and kept the lines of communication open.

None of it had been easy, but I was damned glad I'd dared to run.

# Epilogue

## What came next

When I won that first election in November 2005, it was for the final two-year Elmira mayoral term. A few years earlier, the city council and a voter referendum had extended the terms from two to four years starting in 2008. I fulfilled the two-year term and ran for reelection in 2007. In that race, I was unopposed, though Patsy DiChiara mounted a small write-in campaign and collected a handful of votes. There was no primary and no Republican opponent. A part of me was happy that my work during our first two years in office had deterred others from running to unseat me, but I also was sorry that voters didn't get a choice, as before. I still believed keeping voters—and citizens—engaged was a critical part of running for and holding office. I received just over 3,100 votes in 2007, more than I'd received two years earlier, but overall turnout for the city council races was down significantly.

In that 2007 election, all the incumbents were returned to office. Terry McLaughlin had left his Fourth District seat on council in late 2006 to run for the county legislature, and he was replaced on city council by Democratic Committeeman Mark Hitchcock. Terry won his legislature seat, and in that same election, Andy won his own legislative seat by employing many of the same techniques we'd used in my mayoral campaign. He knocked on a *lot* of doors, a task that was made harder for him because of the sprawling, partly rural nature of his district. He defeated longtime incumbent Sheldon Robinson by twenty-two votes, relying on crossover votes in the Republican-leaning legislative Fifteenth District.

Sharon, who'd been so important to my campaign, left Elmira soon after I entered office when the historic Church Street home she owned and used as a boutique and art studio burned down. Sharon wasn't there at the time and wasn't hurt, but the fire department ruled the fire suspicious because a gasoline can had been found at the scene. The fire marshall never declared it arson, though. The house, which had once been owned by Jervis Langdon, Mark Twain's brother-in-law, was quickly razed and replaced with an empty grass lot. It was a tragic and frightening loss made worse by the indeterminate fire investigation.

A year after my reelection, I decided to run for New York State Senate, taking on longtime Republican incumbent George Winner Jr. Many thought I was crazy for running against him, even suggesting such a race would harm the city's relationship with the state senator, but I tackled it nonetheless. I learned from my first two years in office that the decision-makers in Albany weren't getting it done for cities like Elmira. Everything from state pension contributions, which cost cities more or less each year based on the performance of Wall Street investments, to state road and infrastructure funding were hurting cities. Many people were fleeing New York because of high taxes and low job growth, and I wanted to help change that.

Unlike the city, the state senate race spanned hundreds of miles across the Southern Tier and around the Finger Lakes. It was much harder to win by going door-to-door, but I managed to raise a little over $40,000 and gain support from the Democratic Committees across what was then the 53rd Senate District. I received an endorsement from then-US Senator Hillary Clinton, unions, and many others but, in the end, it wasn't enough. I lost to Winner 53,542 to 43,341, or 56 to 44 percent. He had a lot more money and a lot more connections, so I wasn't too terribly embarrassed by my showing.

George and I had participated in many debates together and we saw a lot of each other that year, and I think spending all that time together—often in contentious situations—actually improved our relationship. Instead of turning against each other in the aftermath of the state senate race, I believe we found a new mutual respect for each other. We'd sometimes meet by chance at the Wisner Park Farmer's Market on Thursdays, and more than once we sat down together to eat lunch. We'd shared a common experience, and we were both better off for it.

By the middle of 2011, I'd decided that six years as mayor would be enough. I'd never intended for it to be a long-term job, and my work in City Hall hadn't changed my mind. I'd always believed elected officials should serve, but not overstay, and I often likened holding political office to a tractor pull: You have just as much energy at the end of a term that you had at the beginning, but then inertia kicks in and creates a drag on the officeholder. I found it to be almost a natural phenomenon. There was still work I wanted to do, and I loved the people I was working with in the city, but I was not convinced that another four years would be good for the city, Elmirans—or me.

Six years in, I'd become a well-known figure in Elmira and certainly wasn't the anonymous newcomer I was in 2005, and I felt the need to move on. It helped that a woman I'd met while working at Syracuse University twenty-five years earlier had reentered my life. I'd first met Gina Granozio, a smart, funny, and outgoing writer, when we worked together in the New Services Office, and we'd become good friends. We never dated back then, though, because shortly after we met, she got engaged and married in 1995. She became Gina Burmeister, had two children, and largely disappeared from my life.

When I ran for state senate, Gina and her then-husband had recently moved to nearby Corning, and she helped out on my campaign. When her marriage ended a couple years later, we started dating and got engaged in March 2011. We were married in a small ceremony with family and friends the following September. Shortly thereafter, I sold my West Gray Street home and moved with Gina and my new stepchildren (and all our cats) to a small village outside Syracuse, New York.

Before I left office, though, Gina and the kids had the chance to walk with me through Elmira in that year's Memorial Day parade. It was the first time I'd walked any parade route without being solo, and I liked it. Aly and Evan were just eleven and seven years old at the time, and I think they enjoyed the parade too. I felt proud of what would soon be my new family, and I looked forward to a new life with them, even though it would take me away from Elmira.

Not long before my second term ended, the *Star-Gazette* continued to shed reporters, editors, and other staff because of shrinking circulation and ad revenue, succumbing to the same challenges facing newspapers across the country. The newspaper started printing each edition at a sister Gannett facility and sold its own press for scrap. Though the newspaper had given me a hard time during the campaign and many of those editors and reporters were gone, I was sad to see the press ripped out and carted off as junk.

A year and a half after I left office, John Burin, now working with Mayor Susan Skidmore, decided to retire. "This is the toughest job I've ever loved," John told the *Star-Gazette* when he announced his retirement. "I just hope that my tenure here will be remembered positively."

I believe it was. John had helped me and the new council navigate through the deficit and restore a healthy city surplus, which topped $6 million when we left. Born and raised in Elmira, John had always maintained a strong love for the city, which showed in the work he did. We had a great working relationship, always able to put everything on the table and grab a beer or a bourbon afterward despite occasionally exchanging some tough words. John had always worked hard to do the right thing. He'd also received a cancer diagnosis eighteen months into my first term as city manager, a diagnosis that took him out of the game for a while and required him to appoint his deputy to fill his shoes for several months. Despite chemotherapy and the need for a feeding tube, John recovered, perhaps gaining a new perspective on life. When he returned to City Hall, he picked up where he left off and never missed a beat.

Like me, John didn't aim for a legacy based on buildings or monuments, but on people. "When I took office, I said one of my goals was to create a government for the future," Burin told the *Star-Gazette*. "My mission was to bring young, talented people to the city government at the time and give them positions of authority. Hopefully, by creating a young, professional core that became decision-makers for our community, it would encourage other young people to stay and make our community home."

He did just that. Jennifer Miller, initially hired as a grant writer, went on to head the city's Community Development office and later became the City of Corning's assistant city manager. Ottavio Campanella, an assistant city attorney, went on to become an Elmira City Court judge and later a Chemung County judge. Kimberly Balok Middaugh became assistant city manager (and filled in when John was sick) and then city manager under Mayor Skidmore, later running for and winning a race to become a judge for the Town of Elmira. There were many others John mentored and trusted, and they all went on to bigger and better things in public service.

"I'm leaving," John told the newspaper, "but the team I'm leaving here to run this city, it's a great team. It's a wonderful team. It's the team of the future."

That team of the future continued to plug away during my successor's term, but the city began to backslide when John and I left. The open communication was less so now, and much of the trust we'd built with the community was lost. That was reflected in results of the 2015 mayoral election, which Skidmore lost to Dan Mandell 2,172 to 736, or 78 to 22 percent. Before I left office, Skidmore, who'd switched from Republican to Democrat in September 2008, had defeated Republican Tim Sullivan 1,607 to 1,430 in the 2011 mayor's race, but she was voted out after one term.

Subsequent elections would continue to see lower voter turnout. The two candidates in the 2011 election received just over 3,000 votes combined, about 2,000 fewer votes than Dan Mandell and I had received in 2005. In 2015, the total votes for both Mandell and Skidmore added up to about 2,900, another dropoff in turnout. Four years later in 2019, Dan Mandell ran for reelection and won with 2,126 votes to Democrat Alex Sweet's 556 votes. Susan Skidmore, running on the Working Families line and attempting a comeback that year, received 203 votes. Mandell won a third term in 2023 with 1,429 votes to Democratic challenger Jim Hassell's 983 votes. The combined total for both candidates was fewer than 2,500 votes.

When I'd first run for mayor, one of my goals was to boost voter engagement and turnout, and that had worked in 2005—even though the newspaper had called it the "quiet campaign." Since that time, Elmira's population had continued to slowly ebb, and voter turnout for city elections has never again been as high. I'm proud of that year's high watermark, but I'm also saddened by the lower and lower election numbers. Back when Jim had first run for mayor, 8,222 of Elmira's nearly 13,000 eligible voters had turned out, or 63 percent.

Eventually, all the members of the city council I served with rolled off. Carol Mechalke lost her bid for a third term when she was defeated by Democrat Brent Stermer in 2011, 134 to 114. Dan Royle attempted a comeback in the Fifth District but lost to Republican Richard Hitchcock Jr. in a close election. Dan would go on to become a full-time painter. Democrat Bill Knapp ran again that same year in the First District but lost by about 35 votes to Republican William Roe. Jim Hare, John Corsi, and Bob Bailey didn't run again in 2011.

It's important to note that long before I left office, my relationship with Jim had returned to something close to the friendliness we'd enjoyed when I'd first met him at that hardware store seven years earlier. To be sure, he caused me quite a bit of agita in my first couple years in office, but I think Jim respected the fact that I worked hard to bring people together, including him. I didn't shut him down or brush him off. He had a lot of experience and broad knowledge that I thought shouldn't be overlooked or dismissed. He was still just as adamant about getting Democrats elected, and when he made another run for a state assembly seat, I set up my voterBase software for him to use. He lost that race, but Jim continued to remain active in politics and the community, including securing a seat on the Elmira Water Board.

In the waning days of my tenure, Jim and I took a moment to talk in the mayor's office on the third floor of City Hall, and he told me, "You were a good mayor." I smiled and told him I really appreciated that. It meant a lot to me that this former mayor and longtime city councillor felt that way. I figured if I could make Jim a fan, anything was possible. We remain friends today.

At the same time, I regularly participated in the local Democratic Committee meetings, lending my voice to their efforts. I thought it was important to be present and help contribute, though I remained strictly nonpartisan as mayor.

In July 2022, John Corsi died at the age of ninety-one. He was a wonderful Italian man and devout Catholic who'd grown up in Elmira, attended Elmira Free Academy, and served in the Marines during the Korean War. He had worked nearly twenty years as the greenskeeper and superintendent of the city-owned Mark Twain Golf Course and then served nine years as the course manager. A year after he retired, he ran for city council and served from 1996 to 2012, the last five years as my deputy mayor. John also was active in the Arctic League, a nonprofit that raised money and collected and delivered toys and other items to needy Elmira children. He was Arctic League president in 1999 and served on a number of community organization boards, including a local museum.

During the city's financial crisis, we proposed selling the Mark Twain Golf Course as a way to generate revenue and reduce the city's operating expenses. Selling the course had been considered before my time as mayor, and it was something John Corsi had always opposed as a member of council. After all, he'd run the place, and it was near and dear to his heart and, depending on the Upstate New York weather, it sometimes turned a profit. Though it was a difficult decision—perhaps the most difficult of his tenure—John voted in favor of selling the course when I was mayor. That took a lot of courage, and I like to think that the openness and trust John Burin and I fostered about the city deficit and the financial dilemma we faced helped convince John Corsi that selling was the right thing to do. In the end, the 2008 real estate market crash resulted in the city holding onto the course, but still John had been willing to make the toughest of calls.

When Terry left and the deputy mayor role opened up in 2006, I'd chosen John Corsi to replace him because he was the senior Republican and I trusted him. It was an easy choice. I knew he'd represent the city well. When I was reelected in 2007, I reappointed him for the next four years.

"Are you sure, mayor?" he asked me about the appointment. "I'm a Republican!"

I laughed and told him, "I don't care about that, John. You're the best man for the job." He was, too, continuing to be a strong advocate for the city he loved and to which he'd committed his life.

When I left office, many people asked if I'd ever run again. I've always demurred. Being mayor had taken me places and introduced me to people I'd never thought I'd meet, but I felt my days in public service were over. I'd done what I'd set out to do, managed to bring people together, and solved some real problems. Still, rubbing elbows with some of the biggest names in politics wasn't something I'd soon forget.

Meeting Eliot Spitzer and having him personally endorse me was a thrill, but unfortunately, his governorship ended prematurely when he was rocked by scandal. In 2006, he'd won the race for New York governor over Republican Nassau county executive Tom Suozzi with 76 percent of the vote. He took office in January 2007 and put Marty Mack, the former mayor of Cortland, in charge of municipal relationships. Spitzer and Mack did a great job in opening lines of communications between cities like Elmira and Albany, and we were all devastated when the *New York Times* reported in March 2008 that Spitzer had patronized high-priced escorts. He resigned ten days later, and Lt. Governor David Paterson became governor.

When I was invited to Paterson's inaugural in the state capitol in Albany a few weeks later, I sat among a veritable who's who of political heavyweights. Next to me sat former New York Mayor Ed Koch, and nearby sat Senator Hillary Clinton, Al Sharpton, Mark Green, and many others. As a reluctant governor, Paterson wasn't the steamroller Spitzer was, and when he decided not to run for reelection, then-Attorney General Andrew Cuomo opened his bid.

During his 2010 race for governor against Western New York Republican Carl Paladino, Cuomo came to Elmira to campaign, and I greeted him at a local gathering. When he was elected later that year by about twenty points over Paladino, Cuomo became the fourth governor I'd work with in five years, a chaotic stretch that made budgeting and other state-city relations difficult.

The first governor I'd met as mayor was Republican George Pataki, who'd come to visit Elmira during my first year in office. Before serving as governor of New York for twelve years, Pataki had been a state senator, state assemblyman, and mayor of Peekskill. He was a tall, somewhat intimidating presence, and before we actually spoke at an informal gathering at the Clemens Center, I noticed the governor eyeing me before eventually coming over to say hello. We shook hands, and he congratulated me on being a young mayor; he'd been about thirty-six when he was elected, two years younger than I'd been. He told me being mayor in the early 1980s was "the toughest job I ever had."

Given that he was now governor, I was a little shocked by that admission, but he was quick to explain. As governor, he said, he got to ride around in big SUVs, always slightly removed from his detractors and the public most of the time. As mayor, he met people every day at the grocery store and listened firsthand to their kudos and gripes. Though I was still new when I met Pataki, over the next six years I'd come to learn exactly what he meant. As mayor, you're always out there, not hidden away, never sheltered. At least that's how it should be and how it was for me. Pataki understood that, and I appreciated that he shared that bit of personal history with me. Republican or Democrat, we were all human.

Besides political stars, I also got to meet some famous Elmirans during my tenure as mayor. Among them were NASA astronaut Eileen Collins, the first woman to pilot and later command Space Shuttle missions, who'd been born in Elmira and had learned to fly there. As a big fan of manned space flight, I was excited to meet her in person.

I also got to know children's author and illustrator Tedd Arnold, who's written more than 100 books and calls Elmira home. I gave Tedd a key to the city, and by way of thanks, he sent me a handmade card with a drawing of his popular character *Fly Guy* holding a skeleton key and speaking a word balloon that read, "Thank you, Mayor Tonello." I still have that framed card hanging in my home.

In my six years as mayor, I'd met great people and had many successes, but I didn't accomplish all I'd set out to do. We'd aimed to do more to fix up neighborhoods and drive growth in downtown business—and we had some successes—but not at the scale I'd really wanted. The Elmira City Police did finally hire two black officers before I left, but it was still not enough.

On the plus side, we did manage to pave more streets by doing what the head of the Department of Public Works called "shaving and paving," a technique that had road crews shave a few inches of tarmac off the worst roads and repave them. I'd learned that the differences drivers saw in citywide paving efforts had not previously been due to a systematic approach, but the result of city councillors separately setting financial priorities for their districts. For some, that meant road repair, others not. We changed that approach by splitting the money for roads evenly among the six city wards, ensuring the worst streets in every part of the city got attention every year.

In City Hall itself, I started a Mayor's Arts Project to fill the third floor's high, empty walls with local artists' work. The revolving collections brightened up the place, highlighted my commitment to the arts, and often sparked conversations among staff and visitors.

I also managed to repeal the city's ill-conceived cat leash law, which had been my predecessors' attempt to reduce the number of stray cats wandering the city. Unfortunately, leashing domesticated cats—most of which are already spayed or neutered—did nothing to reduce the cat population, instead creating an odd burden for responsible pet owners. In repealing that law, we also updated the city code, which still had provisions for how many sheep could be led down a street at one time. That rule dated back more than a century to the city's more agrarian days.

## Tips on governing

Throughout my tenure as mayor, I was determined to do the work and avoid the sash. That is, I didn't want to be like Mayor Quimby on the *Simpsons* television show, who often wore a sash and spouted nonsense. I wanted to do work that mattered and had impact. Much of that related to corralling the members of city council.

To do that, I started right out by communicating *everything*. I made sure we were prolific with our press releases (writing most of them myself) and our internal communications. When John Burin notified me of an issue, I was always quick to share it with all members of the city council. If it was something that affected city staff, I made sure we emailed everyone and encouraged department heads to share that information with staff without regular access to computers, such as public works employees. Some politicians see strength in holding back information. I saw strength in spreading it around quickly, particularly for council members, who needed all the facts to make decisions and explain tough votes to their constituents. As in the campaign, I always wanted to stay out in front to help dispel rumors and make sure everyone had the facts when I had them. The result was frequent agreement—and trust.

Building trust was critical to all the city did during my time in office. After all, one of the reasons I ran was to restore trust in city government that many told me had waned. I made appearances in person and on television, published op-ed pieces, and regularly spoke with television and newspaper reporters to show people exactly what was happening and why. That level of communication was new, and it built a lot of community trust and support.

The same was true with the city council. True to my word, I never held a party caucus or any other Democrats-only meeting to talk about city agenda items or issues. Instead, John and I briefed council members on every decision and vote that would come before them. That enabled me to bridge the party divide, which many said would be one of my greatest challenges when I was first elected. It turned out to be a nonissue because I didn't look at party affiliation. I looked at each council member as a duly elected member of city government with a right to sit at the decision table. I listened to their concerns, and though we didn't always agree, we were able to work together closely and constructively. The key was to have no surprises when we sat down for council meetings—from me or from them. That helped everybody do their work without being blindsided. By the end of my second term, most people were hard-pressed to identify which members of the city council were Democrats and which were Republicans. That suited me just fine.

Trust was particularly important between John Burin and me. It didn't take us long to establish it, and it grew from there. As I mentioned, we could have some *very* frank discussions without holding onto grudges or hard feelings. That became true with the rest of his staff too. We weren't going to pull the rug out from under them on a whim, and they knew it. In return, they ran their departments well, weathered the cuts necessary to balance the budget, and came up with creative ways to solve problems.

I really enjoyed working with city staff members, who worked hard and often earned less pay than they could in private-sector jobs. But in a city-manager/mayor form of government, John Burin was their boss, not me or members of city council. Early on, some council members would go talk directly with department heads, a break in protocol. John and I did a lot to quash that, which staff appreciated, and it led to better operations and far less trepidation. The fact that we held morning workshops on the Thursdays before each Monday council meetings also meant that department heads and staff could all be present during their regular working hours and not have to stay late and endure longer days at the office.

Since members of the media often attended our workshops and council meetings, I used those opportunities to praise staff when they did good work. I wanted them to get the credit, and I wanted the city to know who'd done something on their behalf. Sharing credit is easy when you're not Mayor Quimby, and it paid dividends.

When it came time for criticism, I always did that in private. On the rare occasion when I needed to have a word with a staff member, I'd refer the issue to John Burin, who was their boss. On the even rarer occasions when I needed to have a sharp word with a council member, I did it in private. I did not want to shout down a colleague at a public meeting, which I knew would only lead to more conflict and hard feelings. I tried to remain even-keeled in the hopes that others would follow my example, and most of the time they did. By following the Golden Rule—and the rule of "compliment in public, criticize in private"—I was able to maintain a strong sense of professionalism. That professionalism helped the city solve tough problems that otherwise may have languished.

This approach, which John Burin shared, was why we were able to turn the city's financial crisis around. If our predecessors had been more open and trusting, perhaps the long spiral of a growing deficit might've come to light much sooner. But when people fear repercussions—or even the loss of their livelihoods—they tend to hunker down. It's totally understandable on many levels. John and I never wanted to fall into that same well.

Outside City Hall, I worked hard to be everywhere I could, from church gatherings and festivals to downtown cleanups and local arts events. I wanted to mingle with people from all corners of the city, hear their concerns and take their ideas back to City Hall. I also wanted to avoid fleeting pop-ins and instead really spend time with people in moments that were important to them. I recognized, too, that my presence as mayor could help boost local efforts, such as the annual Buddy Walk for developmentally disabled children and adults. I wanted to draw light to such worthy efforts and the people behind them, not draw attention to myself. As a result, I got to meet hundreds of people and build lasting relationships that gave people hope.

To me, that's what running for office and being mayor were all about.

# Index